DATE DUE

JE 1 8 '93			
MR 6 '97			
DE 6 '99			
DE 20 '00			

DEMCO 38-296

Economic Development
and International Trade

Economic Development and International Trade

The Japanese Model

by Ippei Yamazawa

Translated and revised by Ippei Yamazawa

East-West Center

Resource Systems Institute

Honolulu, Hawaii

First published in the Japanese language in 1984 as *Nihon no Keizai Hatten to Kokusai Bungyō* by Toyo Keizai Inc., Tokyo, Japan.

English-language edition first published in 1990.

Resource Systems Institute, East-West Center, 1777 East-West Road, Honolulu, Hawaii 96848.

Printed in the United States of America.

90 91 92   6 5 4 3 2 1

Library of Congress Cataloging-in-Publication Data

Yamazawa, Ippei, 1937–
    [Nihon no keizai hatten to kokusai bungyō. English]
    Economic development and international trade : the Japanese model
/ by Ippei Yamazawa ; translated and revised by Ippei Yamazawa.
    p. cm.
    Translation of: Nihon no keizai hatten to kokusai bungyō.
    ISBN 0-86638-121-X
    1. Japan—Economic conditions—1945-   2. Japan—Economic
policy—1945-   3. Japan—Commerce.   I. Title.
HC462.9.Y33513   1990
330.952'04—dc20
                                  90-8394
                                      CIP

Contents

Part IV
Japan's Development Experience and Contemporary Developing Countries

Tables and Figures

Figures

Preface

International trade has played a key role in Japan's economic development. Through it Japan has obtained energy and resources unavailable domestically; trade has also introduced new products and technology and has contributed to the development of modern industrial production through import substitution at home and export expansion abroad. As a late-starting industrial country, Japan's industries have typically followed a catching-up product cycle (CPC) process of development.

The catching-up product cycle development process is characterized by import substitution followed by export expansion. Import substitution versus export expansion has become the major choice in development strategy confronting contemporary developing economies. Economists in the developed countries, as well as those at multilateral institutions such as the World Bank, suggest that many developing countries have overemphasized import substitution, which thus hampers export expansion after import substitution is achieved; many of these economists recommend that these countries shift their policies toward export expansion through deregulation and promotion of exports. The CPC development process differs from this orthodox view by stressing the continuity of import substitution while pursuing export expansion.

The term "Japanese model" used in this book describes not so much a development experience unique to Japan but a rational pattern of industrial development and trade in a late-starting industrial country under certain resource and market constraints. This pattern is relevant for contemporary newly industrializing economies (NIEs), and near-NIEs, in spite of the greater technological gap and more severe international market situation confronting them.

What role has the Japanese government played in Japan's successful import substitution and export expansion? Since its first attempts at development Japan has had a strong centralized government staffed by well-trained bureaucrats. Some foreign observers have attributed Japan's success to the foresight and leadership of the government, as in the oft-cited notion of "Japan Incorporated." However, many Japanese economists believe this view overemphasizes the government's role and are inclined to give more credit to private entrepreneurship. Nevertheless, there has long been closer cooperation between government and private business in Japan than in the United States and some European countries, and this does seem to have contributed to Japanese industrial development. This book attempts to present a balanced assessment of the government's role in Japan's economic development.

The Japanese economy managed to overcome the two oil shocks of the 1970s but it has accumulated huge trade surpluses and faces severe trade conflicts with its major trading partners, especially the United States. Japan's main policy efforts have recently been geared toward restructuring its economy and industry so that further growth is compatible with that of its trading partners. Japanese economists are helping to shed light on the changes by explaining these restructuring efforts and how they are being implemented. They can be properly understood only with a precise knowledge of the Japanese policy environment.

This book is organized into four parts. Part I gives a summary of Japan's development process over the long term and analyzes the interaction between production and trade structures with ample consideration given to statistical evidence. Part II analyzes the strategic role of four industries at different stages of Japan's economic development—silk exports during the initial stage; textile and steel industries during CPC development, which is typical of such labor- and capital-intensive industries; and the trading companies in the trade expansion period. Part III focuses on trade and industrial policies adopted by the Japanese government during the pre–Second World War period, the high-growth period of the 1950s and 1960s, and the post–oil shock period. Part IV discusses the relevance of the Japanese development experience to contemporary NIEs and near-NIEs and presents two case studies of the catching-up product cycle and general trading companies in representative developing countries.

This book is based on its Japanese edition (*Nihon no Keizai Hatten to Kokusai Bungyō*), which was published in 1984 and won the *Japan Economic Journal*'s Best Economics Book of the Year Award. However, Chapters 2, 9, and 10 have been revised significantly in order to include the recent changes in Japan's role in the international environment in the 1980s. For other chapters, beyond mere translation into English, explanations and English-language references for English-language readers have been added. Readers with knowledge of the Japanese language should refer to the 1984 edition for Japanese sources that have been omitted from this edition. The interaction between industrial growth and international trade in Japan has occasionally been treated in the English-language economics literature (for example, Lockwood, Allen, Akamatsu, Kojima, Shinohara, Tatemoto-Baba, and Ohkawa and Rosovsky). This author's debt to these studies is great. To these has been added this author's research, which is based on the recent *Long-term Economic Statistics of Japan* series. This book attempts to present a complete picture of the development mechanism and government policies in a long-run historical perspective—this author's version of the Japanese model.

The concept of the catching-up product cycle provides the main analytical framework for Japanese economic development into which such institutional devices as industrial policy and trading companies are incorporated. Although based on Vernon's version of the product cycle, CPC was first proposed by Akamatsu in the early 1940s and is known to Japanese economists as the "flying wild geese pattern" of industrial development. The concept was based on Akamatsu's statistical study of the interrelated development of Japanese industries and trade. The concept was developed further by Kojima and Shinohara. Since introduced by Ohkita at the 4th Pacific Economic Cooperation Conference (PECC) in Seoul in May 1985, the theory has been attracting the attention of economists in the Asia-Pacific region as the theory that best explains industrial transmission among the Asian economies. The phrase "flying wild geese" has become a popular way to describe economic cooperation in the Pacific. This book endeavors to present to English-language readers this Japanese model, with all its implications for the economic development of late-starting countries.

Long-term Japanese economic statistics are used to the fullest extent to describe the process of economic development; these are taken from the coauthored work, *Trade and Balance of Payments* (Yamazawa and Yamamoto, Volume 14 of the *Long-term Economic Statistics of Japan* series) and from other publications in the series, which are available in English translation and may be referred to by interested readers.

August 1990

Acknowledgments

I would like to express my sincere thanks to my long-time friend, Dr. Seiji Naya, Director of the East-West Center's Resource Systems Institute, who encouraged me to translate my 1984 edition into English, offered a month's stay at the Resource Systems Institute to work on the translation, provided me with editorial assistance, and waited patiently for the completion of my manuscript. A former graduate student at Hitotsubashi University, Dr. Gwendlyn Tecson, helped with my translation. I appreciate greatly the Resource Systems Institute's editor, Mr. David Puhlick, for his painstaking efforts to make my English readable and his patience. I also appreciate the help of Dr. Pearl Imada and Ms. Janis Togashi of the Development Policy Program staff, Resource Systems Institute, for their assistance in helping to clarify economic concepts for English-language readers and providing comments that enhanced the overall presentation. I would also like to thank Ms. Ann Takayesu for her editorial support in preparing the manuscript for production. The Graphics and Production Services of the East-West Center designed and typeset this edition.

The publication of the English-language edition would not have been possible without the generous permission of Toyo Keizai, Inc., the publisher of the 1984 Japanese version. I would also like to acknowledge the other sources and publishers upon which parts of this edition were based. The materials in this edition, and the publications in which they appeared, are as follows: Figure 10.2 appeared, in part, as Figure 16.1 in Chapter 16, by I. Yamazawa and S. Tambunlertchai, *Japan and the Developing Economies: A Comparative Analysis,* K. Ohkawa and G. Ranis, eds. (Basil Blackwell, Inc., Oxford, England, 1985). Tables 6.7, 6.8, 10.1, and 10.2 appeared as Tables 18.1, 18.2, 18.3, and 18.5, respectively, in Chapter 18, by I. Yamazawa and H. Kohama, of the same title. Sections of an earlier version of Chapter 5 of this edition appeared as ''Industry Growth and Foreign Trade: A Study of Japan's Steel

Industry," by I. Yamazawa (*Hitotsubashi Journal of Economics,* Vol. 12, No. 2, Feb. 1972, Hitotsubashi University, Tokyo), and an earlier, shorter version of Chapter 7 appeared as "Industrial Growth and Trade Policy in Pre-War Japan," by I. Yamazawa (*The Developing Economies,* Vol. 13, No. 1, 1975, Institute of Developing Economies, Tokyo).

The Japan Foundation provided funding for this edition's publication.

Kunitachi, Tokyo
August 1990   Ippei Yamazawa

Part I

Japan's Economic Development and International Trade

One

Economic Development and Trade Structure: The Long View

At the core of Japanese economic development was Japan's rapid industrialization and great capacity for change. Japan was late in developing, yet Japan's domestic production and trade structures underwent a remarkable change from the period of the introduction of modern industries from the United States and Europe to the period of export-oriented growth. For a country lacking in natural resources—except labor—the strategy of importing raw materials and exporting finished products was most appropriate. Beginning in the Meiji period (1868–1912), the interaction between industrialization and changes in trade structure led to over a century of Japanese economic development, and although severe balance-of-payments constraints characterized Japan's initial period of growth, these gradually eased.

This chapter overviews Japan's development over a century, focusing on the interaction between industrialization and changes in trade structure.[1] This interaction, which is seen through Japan's high capability of transformation, characterizes Japan's economic development. Chapter 2 presents the interaction as a "Japanese model," which provides the framework for the presentation of industry case studies in Chapters 3 through 6. The role of government policy in the process of this successful interaction during the pre–Second World War period, the high-growth period after the Second World War, and the period after the two oil shocks is analyzed. Towards the end of this book it is pointed out, however, that Japan has outgrown this traditional pattern of catching-up industrialization and now searches for a new pattern of economic growth that corresponds to its position as a new industrial leader. Chapter 10 discusses the relevance of the Japanese development experience to contemporary developing countries.

ECONOMIC DEVELOPMENT AND FOREIGN TRADE

Commodity trade grew steadily during the process of Japan's economic development. Columns 1 and 2 in Table 1.1 show changes in total commodity exports and imports. To facilitate observation of such shifts, the pre–Second World War indices have been expressed in terms of overlapping decade averages; the post–Second World War indices have been expressed in terms of

Table 1.1
Development of Japan's Foreign Trade

Period	Exports (1)	Imports (2)	World Trade (3)	Export/GNP Ratio (%) (4)	Import/GNP Ratio (%) (5)
		(1882–91	= 100)		
1874–83	52.7	64.1	—	—	—
1877–86	66.2	69.1	—	—	—
1882–91	100.0	100.0	100.0	—	—
1887–96	143.1	164.3	116.0	3.2	6.0
1892–1901	202.0	275.0	130.6	3.9	8.8
1897–1906	295.7	400.5	159.8	5.2	11.6
1902–11	417.9	487.6	185.7	6.7	12.8
1907–16	643.7	592.8	192:8	9.2	13.9
1912–21	921.2	749.2	192.6	10.6	14.2
1917–26	1,049.1	1,067.9	223.2	10.1	16.9
1922–31	1,297.0	1,375.9	265.2	11.4	19.8
1927–36	2,027.5	1,558.3	251.9	14.9	18.8
1930–39	2,505.1	1,729.0	241.5	16.1	18.2
		(1951–55	= 100)		
1951–55	100	100	100	3.4	4.9
1956–60	284	229	157	6.0	6.8
1961–65	612	485	226	7.7	8.7
1966–70	1,328	900	360	10.0	9.6
1971–75	2,171	1,138	550	11.0	8.2
1976–80	3,242	1,543	729	13.0	8.7

Notes: The indices of Japan's exports (1), imports (2), and world trade (3) are calculated from constant price series; the export (4) and import (5) ratios are calculated from constant price series of exports, imports, and GNP.

Sources: Figures for exports, imports, and world trade are from Yamazawa and Yamamoto (1979a); for GNP, from Ohkawa, Takamatsu, and Yamamoto (1974).

consecutive five-year averages. Both are expressed in constant prices, using as a reference the periods 1882–91 for the prewar series and 1951–55 for the postwar series.

During the 65 years spanning the periods 1874–83 to 1930–39, exports grew at an annual average rate of 6.8 percent compared to a growth rate of 5.8 percent for imports. Between the periods 1951–55 and 1966–70, exports expanded at an average annual rate of 17.2 percent and imports at 14.8 percent. These rates were about double the 8.5 percent growth rate of world trade during the same period. Table 1.2 compares the growth performance of Japan's exports in the principal export markets of Western Europe, the United States, and China during the pre–First World War and interwar years (columns 4 to 5). In all periods or markets, Japan's export and import growth rates were relatively high. Although world trade practically came to a halt or declined during the interwar years, Japan's export growth continued.

Table 1.1 shows the seesaw-like movements in growth of both exports and imports. In the periods 1874–83 to 1882–91, exports were leading; in the peri-

Table 1.2
International Comparison of Trade Expansion:
Average Annual Growth Rates (%)

Period	Number of years	Exports by Japan (1)	Imports by Japan (2)	World Trade (3)	Imports by Western Europe (4)	Imports by the U.S. (5)	Imports by China (6)
1874–83 to 1930–39	57	6.77	5.78	—	—	—	—
1882–91 to 1930–39			49	1.80	1.70	2.59	1.37
1882–91 to 1902–11	20	7.15	7.92	3.09	2.94	3.00	3.04
1922–31 to 1930–39	10	6.58	2.28	−0.94	0.03	−0.72	−3.68
1951–55 to 1966–70	15	17.2	14.8	8.5	—	—	—
1966–70 to 1976–80	10	8.9	3.0	7.1	—	—	—

Notes: The annual compound rates are calculated by dividing the last period values by those of the first period. The periods 1907–16 to 1917–26 are omitted to avoid the influence of the First World War (see Table 1.1).

Sources: Table 1.1, this volume, and Yamazawa and Yamamoto (1979a).

ods 1887–96 to 1902–11 imports were leading, then exports in the periods 1902–11 to 1912–21, imports in the periods 1912–21 to 1927–36, and exports in the periods 1927–36 to 1930–39. During the postwar years, however, the growth rate of exports was consistently higher.

Table 1.1 also shows the movements in commodity exports and imports relative to GNP. At first the import ratio exceeded the export ratio, but as both ratios increased during the entire prewar period, exports overtook imports.[2] Reflecting the movements observed in the export and import growth trends, the import ratio showed a greater increase than did the export ratio during the periods 1882–91 to 1887–96 but was overtaken by the export ratio in the periods 1902–11 to 1912–21. Import ratios again increased by greater amounts during the periods 1912–21 to 1922–31, and export ratios, in the periods 1922–31 to 1930–39. After the Second World War both the export and import ratios were at about the 4–5 percent level, but in the second half of the 1960s the export ratio exceeded the import ratio for the first time.

The rise in the export/GNP and import/GNP ratios followed a general trend observed in the process of modern economic growth in Western European countries. According to Kuznets (1967:18–26), Britain's foreign trade ratio (exports-plus-imports/GNP ratio or X+M/GNP) was 14 percent in the nineteenth century and rose to 43.5 percent in the period before the First World War (1909–13). Similarly, France's ratio was 10 percent in the 1820s and rose to 35.2 percent in the period 1908–10, and Germany's grew from 13 percent in 1840 to 38.3 percent in the period 1910–13.[3] For Japan, the foreign trade ratios were 9.2 percent in 1890 and 23.1 percent in the period before the First World War (1907–16). The ratios rose to 34.3 percent in the period 1930–39. The initial and final levels of the Japanese ratios were thus similar to those of the other developed countries. Although the start of modern Japanese economic growth came 50 to 100 years after that of other developed countries, trade growth after the First World War continued, until in the 1930s it was comparable to the level of trade growth of the developed countries.

Japan, like most developing countries, had a higher GNP growth rate than the developed countries, but what was unusual was that it had an even higher growth rate in trade, particularly exports. Export growth was sustained even in the 1920s and 1930s when other countries' trade either declined or came to a halt. What role did such rapid trade expansion, especially in exports, play in Japan's economic development? What are the implications for the role of trade in the development process as seen in the fluctuation of exports and imports vis-à-vis GNP? Since these questions cannot be answered merely through observation of general trends, an analysis must begin by examining the interaction between changes in the export and import structures and in domestic production.

CHANGES IN THE STRUCTURE OF TRADE

Commodity Composition of Exports

The rapid growth in commodity export and import values was accompanied by significant changes in commodity composition. Table 1.3 shows the dramatic changes in Japan's commodity exports that took place over a period of approximately one hundred years. All primary goods and specific primary goods such as raw silk and copper ingots are included in the data. Note that both of these goods are simply processed from indigenous raw materials and are similar to the processed primary goods exports of contemporary developing countries; they are different from processed goods such as cotton textiles and pig iron, which depend on imported raw materials. At the same time, processed exports of indigenous materials are not limited to these two types of goods. Export goods such as processed food, porcelain pottery, and wooden and straw products also depend on indigenous raw materials but are included in the manufactured goods category. The comparative advantage of these goods in export markets is at the processing stage, since they do not depend as much on the decisive factor of raw material endowments as do raw silk and copper ingots. Although any classification will inevitably be somewhat arbitrary, the special treatment accorded to raw silk and copper ingots is due to their importance as export products.

Aside from raw silk and copper ingots, other principal primary export commodities were tea, marine products, and coal for ships. The share of primary goods in total commodity exports for the period 1874–83 was more than 80 percent, but, except for raw silk, primary goods rapidly became unimportant as export commodities. Among the primary goods, raw silk led export growth and made up one-third of total export value from 1874 to 1896. It was not until the late 1920s that the share of primary goods fell below one-fourth of total exports and became significantly less important than light industry exports such as textiles (particularly cotton fabrics), processed food, and miscellaneous manufactured goods (see Table 1.3). Exports of processed food and other manufactured goods grew rapidly, and both were important export commodities until the Second World War, a period of more than 40 years. The main exports in the heavy industrial category of chemicals, metals, and machinery were primarily such goods as matches and camphor. Exports of more sophisticated heavy industrial goods did not begin until the First World War, after which they grew to replace light industrial goods as principal exports only in the second half of the 1950s. By the latter half of the 1970s, the share of heavy industrial goods in total exports was 87 percent, a rather high percentage, of which two-thirds was represented by machinery exports.[4]

Commodity Composition of Imports

Table 1.4 shows the change in the structure of imports. The most noticeable change in structure is the decline in the share of industrial goods from about 90 percent in the period 1874–86 to 50 percent during the First World War. Another significant change is the rise in the share of imports of primary products from 60 percent in the pre–Second World War period to 70 percent

Table 1.3
Commodity Composition of Japan's Exports (% in market prices)

	Primary Goods[a]			Industrial Goods[b]		
Periods	All primary goods (1)	Raw silk (2)	Copper ingots (3)	All industrial goods (4)	Textiles (5)	Chemicals, metals, and machinery (6)
1874–83	82.4	37.7	2.2	17.6	4.4	5.9
1877–86	79.4	36.8	3.1	20.6	6.1	6.7
1882–91	74.9	36.8	5.1	25.1	8.8	7.2
1887–96	65.5	34.1	5.1	34.5	14.8	8.3
1892–1901	55.1	29.3	4.8	44.9	23.3	8.2
1897–1906	47.7	26.2	4.9	52.3	27.4	9.0
1902–11	45.2	26.2	4.9	54.8	27.7	12.6
1907–16	41.8	24.6	4.9	58.2	28.9	12.5
1912–21	34.2	22.6	2.6	65.8	33.8	16.7
1917–26	36.5	28.4	0.8	63.5	35.2	14.3
1922–31	38.5	31.7	0	61.5	34.1	12.8
1927–36	27.2	20.5	0	52.8	36.3	19.7
1930–39	19.9	13.1	0	80.1	35.0	26.5
1951–55	4.7	—	—	95.3	39.5	39.9
1956–60	4.5	—	—	95.5	32.0	45.1
1961–65	3.5	—	—	96.5	21.3	58.6
1966–70	1.7	—	—	98.3	13.7	71.2
1971–75	1.4	—	—	98.5	7.4	82.9
1976–80	0.9	—	—	99.1	4.7	87.1

Notes: Column 4 includes processed foodstuffs, miscellaneous products, ceramics, and wooden products as well as textiles and chemicals, metals, and machinery.

a. Raw silk and copper ingots are the principal primary goods exports.

b. Textiles as well as chemicals, metals, and machinery are the principal industrial goods exports.

Source: Yamazawa and Yamamoto (1979a: table 1), but adjusted for raw silk. Copper ingots reclassified as a primary good for the years before the Second World War.

Table 1.4
Commodity Composition of Japan's Imports (%)

Periods	Industrial goods			Primary goods					
	Total (2+3) (1)	Industrial goods (2)	Chemicals, metals, machinery (3)	Total (5+6) (4)	Un-processed food (5)	Total (7-9) (6)	Raw materials		
							Textile materials (7)	Metal ores (8)	Fuels (9)
1874–83	91.2	69.9	21.3	8.8	0.7	8.1	0.7	—	5.0
1877–86	89.7	68.4	21.3	10.3	0.8	9.5	1.6	—	6.1
1882–91	81.3	54.7	26.6	18.7	5.0	13.7	5.8	—	6.4
1887–96	71.8	42.8	29.0	28.2	7.1	21.1	14.8	—	4.9
1892–1901	63.6	31.0	32.6	36.5	9.9	26.6	20.8	0.1	4.4
1897–1906	56.9	24.1	32.8	43.1	13.8	29.3	22.9	0.1	4.6
1902–11	54.8	20.5	32.3	46.2	12.5	32.7	25.9	0.2	3.9
1907–16	50.0	15.6	34.4	50.0	10.3	39.7	32.6	0.7	2.7
1912–21	47.4	12.1	35.3	52.6	12.5	40.1	32.4	1.0	2.2
1917–26	45.7	14.9	30.8	54.3	16.1	38.2	29.5	0.8	2.9
1922–31	43.4	17.1	26.3	56.6	18.8	37.8	27.1	0.8	4.3
1927–36	39.0	13.8	25.2	61.0	19.0	42.0	28.6	1.4	5.9
1930–39	42.0	12.3	29.7	58.0	17.5	40.5	25.1	2.6	7.4
1951–55	14.4	4.0	10.4	85.6	25.0	60.6	27.6	6.8	11.0
1956–60	23.3	3.6	19.7	76.7	13.2	63.5	19.3	13.8	15.7
1961–65	27.7	5.5	22.2	72.3	13.5	58.8	12.6	13.0	18.3
1966–70	30.3	7.0	23.3	69.7	12.8	56.9	6.9	13.6	20.4
1971–75	27.2	9.5	17.7	72.8	14.7	58.1	3.8	9.2	33.9
1976–80	25.2	8.9	16.3	75.5	14.3	61.2	2.3	6.4	44.2

Notes: Percentage composition calculated from overlapping decade averages at current prices. (1) + (4) = 100; (2) + (3) = (1); (5) + (6) = (4); but (7) + (8) + (9) < (6), the difference consisting of other agricultural materials, forest products, and other mineral materials.
Source: Yamazawa and Yamamoto (1979a: table 2).

in the postwar era. Thus, over the past century, Japan has undergone a complete transition from an industrial goods-importing country to a primary product-importing country. What is important, however, is the change in the composition of this industrial goods and primary products trade. Light industrial goods represented 70 percent of total imports in the period 1874–83 but rapidly declined thereafter to about 10 percent in the interwar period. In contrast, heavy industrial goods imports rose in importance through the First World War, reaching a maximum share of 35 percent of total imports and falling to about a 30 percent share by the start of the Second World War period.

Figure 1.1 shows the change in composition of industrial goods imports classified according to end use. Beginning with the period 1874–83 consumer goods imports represented close to 50 percent of total imports but rapidly declined to about 10 percent by the interwar period. This declining share was initially replaced by investment goods (producer durables and construction materials), which leveled off at 20–25 percent, and later by intermediate goods imports.

Figure 1.1
Compositional Changes in Imports of Industrial Goods by End Use

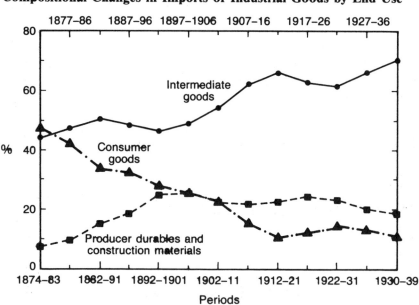

Note: Composition was calculated from the overlapping decade average at current prices.
Source: Yamazawa and Yamamoto (1979a: table 6).

Although consumption goods do not correspond exactly to the light industrial goods category, import substitution in the manufacturing sector brought about growth in essential investment goods imports (mostly heavy industrial goods). The leveling off of the shares of heavy industrial and investment goods imports reflects the import substitution that was simultaneously under way in these industrial sectors.

The growth in primary goods imports was mainly in raw materials. Due to the expansion in textile production in the pre–Second World War period, imports of textile raw materials made up three-quarters of total raw material imports, or one-third to one-fourth of total imports. With the development of iron and steel and other heavy industrial goods production, however, the shares of iron ore, coal, and other mineral product imports began to grow in the 1930s and became the principal raw material imports from the second half of the 1950s. The rapid growth of petroleum imports during the post–Second World War period is particularly evident. In the 1970s, the price of crude oil skyrocketed, and the share of petroleum imports rose to 44 percent of total fuel imports. Because of the increase in total fuel imports, the share of industrial goods declined to about 25 percent of total imports. The other import category that rose in importance during the post–Second World War period was forestry and other agricultural raw material imports (Table 1.1), which together accounted for 13 to 14 percent of total imports, thus demonstrating the trend toward diversification in raw material imports.

The share of basic food imports rose from less than 1 percent in the period 1874–83 to 16–19 percent during the interwar period. Even here, the change in composition of food imports over these periods of time should be noted. The agricultural food imports of the Meiji period fluctuated from year to year. During years of bad harvests and wars (that is, 1879–80, 1890, 1897–98, 1903–13), food imports grew to several times the amounts of the preceding and following years. As a result, the share of food imports during normal years fell far below those shown in Table 1.4. At one point Japan became dependent on Taiwan and Korea for imports of agricultural food products. But in 1912, with the establishment of tariffs on rice and wheat, imports declined. After the First World War, however, agricultural food imports gradually stabilized and represented 16–19 percent of total imports during normal crop years. From 1955 through 1980 the share of food imports in total imports also increased, from about 13 to just above 14 percent, but for the most part this slightly increasing trend reflected import dependence on animal feeds and cereals other than rice.

Geographical Composition

In addition to changes in the composition of trade, there was also a shift in trading partners. Trade began with Western Europe, but East Asia and North

America gradually became the principal trading regions. At the same time, trading regions expanded, first to Southeast and South Asia and the Middle East, and then, after the 1920s, to Oceania, Central and South America, and Africa. Even during the post–Second World War years, the trend toward trade diversification continued, beginning with the decline in importance of East Asia, and, in turn, of Southeast and South Asia and the Middle East; however, the high import shares for North America continued.

Behind these changes in the geographical origins and destinations of exports and imports, a shift in commodity composition is discernable. The first industrial goods imports came from Europe, and as a result of an increase in the volume of raw material imports, diversification of raw material imports took place. Food imports were originally shipped from East Asia in the early 1900s, especially from Japan's colonies. Raw silk was exported to Europe and North America, and other textile products found export markets in Korea, Taiwan, and China, moving gradually to Southeast Asia and to far-flung markets such as South Asia, the Middle East, Africa, Central and South America, and Oceania. Heavy industrial goods, such as iron, steel, and ammonium sulfate, were first exported in the pre–Second World War years to the East Asian colonies and finally to every region of the world during the post–Second World War period.[5]

Colonies such as Taiwan and Korea are usually assumed to have been sources of food and raw material supplies as well as export markets for Japan during the pre–Second World War period, but such a view is not necessarily accurate. At first glance, this assumption fits the British colonial trade pattern and may be considered natural for Japan, which is also a country lacking in raw materials and space. However, although Taiwan and Korea were the major supply sources of food imports, they were not Japan's primary sources of raw material supplies (only 7 to 9% of which was made up of mineral products). Moreover, although these two countries were important export markets for Japan, absorbing about 40 percent of its heavy industrial goods exports, the export/production ratios of chemicals, metals, and machinery were only about 11 to 12 percent—hardly enough to represent the core of pre–Second World War Japan's export-led industrialization.[6]

CHANGES IN THE STRUCTURE
OF INDUSTRIAL PRODUCTION AND TRADE

The shift in the long-term trend of industrial production is demonstrated in Shinohara's overlapping decade average series of industrial production values at constant prices (Shinohara 1972: chap. 2). From the 1870s to the 1930s, the share of the modern sectors—such as textiles, chemicals, ceramics, nonferrous metals, iron and steel, machinery, and printing—grew and the share of the traditional sectors—processed food and wood and miscellaneous products—declined. However, domestic prices in the modern sectors noticeably declined relative to those in the traditional sectors. The data for the relevant years show only small changes in shares, because changing relative prices tended to offset part of the changes in real shares. In the relationship between the expansion of production shares of the modern industrial structure and the decline in relative prices, Shinohara saw proof of Japan's success in achieving comparative advantage in these industries and in import substitution as well as in the export expansion of its products.

Originally termed the "flying wild geese pattern" of industrial development by Akamatsu (1943) and later renamed the "catching-up product cycle" (CPC) by Kojima (1973), the processes of import substitution and subsequent export expansion by the modern industrial sector foreshadow similar developments in major modern industries. These processes provide the basic analytical framework for the following chapters, which begin with an examination of the correspondence of structural changes between industrial output, exports, and imports.

Compositional Changes in Industrial Output, Imports, and Exports

Tables 1.5–1.7 show the trend in composition of industrial output, imports, and exports. For the pre–Second World War period, the overlapping decade average series have been calculated from Shinohara's analysis of the same 13 periods (1874–83 to 1930–39) and the five-year average series for the post–Second World War years (1951–55 to 1976–80). The computed distribution is based on 1934–36 prewar and 1965 postwar price series, because changes in composition based on current year price data might be distorted by changes in relative prices.

As shown in Table 1.5, changes are evident in industrial output in terms of the declining shares of processed food and wood products throughout the entire series, and the declining share of miscellaneous products up to the Second World War. These products were replaced by textiles whose share increased up to 1939. In addition, during the periods 1874–83 through 1907–16 growth begins in the heavy industrial sector in such products as metals and machinery (and later chemicals), and a basic trend emerges in the period 1922–31. Except for the period 1951–55, there is a firming of the trend toward share expansion by the metals, machinery, and chemicals sectors during the postwar period. Among the heavy industrial goods, the expansion of machinery is the most remarkable. While growth problems were encountered in chemicals and metal products during the second half of the 1970s, the assembly industries of the machinery group continued to grow.

Table 1.5
Composition of Industrial Output (%)

Period	Processed food	Textiles	Wood products	Chemicals	Ceramics	Metals	Machinery	Miscellaneous products
1874–83	58.5	10.8	6.3	11.0	1.9	1.4	1.3	8.8
1877–86	56.6	12.5	5.9	11.0	1.5	1.6	1.5	9.3
1882–91	53.4	17.9	4.7	9.5	1.3	1.8	1.4	9.8
1887–96	48.6	24.6	3.7	8.7	1.5	1.7	1.5	9.7
1892–1901	47.3	26.5	3.7	8.6	1.5	1.4	2.2	8.7
1897–1906	45.9	25.1	4.1	9.2	1.6	1.7	3.7	8.7
1902–11	42.1	25.2	3.7	9.7	2.0	2.6	5.6	9.1
1907–16	37.2	27.3	3.1	9.6	2.2	4.3	7.7	8.7
1912–21	32.0	27.6	2.6	9.2	2.1	6.8	12.5	7.7
1917–26	30.9	28.3	2.4	9.2	2.4	8.0	12.2	6.9
1922–31	28.2	29.8	2.6	10.7	2.7	9.0	10.5	6.6
1927–36	21.0	30.4	2.8	13.2	2.6	11.4	12.6	6.2
1930–39	17.3	28.1	2.8	15.2	2.5	13.0	15.5	5.7
1951–55	23.2	14.0	14.5	10.0	4.6	17.6	12.2	3.9
1956–60	18.0	12.3	9.0	13.5	4.2	17.4	19.7	5.9
1961–65	13.6	9.2	5.7	15.9	3.8	17.6	26.4	7.8
1966–70	10.9	7.4	3.9	15.7	3.4	17.9	32.9	7.9
1971–75	8.8	5.9	2.7	15.9	3.0	19.6	36.5	7.6
1976–80	8.1	4.9	2.1	15.4	2.8	18.5	40.2	7.4

Note: Computed from constant price series (base years: 1934–36 (prewar); 1965 (postwar)).

Source: Yamazawa and Yamamoto (1979a).

Table 1.6
Composition of Industrial Goods Imports (%)

Period	Processed food	Textiles	Wood products	Chemicals	Ceramics	Metals	Machinery	Miscellaneous products
1874–83	6.1	65.7	0.1	5.4	1.4	6.0	4.9	10.4
1877–86	7.2	63.0	0.1	5.2	1.4	7.4	7.5	8.2
1882–91	7.8	53.2	0.1	6.0	1.8	9.8	12.9	8.4
1887–96	7.9	44.4	0.0	7.9	1.7	11.9	18.1	8.1
1892–1901	10.2	29.2	0.0	11.9	1.6	13.3	28.1	5.7
1897–1906	10.7	20.2	0.1	15.8	1.9	14.7	32.7	3.9
1902–11	9.6	15.8	0.1	20.3	2.3	17.0	31.5	3.4
1907–16	10.0	11.0	0.1	23.6	2.0	20.2	30.1	3.0
1912–21	11.8	6.8	0.4	25.7	0.9	25.1	27.4	1.9
1917–26	13.0	9.3	2.3	24.4	0.8	23.8	24.8	1.6
1922–31	15.4	10.1	3.6	24.4	1.3	21.3	22.0	1.9
1927–36	18.8	7.5	2.8	27.1	1.5	24.7	15.7	1.9
1930–39	17.4	5.7	1.3	25.1	1.2	34.2	13.5	1.6
1951–55	12.3	5.6	6.0	17.6	1.5	8.9	45.4	2.7
1956–60	6.5	2.4	3.2	21.3	1.6	20.6	41.7	2.7
1961–65	9.7	1.9	3.4	20.4	1.9	16.7	42.5	3.5
1966–70	7.5	3.8	3.3	19.7	3.2	19.8	36.5	6.2
1971–75	4.9	8.3	4.8	18.1	5.8	12.0	36.9	9.2
1976–80	8.6	8.3	5.5	20.0	3.6	9.3	36.2	9.7

Note: Computed from constant price series (base years: 1934–36 (prewar); 1965 (postwar)).
Source: Yamazawa and Yamamoto (1979a).

Table 1.7
Composition of Industrial Goods Exports (%)

Period	Processed food	Textiles	Wood products	Chemicals	Ceramics	Metals	Machinery	Miscellaneous products
1874–83	5.9	59.8	0.3	22.0	1.4	7.2	0.0	3.4
1877–86	5.3	56.0	0.3	22.8	1.6	9.5	0.0	4.5
1882–91	4.0	56.4	0.3	20.3	2.0	11.9	0.0	5.1
1887–96	3.2	59.2	0.5	17.1	2.0	10.9	0.2	6.9
1892–1901	3.6	61.3	1.2	15.3	1.9	7.9	0.3	8.5
1897–1906	6.2	59.2	2.3	13.6	2.3	6.4	0.8	9.2
1902–11	7.2	57.4	3.5	12.3	2.4	6.3	1.6	9.3
1907–16	6.8	56.2	3.0	11.9	2.3	6.4	2.8	10.6
1912–21	7.1	55.1	2.3	11.3	2.4	6.6	5.3	9.9
1917–26	7.1	60.1	1.8	9.9	2.6	5.7	4.5	8.3
1922–31	7.4	62.9	1.3	9.6	3.0	5.2	3.4	7.2
1927–36	7.1	57.4	1.2	10.2	3.3	7.2	6.3	7.3
1930–39	7.1	52.1	1.7	10.8	3.4	7.7	9.5	7.7
1951–55	6.0	41.4	2.0	4.9	5.7	20.6	13.2	6.2
1956–60	6.2	36.1	2.2	6.5	4.5	12.7	23.4	8.4
1961–65	3.6	21.8	1.5	10.1	3.8	18.2	32.6	8.4
1966–70	2.4	14.1	0.8	12.7	2.5	18.1	42.6	6.8
1971–75	1.2	8.6	0.5	13.0	1.4	17.9	53.2	4.2
1976–80	0.7	5.3	0.2	9.8	1.2	14.4	64.9	3.3

Note: Computed from constant price series (base years: 1934–36 (prewar); 1965 (postwar)).

Source: Yamazawa and Yamamoto (1979a).

The change in import structure is even more striking (see Table 1.6). The 66 percent share of textile imports in the period 1874–83 declined drastically to 11 percent by the period 1907–16 and to 2 percent by the period 1961–65. Although its share was smaller, miscellaneous products followed a similar trend up until the Second World War. On the other hand, the shares of three sectors—chemicals, metals, and machinery—grew rapidly, cumulatively reaching 70 percent in the period 1907–16 and leveling off thereafter until the post–First World War years. Processed food, wood products, and ceramics showed a slow but steadily rising trend.

The change in the export structure before the First World War is not as remarkable as the changes that occurred in the import and output structures (see Table 1.7). Up to the period 1922–31, the structure of industrial goods exports changed relatively little. Textiles maintained its share between 50 and 60 percent; the share of chemicals showed a steady decline. After surging in the periods 1877–86, 1882–91, and 1887–96, the share of metals dropped dramatically in the period 1892–1901 and did not regain its 1874–83 share until the period 1927–36. The shares of wood products, processed food, and miscellaneous products gradually rose. However, a significant change took place in textiles—the share of raw silk fell during the periods 1874–83 to 1930–39 from 38.3 percent to 12.1 percent of total industrial exports (raw silk is included in industrial exports in Table 1.7), but that of other textile products (mainly cotton fabrics) rose from 21.5 percent to 40.0 percent.

Beginning in the period 1922–31 and continuing through the post–Second World War years, the combined share of chemicals, metals, and machinery exports rose and eventually replaced that of textiles in the period 1956–60 (see Table 1.7). This change occurred as the share of textiles declined from 63 percent (1922–31) to 52 percent (1930–39) to 14 percent (1966–70), while the share of chemicals, metals, and machinery rose from 18 percent to 28 percent to 73 percent in the same periods. The decline in the share of textiles from the periods 1922–31 to 1930–39 was primarily due to the decline in the share of raw silk (the remaining share of textile products plunged during the post–Second World War years). Likewise, miscellaneous products, processed food, and wood products held a 20 percent share in the periods 1902–11 to 1912–21; this was halved to 10 percent by the period 1966–70.

It is inaccurate to assert that import substitution and export expansion proceeded in all modern industrial sectors before the Second World War by merely comparing the situations in the periods 1874–83 and 1930–39. Whereas import substitution was completed for textile products by the period 1907–16, for chemicals, metals, and machinery import substitution occurred after the period 1912–21. Although chemicals, metals, and machinery maintained a combined share of 70 percent of total imports in the postwar period, it should be noted that the share of industrial goods sharply declined as a percentage of total imports. As Table 1.6 shows, after the period 1956–60 the shares of other industrial goods imports such as textiles, processed foods, and miscellaneous products began to rise.

Beginning in the period 1882–91, the share of other textile products (except for raw silk) grew, rising to 40 percent in the period 1930–39. Again, this share was displaced in the postwar period by those of chemicals, metals, and machinery combined, whose shares began to grow after the period 1922–31. Within this group, the growth in machinery exports, beginning in the 1970s, was indeed remarkable. Thus, although occurring at different times, expansion in the shares of light industrial goods (particularly textile products—except raw silk) and heavy industrial goods (such as chemicals, metals, and machinery) constituted the two largest shifts in structure, each following the sequence of imports, production, and exports. Kojima referred to this as "import-led structural change" (1958: chap. 3).

Interaction between Production and Trade

The change from import substitution to export-led growth should be considered not in terms of composition but, rather, in terms of the relationship between exports and imports, domestic production, and domestic demand. Figure 1.2 shows the change in import dependence—that is, the ratio of imports to domestic demand—and the change in the export/production ratio of textile products (except raw silk) as well as chemicals, metals (except copper ingots), and machinery. As is shown in Chapter 2 (see Figure 2.1 (B)), the decline in import dependence signals the advent of import substitution, and the rise in the export/production ratio indicates development of the export stage. When the export/production ratio exceeds the import/demand ratio, the sector moves to the position of being a net exporter; this is the demarcation point between the import substitution and export stages (see Figure 2.1). Using this standard, the two graphs in Figure 1.2 show that import substitution in textile products progressed during the periods 1874–83 to 1892–1901, and the export stage was reached by the period 1892–1901. In the other industries—chemicals, metals, and machinery—the import/demand ratio continued to increase, reached a plateau during the periods 1892–1901 to 1902–11, and rapidly declined thereafter. It was not until the post–Second World War years that the export/production ratio was greater than the import/demand ratio in these industries. Thus, it appears that although import substitution in heavy industrial goods grew from 1900 to the Second World War, the export stage emerged only after the Second World War.

However, the export/production ratio of machinery alone has tended to outstrip those of chemicals and metals in the 1970s. In the periods 1971–75 and 1976–80, the export/production ratio for machinery alone was 19.0 and

24.6, respectively, whereas for chemicals and metals as a group the export/production ratio was 9.6 and 8.0 in the same periods (Yamazawa and Yamamoto 1979a). This reflects the shift in Japan's comparative advantage after the first oil shock in 1973 from the basic materials-producing sectors to the processing-assembly sectors. Moreover, even within the machinery group the emphasis shifted away from the highly labor-intensive industries such as shipbuilding and radio assembly to the technology-intensive industries such as production of automobiles, video cassette recorders (VCRs), and industrial machinery. Eventually, this might be referred to as the third stage of structural change.

Figure 1.2
Import Substitution and Export Expansion of Two Major Industries

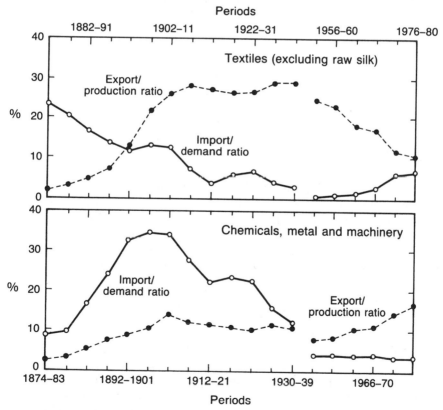

Note: Overlapping decade averages.

Sources: Calculated by the author from Yamazawa and Yamamoto (1979a: tables 1-13, 1-15, 1-17) and Shinohara (1972: table 1).

The import/demand and export/production ratios of such sectors as processed food and wood products have remained low. These are sectors that strongly depend on indigenous raw materials and for which domestic demand absorbs the major portion of domestic production. To a certain extent, this could also be said of ceramics and miscellaneous products. The trend in the import/demand and export/production ratios for all industrial goods is the aggregate of the different trends in these three product categories (light and heavy industrial goods, food and wood products, etc.), but the trend becomes ambiguous and is generally lower, a reflection of the overwhelming share of food-processing.

Import substitution and export expansion did not occur at once over the entire range of modern industries. Import substitution began with light industrial products, such as textiles, and was gradually expanded from one industry to the next to include heavy industries such as chemicals, metals, and machinery. Successful import substitution was then followed by export expansion. Fundamentally, the change in Japanese trade can be summarized as the movement from import substitution to export expansion, first in the light industries, then in the heavy industries. Thus, changes in industrial production follow a predictable pattern.

Three stages in Japan's pattern of trade can be identified. The first stage consists of the export of primary products and the import of light industrial goods. The second consists of the export of light industrial goods and the import of heavy industrial goods as well as raw materials. The export of heavy industrial goods and import of raw materials characterize the third stage.

In the first stage, as a result of primary product exports, import substitution of light industrial goods could proceed. In the second stage, as light industrial goods are successfully exported, import substitution in heavy industrial goods takes place. In the third stage, the export of heavy industrial goods is achieved. There is some overlap between stages, and in every stage, a fundamental and discernible pattern of trade emerges.

In attempting to delineate these stages, the point in time marking the transition between stages one and two could be set at 1895 and that between stages two and three at 1955. This can be seen in Table 1.4, where in the first half of the 1890s the import share of light industrial goods and the export share of primary products was large (see Table 1.3). Then, around 1895, the export/production ratio of textile products began to exceed their import/demand ratio, delineating the start of stage two. The early 1950s saw the advent of stage three, when raw material imports exceeded heavy industrial goods imports and claimed a large share of total imports. During the first half of the 1950s, the export share of light industrial goods was about equal to that of heavy industrial goods. However, the export/production ratios of chemicals, metals, and machinery finally exceeded their import/demand ratios in the second half of the 1950s.[7]

INDUSTRIAL EXPORT GROWTH
AND THE TRADE BALANCE

The relationship between changes in the industrial output structure and changes in the trade structure has been demonstrated, and the mechanism (the catching-up product cycle) through which these large structural changes occurred has been highlighted. It has been shown that there is a 30- to 40-year lag between light and heavy industrialization. To summarize, there were shifts over time in four variables—output, exports, imports, and the raw material imports that were inputs to industrial production. Figure 1.3 shows the trends for these four variables in constant 1934–36 prices. Because the data are plotted on a semi-log graph, the slopes of the lines can be interpreted as growth rates.

Except for small undulations, the monotonic growth of industrial output during the period up to the Second World War is obvious. The trend continues in the post–Second World War period and exhibits an even steeper rate of increase. In contrast, increases in raw material imports initially exceeded that of output, and after reaching a tenth of output value in the 1900s, changes in raw material imports gradually began to synchronize with output. This trend continued into the post–Second World War period. Industrial imports also grew faster than output until around the first decade of this century, when the rate of growth settled into a slow yet steadily rising trend that, except for a spurt of growth after the First World War, has been maintained in the postwar period. Moreover, during the early years industrial exports initially grew at the same rate as imports. After 1925, industrial exports were higher than industrial imports. In the periods both before and after the Second World War, growth of industrial exports was higher than growth of industrial output.

The relationship between the long-run trend in industrial production and raw material imports is important, as the latter constitutes indispensable inputs to the former. The elasticity of industrial output with respect to raw material imports was 2.6 in the period before the First World War. The elasticity dropped to 0.7 during the interwar period and rose to 0.9 in the period after the Second World War.[8]

The abnormally high elasticity for raw material imports in the period 1874–83 may be explained by the shift from domestic to imported raw material inputs. For instance, in this period the use of domestic cotton in cotton production failed, and a shift to dependence on imported raw cotton took place. This was also the case for iron ore and coal in the decade after the turn of the century. The low value of imported inputs in the interwar period reflects the difficulty of importing during the second half of the 1930s, which resulted from the mounting tensions between Japan and the United States. After the Second World War elasticity remained close to 1.0; thus, raw material

Figure 1.3
Industrial Output, Exports, Imports, and Raw Material Imports

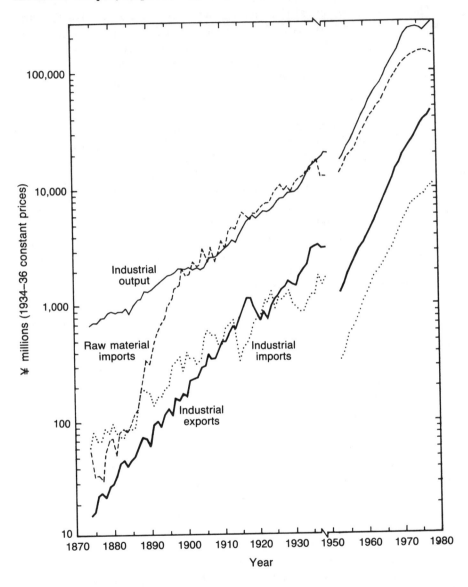

Notes: In seven-year moving average. Raw material imports are plotted at ten times the scale of industrial output, industrial imports, and industrial exports.

Sources: Yamazawa and Yamamoto (1979a: tables 1-3, 1-4) and Shinohara (1972: table 2).

imports grew in proportion to the increase in production, which is to be expected under the assumption of fixed commodity composition and technological coefficients. In reality, however, large shifts were observed in both commodity composition and technological coefficients, and their influences must have offset each other as the trend seems to indicate. After the two oil shocks of the 1970s, the degree of output responsiveness declined due to the decrease in the number of raw material-consuming industries and the technological changes that led to conservation of raw material inputs.

The movements in industrial imports, exports, and raw material imports relative to industrial output can be analyzed to determine the trend of the trade balance. Figure 1.4 shows the seven-year moving average of the ratios of industrial exports to the sum of industrial commodity and raw material imports, as well as the ratios of current account receipts to payments (a five-year moving average is used for the post–Second World War period). Since the former is directly related to the trade balance, it is simply referred to as the industrial trade balance. When the ratio is equal to 1.0, trade is said to

Figure 1.4
Long-Term Swings in the Balance of Payments

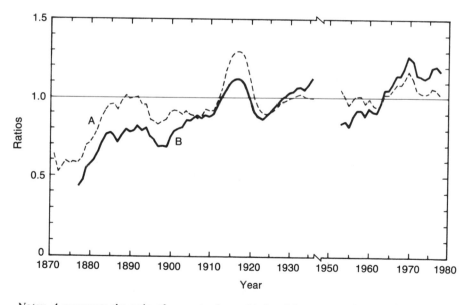

Year

Notes: *A* represents the ratio of current values of industrial exports to the sum of industrial imports plus raw material imports. *B* represents the ratio of total receipts to total payments in the current accounts. Both series are smoothed by seven-year moving averages (five-year for post–Second World War years).

Source: Yamazawa (1984).

be in balance, and when it is greater (less) than 1.0 there is a surplus (deficit). In the periods both before and after the Second World War, the industrial trade balance, although exhibiting cyclical behavior, nevertheless showed a strongly rising trend overall (that is, an improvement in the balance of trade).

This long-run rising trend corresponds to the upward trend in the long swings of the industrial output growth cycle. Thus, the growth rate of industrial output accelerated as the structure was shifting from light to heavy industrialization. Meanwhile, the growth in raw material imports, although undergoing similar undulations, was decelerating. Moreover, the growth in imports of industrial goods—except for the import rush of the First World War—was also weakening as import substitution was being achieved in textiles and in heavy industrial goods. The result was a steady improvement in the industrial trade balance. From a trade deficit in most of the preceding period, the trade balance ratio finally exceeded 1.0 around 1930; the same scenario repeated itself in the post–Second World War period, so that in the latter half of the 1960s continuing surpluses resulted. Whereas the problem of international trade deficits plagues the industrialization drives of contemporary developing countries, industrial growth seems to have been self-reinforcing for Japan.

The critical components in Japan's current account balance are exports and imports of industrial goods and imports of raw materials, although trade in services and primary goods other than imports of raw materials are also included. (The industrial goods trade balance outweighs by far the services trade balance.) Trade balances in other primary goods as well as the trade in services balances showed surpluses until 1925 and from the Second World War until 1963, but from 1925 to the Second World War and after 1963 they posted deficits. Between 1925 and the Second World War, the deficits were caused by problems in the export of primary goods and increases in food imports. In the case of the post-1963 deficit, the trade in services deficit was responsible. These can thus be considered changes in trends rather than cyclical changes.

Japan's current account balance shifted from a deficit to a surplus position as its economy developed. Its long-term capital balance tended to offset the current account imbalance, resulting in an equilibrium of its basic balance (current account balance plus long-term capital balance). The long-term capital inflows of the period 1895–1914 were partly encouraged by the government to finance the persistent current account deficit during the period. But to continue long-term capital inflows (issues of bonds by local governments and public enterprises), the government would have to tighten its money supply (under the gold standard) and decelerate the heavy industrialization. On the other hand, long-term capital outflows were large (1) during the First World War, (2) after the end of the 1920s, and (3) after 1965. The first and third outflows came from large current account surpluses and did not cause any payment difficulties. The second outflow (investment in Manchuria in the 1920s) exceeded the current account surplus and led to deficits in the basic balance, but since investment was undertaken within the yen bloc, it did not lead to balance-of-payments constraints.

CHARACTERISTICS OF JAPANESE ECONOMIC DEVELOPMENT AND INTERNATIONAL TRADE

With regard to the long-term trends in Japanese economic development and trade growth, the following characteristics have been observed:

1. Rapid industrial growth lay at the core of Japan's economic development and was accomplished by an even greater expansion in exports and imports, reflecting Japan's resource endowment conditions.

2. The industrial growth process illustrates the CPC model of development, wherein several modern industries introduced from abroad first achieved import substitution and later developed into export industries. This can be considered a suitable development strategy for later-developing countries.

3. As a result of CPC development in individual industries, remarkable structural changes in the economy took place in terms of the domestic output structure and the export and import structures.

4. The sequencing of CPC development from light to heavy industries made possible the long-term positive trend—that is, the accumulation of surpluses—in the trade balance, thereby avoiding the balance-of-payments constraints in the latter stages of the development process.

Chapter 2 examines the mechanism behind each of these characteristics more closely and presents a Japanese model of economic development and trade.

Two

Interaction Between Trade
and Development: A Japanese Model

The previous chapter overviewed the long-term trends of Japan's economic development and identified some characteristics of industrial development and the expansion of international trade. Unlike the one-way cause and effect often assumed in international economics textbooks, a two-way interaction has been observed between the two—that is, a close association between changes in the industrial structure and changes in the trade structure, each promoting the other in the process of economic development.

Long-term industrial development was successfully achieved in Japan through the interaction of trade and production. This interaction between trade and production forms the basis of what can be called a Japanese model of development. However, this interaction is not unique to Japan; thus, the development strategy adopted by the Japanese may be regarded as a suitable development strategy for newly industrializing economies (NIEs) today. The principal task of this book is to describe the Japanese model in detail and clarify its underlying mechanism. The *catching-up product cycle* (CPC) model describes industrial development through the interaction of trade and production. The chapters that follow exemplify the CPC model in a few major industries and clarify the roles played by firms and the government. This chapter provides a schematic representation of the CPC model and substantiates its use in the chapters that follow. In the latter part of this chapter, the model is extended to analyze the interaction of production and trade at the aggregate level.

CATCHING-UP PRODUCT CYCLE: THE BASIC TYPE

For countries that began their industrialization later than the United Kingdom, France, the United States, Germany and Russia (hereafter referred to as late-starting countries), the development of modern industry typically began with the import of a new product from more advanced countries, followed by import-substituting production, and finally progressed to production for export abroad. The growth sequence of imports, production, and exports was first highlighted by Kaname Akamatsu (1943 and 1961) in his statistical study of trade and production of a few modern industries in Japan before the Second World War. It was Akamatsu who first used the term *flock formation of flying wild geese pattern* of industrial development to describe the shape of import, production, and export growth curves and who pointed out that the pattern was typical of industrial development in a NIE, particularly Japan.[1]

This pattern has been empirically substantiated in many major manufacturing industries in Japan and has often been cited in studies of Japan's economic growth (Kojima 1958; Shinohara 1962; Baba and Tatemoto 1968; Yamazawa 1972, 1984). Akamatsu's thesis was first translated into English in 1956 and was introduced to Western Europe by Sautter (1973). Kojima (1973) renamed the pattern the *catching-up product cycle* (CPC) after its association with the *product cycle* model of Vernon (1964). The new name conveys more precisely the mechanism of industrial development that has been adopted in this study, but the original name has remained popular. Yamazawa (1984), Pasha (1987), and Chen (1989) have further extended the pattern to include the transfer of modern industries to East and Southeast Asian countries. The pattern has also been frequently cited in trade policy discussions on Pacific economic cooperation (Kojima 1973; Ohkita 1987; Yamazawa 1988b).

CPC—that is, the sequence of imports, production, and exports—may at first appear to be self-evident and require no further investigation. But there are many questions about the CPC process that need to be answered. For example, why does the CPC process start earlier in one industry than in another? Why do certain industries succeed in import substitution and export promotion more quickly than others? Why do some industries fail to follow CPC? Under what conditions is the growth of an industry preceded by imports and followed by exports, and what factors determine the speed of import substitution and export expansion? The answers to these questions are not self-evident and require theoretical explanation with empirical verification as is attempted in this book.

Two extensions to Akamatsu's original CPC model are developed to explain the new problems arising after the Second World War. First, with many Japanese industries reaching the export stage after the Second World War, there was concern over what stage should come next. International specialization grew beyond the confines of commodity trade to include technology transfer and direct foreign investment (DFI). Second, the CPC model has spread to East and Southeast Asian countries, enabling their rapid industrialization over the past two decades. This chapter also attempts to incorporate these new situations into the schematic outline of the CPC model.

Panel A in Figure 2.1 illustrates the CPC model of a modern industrial product with four growth curves representing imports (M), domestic production (S), domestic demand (D), and exports (X). Theoretically, the growth of domestic demand leads CPC development. Statistically, domestic demand

Figure 2.1
Schematic Diagram of the Catching-Up Product Cycle Development of an Industry

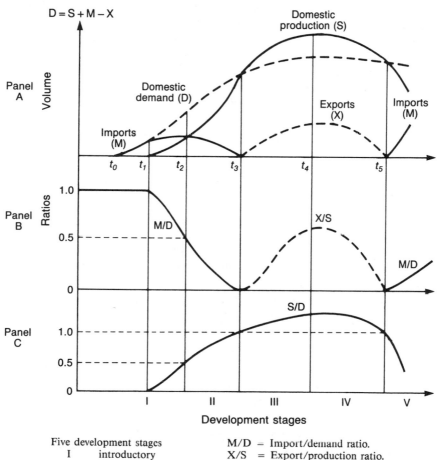

Five development stages
I   introductory
II   import substitution
III export
IV   mature
V   reverse import

M/D = Import/demand ratio.
X/S = Export/production ratio.
S/D = Production/demand ratio.

is defined to be production plus imports minus exports (D = S + M − X), but its growth curve determines the basic pattern of development for a particular industry. Panel B illustrates the change for the two key ratios, the import/demand ratio (M/D) and the export/production ratio (X/S), in the process of CPC development. The two ratios are often used to measure the progress of import substitution and export expansion, respectively. In this schematic diagram, exports begin only after imports cease. In reality, however, products are differentiated within the same category, and the export of lower-quality products can occur at the same time that import of sophisticated or higher-quality ones continues.

Panel C in Figure 2.1 illustrates the CPC with a single growth curve that represents the production/demand ratio (S/D). Five development stages— *introductory, import substitution, export, mature,* and *reverse import*—are distinguished by the specific values of S/D, namely, 0.5, 1.0, and, again, the maximum, 1.0. Although the values are arbitrary, distinguishing the stages remains useful in describing the life cycle of an industry. The main characteristics of these five stages are described below.

At the *introductory* stage, a new product is introduced via imports from advanced countries, and domestic consumption of the product increases gradually. Domestic production begins through imitation or borrowed technology, but the domestic product cannot compete with the imported product because of the inferior quality and high production costs of the domestically produced good.

In the *import substitution* stage, domestic consumption increases rapidly, which encourages production to expand at a faster rate than demand, thereby decreasing the share of imports in the domestic market. Production technology is standardized, and large-scale production becomes possible, with the domestic product gradually replacing the imported one. Product quality improves and the price falls below the price of the imported product.

In the *export* stage, the domestically produced good begins to be exported. The growth of domestic demand slows down, but with the increase in export growth, the increases in production can be maintained.

In the *mature* stage, both domestic demand and exports slowly decrease, preventing further expansion of production. Exports begin to decrease when the domestic product fails to compete with similar products from late-starting countries.

Finally, in the *reverse import* stage, products of late-starting countries, which are cheaper and of no less inferior quality, begin to be imported and gradually replace domestic products in the domestic market, which contributes to the accelerating decline of domestic production.

The five stages describe the life cycle of an industry's development, but what mechanism underlies the shift from one stage to the next? At the introductory stage, the learning-by-doing effect in both consumption and production plays an important role. As consumption of the new product grows, market conditions are right for domestic entrepreneurs to begin production. As production experience accumulates, domestic producers gradually improve quality and reduce costs. Factors common to both the import substitution and export expansion stages help to make the shift from one to the other a continuous process. In particular, the growth of domestic and foreign demand for the good enables substitution of the domestic product for foreign products in the domestic market (import substitution) initially, and then in foreign markets (export expansion). Decreasing unit costs are later realized through operating on a larger scale, adoption of better technology, and accumulated experience in both labor and management, all of which are made possible through the expansion of production and increasing capacity investment.

Entrepreneurship and the accumulation of managerial resources specific to an industry underlie capacity investment and decreasing unit costs in the process of CPC development. Managerial resources include not only capital for capacity investment, but also production and marketing technologies specific to the industry, as well as managers, engineers, foremen, and other skilled workers embodying industry-specific technology. Domestic production is initiated by an entrepreneur who, with foresight, observes the increase in demand for the new product in the domestic market and realizes the profitability of import substitution. He may be handicapped by the inadequate availability of managerial resources but will gradually accumulate them as he produces and sells his product. The learning-by-doing effect in production and the increased competitiveness of domestic products both reflect the achievement of accumulated managerial resources.

The shift from the export to the mature stage is caused by stagnant demand growth, which discourages capacity investment and further cost reductions. As long as export growth steadily increases, it will offset stagnant domestic demand and lead to further expansion of domestic production, thus postponing the mature stage. However, producers often lack knowledge of market conditions abroad, and their decisions to invest in capacity expansion tends to be influenced by domestic demand. It is akin to the emphasis Linder (1961) places on the domestic market. On the other hand, as import substitution occurs in late-starting countries, the domestic demand of these late-starting countries begins to be met by their own production and the exporting country will have to decrease its production of the good. The process of decreasing exports will continue to the point when exports cease altogether. Imports will begin again, initiating the reverse import stage. These last two stages are continuous and are moved by a common factor, which is a decrease in competitiveness resulting from the entry of products from late-starting countries into the domestic markets of exporting countries.

How do government policies affect CPC development? They can either accelerate or decelerate CPC at each stage of its development. During the introductory stage, governments can encourage local or foreign firms to initiate new industries by means of subsidies or tax exemptions. A government may even establish a state enterprise to begin a new industry and finance losses for a fixed period of time, as is often the case in strategic industries such as iron and steel. During the two import stages, import substitution and reverse import, a government can support domestic production by affecting the competition between the domestic product and the imported one. The aims of government policies in the two different import stages, however, are not the same. In the import substitution stage, import substitution is promoted through government policies that restrict imports or subsidize domestic producers. This is typically done to protect infant industries. On the other hand, during the reverse import stage, a government assists domestic production by slowing the inflow of or restricting imports or by subsidizing production. In this case, protection is usually implemented to avoid the high social and economic costs of adjustment in declining industries. However, the increase in imports should not be restricted too long.

During both the export and mature stages, a government's ability to affect the CPC is reduced. Some governments promote the initiation of new product exports with subsidies, but continuing export subsidies indefinitely is costly. Thus, the main mechanisms for these stages in CPC development are market forces such as growth in demand and decreasing costs.

It has already been confirmed that the major modern industries of Japan followed CPC development. It is never easy to match production and trade data for well-defined homogeneous products. For broadly defined products, the difference in product mixes among production, imports, and exports should be considered and price indexing should be employed to obtain series at constant prices.[2]

It is not sufficient to construct CPC curves for individual industries; analysis of the development of selected industries in the chapters that follow also considers the other relevant variables. Chapters 4 and 5 analyze the CPC of two major industries, textiles and steel. Chapter 5 presents a simple econometric model that incorporates such variables as domestic and foreign income and relative domestic/foreign prices. The model is extended to simulate the alternating performance of import substitution and export expansion under some counter-factual assumptions. The two industries illustrate successful CPCs with and without government protection. Chapters 7 to 9 analyze policy aspects of CPC development, and Chapter 10 looks at the relevance of the CPC model to contemporary developing countries.[3]

Variation 1: Linkage to Other Industries

Akamatsu (1943) observes CPC development in a succession of industries. Diagrammatically, the CPC development of other industries can be illustrated by superimposing import, production, and export curves (as in Panel A of Figure 2.1) as well as other industry life-cycle curves (S/D curves [as in Panel C of Figure 2.1]), over the observed set of curves of the first industry (with some time lags) along the same time scale (overlap is illustrated in Figures 5.3 and 10.1). Akamatsu describes the overlap of curves as a variation of the CPC model. The resulting diagram bears a resemblance to a flock formation of flying wild geese, but the relationship between the first CPC and succeeding CPCs has deeper economic meaning than its mere resemblance in shape. The linkage between the industry curves reflects the mechanism underlying the diversification of the production structure in the process of industrialization.

Four identifiable forces affect the diversification of industrial structure. The first force is the increased availability of capital. The factor proportion theory (or Heckscher-Ohlin theory) of international economics is applied to the process of structural change in production and trade as industrialization proceeds. Industrial production is mobile and can be located in any country by importing material inputs unavailable domestically. The final output is produced by combining labor and capital with materials. Individual industries differ in their capital and labor composition; light manufacturing industries require relatively more labor, whereas heavy manufacturing industries require relatively more capital. The two-commodity, two-factor model of the factor proportion theory determines the output composition of two industries, so that all available capital and labor are fully employed. In Japan, where labor was abundant at the early stage of industrialization, light industry was relatively larger than heavy industry, but as Japan accumulated capital the share of heavy industry increased.

The statistical classification of *light* and *heavy* industry does not coincide exactly with the distinction between labor- and capital-intensity in the factor proportion theory. Although metal refining and petrochemicals production, which are classified as heavy industries, require relatively few laborers to maintain and operate capital equipment, the assembly of machinery, which is also considered a heavy industry, requires many, especially skilled laborers. On the other hand, light industry requires relatively more unskilled laborers and is characterized by small-scale operations and technology that is easily absorbed even in modern factories. H. G. Johnson's (1968) capital-theoretical approach resolved this discrepancy between theory and statistics. In addition to physical capital such as machinery and equipment, both the skill and technological know-how embodied in laborers and engineers are considered to be forms of capital. If only unskilled labor is defined as labor and all forms of capital are broadly defined as capital (including managerial resources), then the factor proportion theory serves well to explain heavy industrialization in the process of capital accumulation.

Thus, the two-factor, two-commodity model explains how capital-intensive production expands—that is, how the industrial structure is diversified—so that accumulated capital is fully employed. If the industries are disaggregated, the different forms of capital and technology specific to individual industries have to be distinguished in order to explain the actual process of industrialization; this forms the basis of the multi-factor, multi-commodity model. It is well known that there is no unique allocation of the many factors among the many industries in such a model (Caves and Jones 1973: chaps. 7 and 8). That is, changes in production and the trade structure cannot be determined by full employment alone. Additional factors have been introduced in order to determine the diversification of the industrial structure (see the sectoral models of Kojima [1958: chap. 7], Inada et al. [1972], and the nuclear sector model of Bensusan-Butt [1954]). The accumulation of capital provides, then, the first explanation for the broad diversification of the industrial structure, but it must be supplemented by additional factors affecting actual diversification at a more disaggregated level. The CPC model meets this need.

Entrepreneurship is viewed as the force behind the decision to begin a new industry. The basic CPC model reveals a few important determinants for the expansion of production in a newly introduced industry: growth of domestic demand, realization of decreasing unit costs as production expands, and protection provided by government. The entrepreneur's decision to begin a new industry is affected by the expected value of these variables but these variables do not explain the situation fully. Educational background and business acumen, for example, help shape decisions (Yamazawa and Tambunlertchai 1985). Chapter 6 analyzes the CPC model for trading companies and a service industry handling foreign transactions; Japanese trading companies that have helped manufacturers determine advantageous shifts in comparative advantage are also discussed.

Forward and backward linkage effects assist the transfer of CPC from the first industry to the others. In forward linkages, industries relying on the input of the first industry's output are assisted by following the CPC model, and in backward linkages, industries supplying inputs to the first industry benefit from increases in demand. Chapter 4 provides two econometric examples of backward linkages in the cotton textile industry, and Figure 5.5 shows an overlap of CPC curves, which reflects industrial diversification. Chapter 3 analyzes the export growth of the silk industry, which, although it was the first modern manufacturing industry established and the biggest earner of foreign exchange in its first few decades, neither followed CPC development nor benefited from linkage effects.

The learning-by-doing effect helped the transfer of one industry's CPC to the other. CPC development is generally achieved first in goods for which production is standardized and then in goods requiring more sophisticated production processes. This process has been observed most clearly in the production of low-count and high-count cotton yarns, and black-and-white and color televisions. However, owing to elements common to both production and marketing technology for each pair, the CPC of sophisticated products may be cut short because the know-how gained in the production of less sophisticated products can reduce the need for the trial and error method in both the introductory and import substitution stages. Production can then be geared to the export stage from the beginning.

Variation 2: International Transfer of CPC, Direct Foreign Investment, and Technology Transfer

The transfer of CPC from one country to another can result in variations of the CPC model; the overlap of an industry's life-cycle curves among countries at different development stages illustrates variations of flock formations of flying wild geese (see Figure 10.1). This can be explained by the basic type of CPC in a late-starting country, which is also affected significantly by the transfer of managerial resources from an early- to a late-starting country. Managerial resources can be imported from abroad rather than generated and accumulated locally to hasten CPC development.

In many industries in Japan, indigenous firms accumulated their own managerial resources through trial and error, using domestic capital and relying on imported machines, equipment, and materials. In a few industries, however, CPC was hastened by introducing managerial resources from abroad. New technology was introduced under licensing agreements (technology transfer) or, if foreign suppliers of technology insisted, through investment in kind under joint-venture agreements with the foreign firms (direct foreign investment—DFI).

Inward DFI and technology transfer have been observed in the introductory and import substitution stages, but in the export and mature stages outward DFI and technology transfer can occur and tend to accelerate CPC development in the investing country. Outward DFI and technology transfer occur only after enough managerial expertise has been acquired. Outward DFI is further distinguished between the export and mature stages. Export stage DFI primarily supports export marketing and aims to secure a share of export markets. Thus exports and DFI increase in a parallel manner. On the other hand, during the mature stage, DFI can be used to relocate domestic production abroad to take advantage of cheaper input prices or further market expansion: in this case, DFI is a substitute for domestic exports.

DFI and technology transfer accelerate import substitution in host, late-starting countries, as has been frequently observed in East and Southeast Asian countries for the past two decades. Both DFI and technology transfer have enabled rapid catching-up industrialization in these countries. Host countries and domestic policies on DFI and technology transfer may encourage or restrict them. However, such policies are often influenced by policy objectives other than trying to deliberately control CPC, including correcting the balance of payments or providing employment.

Domestic production sometimes begins entirely with foreign entrepreneurs who control 100 percent of the equity shares and with imported managerial resources, which is consistent with the product cycle model proposed by Vernon (1964). In this situation, the trial and error method can be avoided, much of the learning-by-doing process in the product cycle model can be shortened, and the foreign firm can begin to export immediately, thus cutting short the CPC. However, only a minimum of managerial resources is usually transferred to the host country, and the industry is never able to produce new products or employ new processes on its own. Every new product or process has to be introduced from abroad—a situation that does not fit the definition of a transfer of new industry.

The transfer of new products and new technology from advanced countries in one form or another is indispensable for the start of CPC in a late-starting country, but the manner in which this transfer occurs significantly affects the later performance of CPC. The manner of technology transfer is determined by the entrepreneurial skills of local firms and the negotiations between local and foreign firms. The last section of Chapter 7 explains how Japanese electrical appliance firms began as joint ventures with American and European firms but quickly evolved into independent enterprises in the 1920s. Tran (1988) analyzes the similar experience of Korean synthetic fiber producers in the 1970s. Chen (1989) extends the CPC model to promote the transfer of the electronics industry among the Asian NIEs and ASEAN members in such a way that industrial adjustment is coordinated in the region.

EFFECT OF TERMS OF TRADE ON CPC DEVELOPMENT

A necessary condition for successful CPC is the realization of decreasing costs in the expansion of production, which makes domestic products cheaper relative to foreign products both in the domestic market (through import substitution) and in foreign markets (through export expansion). In order to examine this mechanism, it is necessary to investigate changes in prices. In Japan, it was, of course, the declining relative prices of domestic to foreign products that promoted substitution, while all absolute prices, both domestically and in foreign markets, moved parallel with one another and showed a common trend, rising slowly in the period before the First World War, rising steeply during the war, and steadily declining throughout the 1920s (Yamazawa and Yamamoto 1979a: chap. 1).

Figure 2.2 shows four types of relative price changes. The commodity terms of trade (TT in Figure 2.2) is defined as the total export price index divided by the total import price. Since this ratio gives the amount of imports that could be exchanged per unit of exports, it is often used as an indicator of changes in the gains from trade. The effect of the terms of trade on Japan's export expansion in the pre–Second World War period has been widely debated. Over the entire prewar period, Japan's terms of trade decreased. According to Shinohara (1962: chap. 10), this decline enabled the expansion of Japan's exports, but Kojima (1958: chap. 3) claims that the decline in the terms of trade contributed to export growth mainly during the interwar period. A new estimate by Yamazawa and Yamamoto (1979a), shown as TT in Figure 2.2, seems to support Kojima. The declining trend in the terms of trade is clear and is, without doubt, related to the export growth during the periods 1908–18 and 1924–36, but not during the period of rapid export expansion before 1900. On the other hand, during the high-growth period after 1945, the terms of trade were stable, declining steeply only during the period after 1973 when the price of oil and other raw materials increased dramatically.

The factoral terms of trade (FTT) are derived by introducing labor productivity in the export industries (e.g., manufacturing) into the terms of trade calculation. FTT measures the volume of imports that could be exchanged per man-hour of labor input in the export industry and complements the commodity terms of trade figure. FTT increased even before 1908 and rose steeply in the 1920s and after the Second World War. The sharp increase in the last two periods was the result of a remarkable increase in labor productivity.

The other two price indices in Figure 2.2 offer a better means to measure real price effects because they compare prices of Japan's exports and domestic prices with comparable world prices. The relative export price (REP) compares manufactured export prices in Japan (P_x in yen) with the corresponding world market prices (P_w in U.S. dollars), adjusted by the exchange rate (R = yen/US\$). Represented as $(P_x \cdot R)/P_w$, this equation measures the competitiveness of Japan's exports abroad. The other index, the relative import price (RIP), compares domestic and import prices (P and P_m in yen) of manufactures in the domestic market (P_m/P). Extending back to 1898 and including the whole post–Second World War period, the REP shows a longer declining trend than do the terms of trade. The RIP, on the other hand, exhibits more variability with an overall declining trend that is offset by increases during the periods 1906–17 and 1922–36.

Figure 2.2
Terms of Trade, and Relative Export and Import Prices: 1885–1980

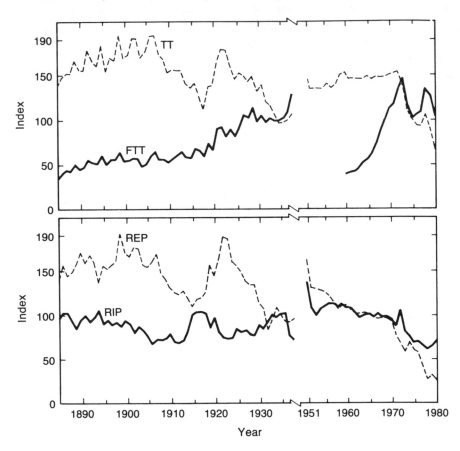

Notes:

TT: Commodity terms of trade (total export price divided by total import price).

FTT: Factoral terms of trade (terms of trade multiplied by productivity index in the export sector).

REP: Relative export price $((P_x{\cdot}R)/P_w$: Japan's export price of manufactures, P_x in yen, divided by corresponding world market price, P_w in U.S. dollars, adjusted by the exchange rate, R, yen/US$).

RIP: Relative import price $(P_m/P$: Japan's domestic price of manufactures in yen divided by the import price of manufactures in yen).

The base period is 1934–36 for all four series before the Second World War, but 1965 for the REP and RIP series and 1975 for the TT and FTT series after the Second World War.

Source: Yamazawa and Yamamoto (1979a: chap. 2).

The lack of an obvious trend of the RIP partly results from the combined effects of diverse price movements in different manufacturing industries. Against the overall trend of rising prices, there emerges a clear pattern that shows modern industries had only small price increases, whereas in traditional industries such as food processing and wood products prices increased steadily. Because traditional industries generally did not have declining unit costs as did import substituting industries, and because traditional industries occupied a greater share of manufacturing, the overall trend of the RIP is obscured. On the other hand, within modern industries such as textiles, metals and chemicals, which chose import substitution and export expansion as the means to growth, domestic prices declined relative to import prices, thereby increasing the RIP.[4]

Despite the ambiguities of the movement of aggregate relative prices, it is worthwhile to investigate their effects on the CPC development of the Japanese manufacturing industry as a whole. Table 2.1 shows the estimation of export and import equations for manufactures for three separate periods. Both equations follow the usual specification and include income and price variables. The RIP is multiplied by the sum (1 + the average tariff rate) in order to include the effects of tariff protection. The First World War years are excluded from the estimation of exports because of the unavailability of statistics for world trade volume and prices. These years are, however, included in the estimation of imports. A First World War dummy variable has been included so that the limited availability of manufactured imports during the war can be taken into account. All coefficients but one (the price coefficient in the import equation after the Second World War) are significant and consistent with theoretical expectations. These findings support the theory that changing relative prices associated with the decreasing costs from import substitution and export expansion have a significant impact on industrial development. It should be noted that the price effect prevails over the income effect in the export equation in the second and third periods. The actual price effect, which is measured by multiplying the coefficient by the relative price change, was more significant in export expansion during the interwar period when world trade stagnated.

On the other hand, raw material imports (equation 3) are related to manufacturing production, although with decreasing impact in later years, as is evidenced by a coefficient less than unity. Any increase in manufacturing production would therefore lead to a less-than-proportionate increase in raw materials imports. This tendency partly contributed to the balance-of-trade surplus at later stages of industrial development.

Equations 4 and 5 support the preceding discussion of the effects of domestic and export prices of manufactures. Domestic prices were affected positively by the wage rate and raw materials prices, but were affected negatively by productivity increases. Export prices increased less than domestic prices in the period of overall rising prices (with elasticity less than unity before 1913 and after the Second World War). Furthermore, the export prices tended to lag behind domestic prices, as is evidenced by the negative time-trend coefficient, which implies higher productivity increases and decreasing costs in export production than in the rest of manufacturing production.

LONG SWINGS AND STRUCTURAL CHANGES

The export and import equations for total manufacturing only provide empirical verification of the importance of changing relative prices at best, because they represent the aggregate effects of CPC development of individual manufacturing industries. The composition of industries within total manufacturing changed as individual industry CPCs proceeded at different times. The changes were not smooth but were characterized by long swings associated

Table 2.1
Estimation of Equations for Export, Import, and Related Variables

1. Export of Manufactures

Period	Constant	World trade volume	Relative export price	$\bar{R}^2$ (DW)
1885–1913	7.07	2.73 (20.4)	−0.98 (3.0)	0.971 (1.59)
1921–38	7.73	1.18 (3.4)	−1.79 (10.1)	0.925 (0.69)
1953–70	7.92	1.50 (15.3)	−2.13 (5.4)	0.997 (1.06)

2. Import of Manufactures

Period	Constant	Japan's GDP	Relative import price including tariff	First World War dummy	$\bar{R}^2$ (DW)
1885–1913	−12.52	2.08 (9.1)	−1.83 (3.6)		0.958 (1.49)
1914–38	−4.04	1.15 (8.7)	−1.43 (7.3)	−0.17 (2.1)	0.968 (1.94)
1953–70	−10.58	1.70 (14.5)	−0.48 (0.5)		0.979 (0.43)

3. Import of Raw Material

Period	Constant	Manufacturing output	Relative import price of raw material	First World War dummy	$\bar{R}^2$ (DW)
1885–1913	−15.03	2.57 (15.4)	−1.96 (4.3)		0.979 (0.84)
1914–38	0.92	0.66 (10.1)		−0.19 (2.9)	0.961 (1.51)
1953–70	−1.87	0.91 (44.9)			0.996 (1.84)

with fluctuations in industrial activity. Figure 2.3 shows the growth cycle of Japan's manufacturing output (A) and the corresponding moving average of the coefficients of structural change in manufacturing output (B). The output growth cycle shows a long swing of around 20 years' duration and a clear upward trend through swings (connecting one peak with the next, and one trough with the next) until the early 1970s when it declined abruptly (Ohkawa and Rosovsky 1973).

A relationship between curves A and B can be observed by comparing the peaks in curve A with the peaks in curve B at least until 1970. If an industry's share increases steadily by say 2 percent every year, curve B will be flat. But if the industry's share increases rapidly for several years and then ceases for another several years, curve B will peak, which indicates a boom in industrial activity. During industrial booms (peaks of the growth cycle), all industries do not expand simultaneously. Some industries expand more than

Table 2.1 Continued.

4. Domestic Price of Manufactures (P)

Period	Constant	Wage	Labor productivity	Material price	$\bar{R}^2$ (DW)
1885–1913	0.75	0.77 (10.2)	−0.16 (1.2)		0.985 (0.83)
1914–38	0.33	0.16 (2.6)	−0.24 (3.0)	0.63 (7.6)	0.924 (1.29)
1953–70	0.08	0.29 (5.2)	−0.09 (1.8)	0.35 (5.5)	0.986 (1.84)

5. Export Price of Manufactures

Period	Constant	Domestic price manufactures	Time-trend	$\bar{R}^2$ (DW)
1885–1913	0.56	0.90 (3.5)	−0.011 (1.1)	0.902 (0.63)
1914–38	1.31	1.06 (11.3)	−0.026 (7.9)	0.982 (0.90)
1953–70	1.03	0.71 (4.9)	−0.015 (7.2)	0.873 (1.52)

Notes: The relative export price is Japan's price of manufactured exports divided by the world price of manufactures and adjusted by exchange rate changes. The relative import price of manufactures and that of raw materials are Japan's import price of manufactures and raw materials, respectively, divided by the domestic price of manufactures.

All equations are estimated using the ordinary least squares method in natural log-linear form. Thus the estimates give the contribution of the rate of changes in individual explanatory variables on the right-hand side to the rate of changes in explained variables on the left-hand side despite different units of measurement of individual variables. Figures in parentheses after coefficients are t-statistics. $\bar{R}^2$ is the coefficient of determination adjusted for degrees of freedom, and DW is the Durbin-Watson statistic.

Sources: Ohkawa, Takamatsu, and Yamamoto (1974); Shinohara (1972); and Yamazawa and Yamamoto (1979a). See Shionoya and Yamazawa (1973) for further technical details.

Figure 2.3
Long Swings in Manufacturing Output: Growth and Structural Change

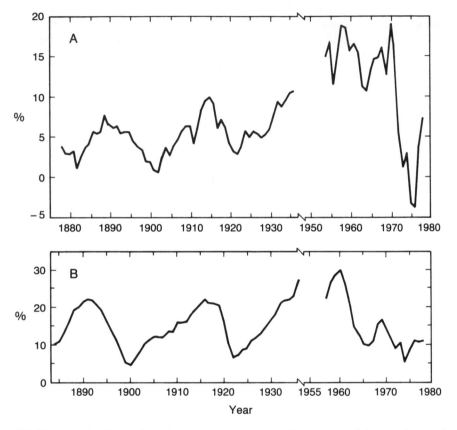

(A) Growth cycle of manufacturing output: seven-year moving average of the growth rate of manufacturing production to previous years calculated from 1934-36 constant price series. Five-year moving average after the Second World War.

(B) Seven-year moving average of the coefficient of structural change as defined below. Five-year moving average after the Second World War.

$$v(t) = \sum_j |s(t,j) - s(t-7,j)|,$$

s = the percentage share of industry j in total manufacturing.

Sources: Yamazawa and Yamamoto (1979a: chaps. 1 and 4).

others, thereby enlarging their shares, and this causes curve B to peak.

Figure 2.3 shows the long swings in manufacturing output, which can be related to the structural changes of industrial composition. The 1889 peak corresponds to the expansion of textile production while food processing and other sectors decreased; the 1915 peak corresponds to the expansion of metal, chemical and machinery manufacturing, as well as textiles, while food processing and other sectors decreased further; and peaks in 1936 and around 1960 correspond to the expansion of metal, chemical and machinery manufacturing at the expense of textiles and food processing production.

The correspondence of the growth cycles of trade to the output growth cycle reveals the interaction between trade and production. A clear relationship between changes in the production and imports of both raw materials and manufactures has been observed, which is consistent with the estimation of significant income effects in import equations 2 and 3 of Table 2.1. That is, the manufacture of industrial products and the growth of GDP strongly induced imports of raw materials, machinery, and intermediate goods.

On the other hand, the cause and effect relationship between production and exports is reversed in theory, which argues that exports, an important element of aggregate demand, induce output growth. The data generally support the theory, showing, for the most part, steady export growth relative to the output growth cycle, although the relationship was obscured during the First World War and in the early 1930s.

The correspondence between the growth cycle and structural change coefficients has been observed in manufactured exports and imports as well (Yamazawa and Yamamoto 1979b). Moreover, the correspondence between structural change coefficients of both exports and imports and output cycles provides further evidence of a peculiar characteristic of structural changes in Japan's production and trade; that is, the same change, beginning with light industrialization and moving to heavy industrialization, first occurred with imports, then with production, and ended with exports. These all show that the CPC development of textiles, metals, chemicals, and machinery production were the underlying mechanisms behind the expansion of and interaction between production and trade in Japan.

BALANCE-OF-PAYMENTS CONSTRAINT ON INDUSTRIAL GROWTH

Why did the process of light and heavy industrialization not continue its steady growth? Why was this process interrupted by more than one industrial boom? The most important constraint to steady growth was a deterioration of the balance of payments. The relationships between output cycles and trade described above affect the balance-of-payments situation, which, in turn, either constrains or encourages output growth.

The effect of an industrial boom depends on whether it is led by growth of domestic demand or by growth of exports. In the rising phase of long swings that are initiated by some domestic incentive to increase output, import growth tends to exceed export growth, thereby decreasing the export/import ratio. The resulting balance-of-payments deficit triggers monetary contraction, which restrains investment and other economic activities, and thus slows output growth. In the declining phase of long swings, import growth falls short of export growth, thereby increasing the export/import ratio. The improved balance of payments helps ease credit, and investment resumes to increase output, initiating a new rising phase in the long swing. Figure 2.4 (A) shows the interaction of production, trade, and the trade balance over the rising and declining phases of a long swing. A solid line added to the export/import ratio represents the critical trade balance ratio. The long swings of the export/import ratios lead those of manufacturing production by about a quarter cycle, as shown in (A). This is essentially what happened in the pre–First World War and post–Second World War long swings.

During the export-led booms of the First World War and the early 1930s, export growth induced output expansion directly. Since export growth exceeded import growth, the export/import ratio increased and the balance of payments ran a surplus. Output expansion stopped only after the export booms were ended by exogenous factors, including the end of the First World War and the worldwide prevalence of bloc economies in the 1930s. As a result, import growth then exceeded export growth and caused a deterioration in the balance of payments. In this case, long swings in the export/import ratio

Figure 2.4
Schematic Diagram of Alternative Correspondence among
Production (S), Trade (X and M), and the Trade Balance (X/M)

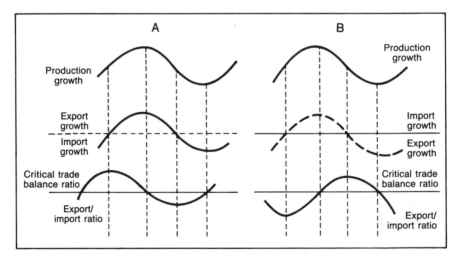

(A) Domestic demand-led growth.
(B) Export-led growth.
Source: Yamazawa and Yamamoto (1979b: figs. 7.3, 7.4).

tended to lag behind exports and manufacturing production by about a quarter cycle, as shown in Figure 2.4 (B).

Figure 2.4 is an oversimplification of reality, and the correspondence between the growth cycle and balance of payments (export/import ratio) is actually more complicated. In long swings, the actual, observed rising and falling phases are not of the same length, and the degree of monetary contraction brought about by the decreasing export/import ratio will vary depending on the prospects for capital inflows and with different exchange rate systems. Comparing (A) in Figure 2.3 with Figure 1.4 (keeping in mind the schematic correspondence of Figure 2.4) is worthwhile. Long swings in the export/import ratio appear to have led the growth cycle of manufacturing production by two to three years before the beginning of the First World War and after the Second World War, while it was synchronous or tended to lag behind during the interwar period. Decelerating trends of imports of materials and manufactures relative to the high, steady growth of exports produced a strong upward trend in the export/import ratio, and this resulted in a persistent surplus during the 1930s and the late 1960s. Long swings of accelerated growth of manufacturing production corresponded to strong improvement in the long swings of the balance of payments (steep upward trend of curve B in Figure 2.4).[5]

The international monetary system played a key role in determining how quickly a deteriorating balance of payments would negatively affect industrial growth. Under the gold standard between 1897 and the First World War, and under the pegged exchange rate system in the 1950s and 1960s, the deterioration in the balance of payments triggered monetary contraction, which restrained investment and other activities, and slowed industrial growth. However, as long as foreign capital inflows were available, the effect of a deficit in the balance of payments was delayed and structural change could continue uninterrupted. But, when the yen depreciated in 1932, a balance-of-payments deficit resulted; nevertheless, exports expanded, producing an industrial boom in the early 1930s.

CONTRIBUTION OF FOREIGN CAPITAL

Another characteristic of the Japanese model is that domestic saving financed a major portion of Japan's domestic investment before the Second World War. During a few periods, foreign capital made significant contributions to domestic investment and eased the balance-of-payments constraint to industrial growth (Yamamoto 1969; Key 1970). Table 2.2, which shows the balance of payments of Japan, breaks down the inflow of foreign capital by flow type and provides three alternative measures of the net flow of foreign capital. The first measure is the most broadly defined and includes transfer

Table 2.2
Japan's Balance of Payments

	1886–93	1894–1903	1904–13	1914–19	1920–31	1932–36
1. Commodity trade balance	−24.8	−399.1	−552.6	1,333.7	−4,737.3	−818.9
2. Service trade balance	8.5	−14.3	−445.6	1,595.9	2,092.5	−118.6
3. Net transfer payment	17.7	436.4	75.1	150.9	242.9	416.7
4. Net long-term capital balance	−6.6	156.4	1,254.5	−1,668.5	−1,720.2	−2,850.0
4.1. Increase in external debt	—	170.0	1,600.0	−246.0	524.0	—
4.2. Direct investment	—	—	70–100	—	145.0	—
5. Net short-term capital balance	24.9	−165.7	−97.2	343.3	2,726.5	1,712.5
6. Specie movement and changes in specie held abroad	−19.7	−13.7	−234.2	−1,775.3	1,395.6	1,658.3
7. Current surplus/GDCF (%)[a]	1.5	12.0	15.2	−29.1	8.0	3.3
8. Current surplus/GDS (%)[a]	1.5	13.4	20.2	−24.0	9.6	4.5
9. Transfer and capital balance/GDCF	3.3	12.4	18.7	−11.6	3.8	−2.6
10. Transfer and long-term capital balance/GDCF	1.0	17.2	20.2	−15.1	−4.5	−8.1

Notes: The sum of lines 1 to 6 is 0.

Line 7 $= -\{(1) + (2)\}/\text{GDCF}$.
Line 8 $= -\{(1) + (2)\}/\text{GDS}$.
Line 9 $= -\{(3) + (4) + (5)\}/\text{GDCF}$.
Line 10 $= \{(3) + (4)\}/\text{GDCF}$.

a. Reparation payments are not included in the current account because they served as capital inflows during these periods in Japan.

Sources: Based on Yamamoto's estimate in Yamazawa and Yamamoto (1979a); GDCF and GDS are from Ohkawa, Takamatsu, and Yamamoto (1974).

payments of grants from abroad and reparation payments, short- and long-term capital flows, and exports of specie—the sum of lines 3 to 6.

The second measure is the sum of lines 3 to 5. It excludes specie movement and changes in specie held abroad. A substantial share of Japan's foreign exchange reserve was held in the form of specie deposits at banks in London during the years 1900–1930. Annual capital flow data (line 4) clearly show a change from a net inflow over a period of consecutive years to a net outflow over the next period, followed by another period of net inflows and then outflows. These flows correspond to the periodization in the table.

The third measure has the narrowest definition and includes only the flow of funds of a long-term nature—lines 3 and 4. They are divided by either gross domestic capital formation (GDCF) or gross domestic saving (GDS) to indicate their relative contributions.

Significant capital inflows were recorded for two periods, 1894–1903 and 1904–13. In terms of the third measure, it contributed 17 and 20 percent to the GDCF, respectively. Whereas the capital inflow in the first period was from the reparations paid by China (1896–98) after the Sino-Japanese War, in the second period it was from loans floated in London and New York. Japan adopted the gold standard from 1897 to 1917, during which time persistent trade deficits reduced the specie held abroad, thereby setting the stage for monetary contraction and depressed industrial activity. On the other hand, a huge amount of specie was accumulated in London banks during the export boom of the First World War. After the First World War (1921–31), capital flows into Japan came from both foreign portfolio and direct investment. But the inflow of capital was largely offset by Japanese investment in Manchuria, and for this reason, the third measure shows a net outflow.

Incidentally, after the Second World War only a small percentage of net inflow was recorded. The equivalent to line 10 in Table 2.2 for 1962–64 was 2.2 percent, showing that the rapid growth was mainly financed by domestic savings.

The model as discussed thus far shows how major modern manufacturing industries followed CPC development and how both the industrial and trade structures changed drastically as CPC development was accomplished. In macroeconomic terms, the accelerated trend of industrial growth was accompanied by both a steady expansion of manufactured exports and a deceleration of imported raw materials and intermediate manufactured goods, thereby improving the industrial trade balance over time and achieving persistent trade surpluses in the 1930s and again after the mid-1960s. Japan's industrial growth was continuously severely constrained by balance-of-payment deficits for the first 50 to 70 years of industrial development but these were corrected eventually.

Japanese industries have outgrown the CPC model as a means for development. The successful CPC development of major industries has resulted in an industrial complex with a high degree of self-sufficiency except in its needs for raw materials. This success now generates persistent trade surpluses which have become a major source of friction with Japan's major trading partners. Some industries are at the forefront of technology development and are no longer in a position of catching up; therefore, the development and growth of these industries is more consistent with the product cycle model. However, the CPC model still remains useful in explaining the industrialization of East and Southeast Asian countries. While the CPC model was developed from Japan's special situation in the late nineteenth and early twentieth centuries, its extension to late-starting countries under severe resource constraints as a strategy of industrial development should be carefully considered. This is discussed further in Chapters 9 and 10.

Part II

Industry Growth and International Trade

Three

Raw-Silk Exports and
Japanese Economic Development

There are numerous instances of countries in which foreign trade generated a surge in economic growth. Canada is a well-known example of a country whose growth experience can be represented by the "staple theory of growth." In the case of Japan, it has been argued that raw-silk exports spurred the country's economic takeoff. However, closer examination shows that Japan's experience with growth due to raw-silk exports differed from the staple theory in several ways. Moreover, the expansion of export-oriented raw-silk production exhibits the characteristic features of Japanese industrial development by which Japan has become known as the pioneer of the so-called export-led growth strategy, now the model for small, resource-poor, newly industrializing economies (NIEs). Thus, an analysis of Japan's raw-silk export growth is relevant to current economic events. However, because of inherent limits in domestic demand expansion, scale economies, and technological progress, the silk industry did not become the core of Japan's economic growth. Rather, sustained industrialization only became possible with the type of CPC growth that characterized the cotton industry.

STAPLE GOODS EXPORTS AND
THE SURGE IN ECONOMIC DEVELOPMENT

In the nineteenth century, the United States and Canada expanded their exports to Europe with such goods as lumber and wheat, which led to the inflow of additional capital and labor to the United States and Canada. As demand for export production and consumption goods expanded, and as the population increased, production of intermediate and capital goods was also stimulated. Thus, according to the staple theory of growth, foreign demand stimulated expansion in the production of staple goods and ultimately brought about economic growth in the sparsely populated, newly opened countries of North America.

However, production of staple exports in response to foreign demand has not always led to economic growth. For example, during the same period, the Southeast Asian countries' exports of rice, rubber, and tin did not result in a similar development process. The abundance of natural resources in Southeast Asia that were suitable for production of staple goods were used merely to meet the small domestic demand, and many resources were left unexploited. With the opening of foreign trade, a demand for exports was generated and capital and labor were channeled to export production. However, this growth in the production of staples merely led to the utilization of heretofore idle resources, but did not bring about sustained economic growth. In this sense, exports became merely a surplus outlet (vent for surplus theory). The Southeast Asian experience points out that the resource endowments of a region and the characteristics of the goods themselves determine whether staple goods exports will lead to sustained economic growth.[1]

In Japan, too, export-oriented domestic production began with the export of staples such as raw silk, coal, and copper and grew with the opening of foreign trade in 1858. Raw silk was considered an important commercial item, both in terms of its export value as well as its prospects for long-term growth. For this reason, Baba and Tatemoto (1968) and Henmi (1969) view raw-silk exports as Japan's version of a staple export that induced the country's sustained economic growth.

Indeed, this view is supported by the following considerations:

1. Raw silk was one of the specialty goods that was indigenous to resource-poor Japan.

2. Because of the limited domestic market for silk, which is a luxury good, most of Japan's production of raw silk was destined for export markets. At the time, export expansion was enhanced by favorable conditions such as the development of the U.S. weaving industry, which increased demand for raw silk, and the silkworm disease epidemic in Europe, which reduced the worldwide supply of raw silk.

3. Exports of raw silk became an important source of foreign exchange for Japan and made possible the financing of essential imports required in the initial stages of economic growth. During the first three decades following 1858, raw-silk exports made up a third of Japan's total exports.

However, Japan's silk exports did not conform precisely to the schema of the vent for surplus theory. In response to the growth of the silk-reeling industry, sericulture also grew but did not absorb all of the idle land and labor resources. Wheat production competed for the land needed for mulberry trees and for the labor required in silkworm breeding.

In addition, closer examination of the three points raised above shows that raw-silk exports did not perfectly conform to the staple theory of growth:

1. Export growth did not come about merely as a result of the growth in foreign demand for Japanese silk. Even within the growing U.S. market, Japanese raw-silk exports were able to take away an increasing share of the market from Italian and Chinese exporters because of lower prices.

2. At the time there was little left in the way of unutilized resources in densely populated Japan, and the sericulture industry had to vie with the more developed areas of wheat agriculture for resources. This resource limitation was overcome by technological progress and increased labor productivity in the sericulture and silk-reeling industries, leading to further export expansion.

3. Though the effect on foreign exchange earnings was undoubtedly great, because silk was a luxury consumer good, its scale of production remained small. Furthermore, since production of silk relied in part on traditional technology, its ability to induce the development of other industries or to generate a surge of modern economic growth was limited.

Because of the expansion of demand for silk resulting from the export trade and the subsequent growth in production, technological progress and productivity improvements were realized. This demonstrates the dynamic effect of trade, which is strongly evident in the case of Japan's raw-silk export growth. Such effects were subsequently realized in the development process of the silk-weaving and textile industries. Moreover, if one considers the considerable effect on foreign exchange earnings as well as the peculiarities of the industry in terms of productivity growth and technological progress under conditions of resource constraints, then the industry may be considered the forerunner of the export-oriented industrialization strategy.

Although Japanese silk exports continued to grow—even to the extent of gaining a monopoly position in the U.S. market in the 1920s—their role in Japan's economic growth began to decline after 1910. The analysis presented here therefore considers silk exports only until 1910.

THE PROCESS OF RAW-SILK EXPORT GROWTH

Japan began exporting raw silk in response to strong demand from the European silk-weaving industries that were plagued by an insufficient supply of raw silk due to the silkworm disease that had ravaged the sericulture industry in Europe. The composition of Japanese silk exports changed considerably over time. In the second half of the 1860s, 40 percent of silk exports were in the form of silkworm eggs and cocoons, but the share of these exports declined thereafter to a minimal share by 1885. Excluding this initial period, silk exports consisted mainly of raw silk, and between 1870 and 1910 raw-silk exports continued to grow at an annual rate of 8.7 percent (as measured in yen). During this period, the export price of raw silk rose at an annual rate of 2.2 percent while export volumes expanded at about 6.5 percent.

In the second half of the 1870s, the United States became a major importer of raw silk due to the rapid development of its domestic silk-weaving industry. At the time, only a small share of Japan's raw-silk exports was destined for the U.S. market. However, the U.S. share of raw-silk exports from Japan rose to 42 percent during the first half of the 1880s, to 57 percent in the latter half of the 1880s, and eventually reached 71 percent in 1901 (see Table 3.1). In contrast, exports of silk fabrics to the United States, which expanded rapidly in the second half of the 1880s, at best represented only a third of the total value of Japan's raw-silk exports. (As silk yarn export volume was insignificant, it is not discussed here.) This was partly due to the U.S. tariff structure, which caused the volume of silk yarn and silk fabric exports to remain small relative to that of raw-silk exports to the United States. Under the Tariff Law of 1883, raw-silk imports could enter duty-free, but silk fabrics and silk yarn could only be imported at a general ad valorem tariff rate of 50 percent and 30 percent, respectively (Mason 1910).

From 1870 to 1908, a change occurred in the composition of the U.S. silk import market with regard to the composition of market shares held by the principal exporting countries (see Table 3.2). The opening of the transcontinental railway in 1879 in the United States lowered the export freight rates of Asian raw-silk exports to the silk-weaving industries of the East Coast, leading to market share increases for China and Japan. In addition, during

Table 3.1
Direction of Japan's Raw-Silk Exports (%)[a]

Years	United States	France	United Kingdom	Others	Total
1873–75	1.7	42.0	41.4	14.9	100.0
1876–80	19.1	47.5	27.5	5.9	100.0
1881–85	42.2	46.4	10.7	0.7	100.0
1886–90	57.7	36.6	3.5	2.2	100.0
1891–95	56.0	37.6	1.5	4.9	100.0
1896–1900	59.2	32.5	0.6	7.7	100.0
1901–05	65.4	19.8	0.2	14.6	100.0
1906–10	71.1	18.7	0.1	11.1	100.0

Note:
a. In terms of value of exports.

Source: Computed from Ministry of Finance (Okurasho), *Dainihon Gaikoku Boeki Nempyo* (Foreign Trade Annual of the Empire of Japan), various issues.

the period between 1870 and 1880, the share of Japan's exports grew rapidly at the expense of China's share, mainly as a result of changes in the pattern of U.S. demand. In the United States, technological progress had occurred in the reeling and weaving stages, including a shift from hand to power looms. In addition, consumer demand shifted to broad fabrics, which called for raw silk of a better, standardized quality. Although European steam filature was best suited to meet these requirements, an increase in the European export supply would not have been possible without a price increase since the industry had to compete for scarce labor. As a result, the growth of European countries' share in the U.S. market was minimal.

At the same time, rapid technological innovations in the sericulture and silk-reeling industries in Japan helped to increase the competitiveness of Japan's raw-silk exports. Technological innovations, such as those allowing for silkworm breeding in the fall as well as in the spring and for the artificially controlled environments appropriate for silkworm breeding, began to be devised in the late 1870s and spread rapidly. Thus, by the early 1880s the cocoon requirement per unit of filature—one measure of raw-silk export costs—was reduced by about 30 percent.[2]

Other improvements contributed to the increased productivity of Japan's silk industry. In the silk-reeling industry, the traditional hand and sedentary machines gave way to threading machines. Moreover, steam-filature technology was introduced from Europe and assimilated into the Japanese mode of production, quickly surpassing hand filature by the end of the 1890s. The share of steam filature in total production in 1890 was 40 percent but rose to 70 percent by the middle of the next decade. Since steam-filature output was, for the most part, destined for the export market, its share of Japan's total raw-silk exports was 70 percent in the mid-1890s, rising to 90 percent in the early 1900s. In contrast, Chinese producers continued to rely on traditional hand-loom technology and were late in introducing the steam-filature

Table 3.2
Sources of U.S. Silk Imports (%)[a]

Years	Japan	China	Italy	France
1870–71	11.0	28.5	—	7.1
1879–81	28.6	54.7	0.1	9.6
1889–91	53.9	22.1	16.5	4.4
1906–1908	56.5	18.7	21.8	3.0

Note:
a. In terms of volume.
Source: Mason (1910).

technique. As a result, the share of steam filature in China's raw-silk exports only rose from 35 percent in 1898 to 42 percent in 1908.

A CONSTANT MARKET SHARE (CMS) ANALYSIS OF EXPORT GROWTH

In the following sections, the growth mechanism of Japan's silk exports to the United States (discussed above) is analyzed. By disaggregating Japan's total volume of raw-silk exports to the United States (X) into hand-filature exports (X_1) and steam-filature exports (X_2) and denoting their shares as s_1, s_2, respectively, in total U.S. silk import volume (M_1, M_2), the following equation can be derived:

$$X = X_1 + X_2$$
$$= s_1 M_1 + s_2 M_2$$

Given the change in exports between time 0 and 1 (that is, $\Delta X = X^1 - X^0$), the above equation can be rewritten as follows:

$$\Delta X = \sum_{i=1}^{2} s_i^0 \Delta M_i + \sum_{i=1}^{2} M_i^0 \Delta s_i + \sum_{i=1}^{2} \Delta M_i \Delta s_i \qquad (3.1)$$

$$= s^0 \Delta M + \left(\sum_{i=1}^{2} s_i^0 \Delta M_i - s^0 \Delta M \right) + \sum_{i=1}^{2} M_i^0 \Delta s_i + \sum_{i=1}^{2} \Delta M_i \Delta s_i$$

where ΔM and Δs are changes in import volume and import shares, respectively, and where $M = M_1 + M_2$ and $X = sM$.

The first term on the right-hand side of equation 3.1 ($s^0 \Delta M$) represents the market-demand-growth effect—that is, under the assumption of constant Japanese shares, exports increase as a result of an increase in total U.S. imports of a given commodity. The second term ($\sum_{i=1}^{2} s_i^0 \Delta M_i - s^0 \Delta M$) represents the commodity-composition effect, where even assuming constant shares of hand and steam filatures in the U.S. market, an increase in import demand for silk is greater than demand for total imports, thereby inducing an increase in Japan's silk exports. The third term ($\sum_{i=1}^{2} M_i^0 \Delta s_i$) shows the competition effect—that is, in the absence of any increase in U.S. imports of the product, an increase in the share of Japan's exports will increase total silk exports. The fourth term ($\sum_{i=1}^{2} \Delta M_i \Delta s_i$) represents the interaction term—that is, the effect of the combination of changes in Japan's share and changes in U.S. import demand. However, the fourth term, like the third term, may be considered a competition effect, since its value increases whenever an increase in Japan's share accompanies a large increase in U.S. market demand.

Using equation 3.1, the growth of Japan's raw-silk exports to the U.S. market can be disaggregated into the market-demand-growth effect, the commodity-composition effect, and the competition effect. Since the effects are differentiated according to whether market shares are assumed to be constant or variable, this approach is referred to as the constant market share (CMS) analysis.[3]

Table 3.3 reveals certain trends in the five-year average of Japan's silk exports to the United States and of total U.S. silk imports from 1876 to 1910. In analyzing these fluctuations the focus is long-term trends; short-term changes are disregarded. Notwithstanding the arbitrary nature of the five-year divisions, the sources of export growth can be identified. To do this, assumptions had to be made with regard to the published data on total silk exports when disaggregating them into hand- and steam-filature exports.[4]

Beginning in the second half of the 1870s and continuing through the first half of the 1880s, U.S. silk imports grew at a rapid rate of 12.5 percent per year. In subsequent years, growth of U.S. silk imports stabilized at 6 to 8 percent annually. However, during the same time period the share of steam filature rose from 14 to 86 percent of total silk imports, indicating that hand-filature imports were being rapidly crowded out of the market.

During this period, Japan's share of U.S. silk imports rose from 29 to 56 percent. Furthermore, in response to the dramatic change in U.S. import demand (which was mentioned above), Japan's steam-filature export share climbed from 18 to 95 percent. Still, Japan's export growth did not proceed smoothly. Until the second half of the 1880s, annual export growth rates as high as 15 to 19 percent were posted, but in the following ten-year period (1886–95), annual export growth declined to 4 to 5 percent. During the period 1896–1900, the annual growth of exports climbed back to 8 percent. There were several factors behind these fluctuations in the growth of exports to the U.S. market.

Applying the data in Table 3.4 to equation 3.1, a CMS analysis was conducted for each period. It is evident that over the entire period from 1876 to 1910, the market-demand-growth effect was large and represented about half of Japan's export increase. This means that the growth in U.S. import demand induced a major part of the growth of Japan's raw-silk exports to the United States during that period. Thus, the slowdown in growth of the U.S. import market in the 1890s was one of the causes of the sluggishness of Japan's export growth. There were, however, other forces at work.

The commodity-composition effect became positive and remained that way from the first half of the 1880s to the 1890s. Since the growth in U.S. silk imports mainly reflected the growth of steam-filature imports, this effect was positive during the period when Japan's share of steam filature exceeded that of hand-filature imports. In contrast, the commodity-composition effect was negative in the 1880s when the share of hand-filature imports rose. After 1890,

Table 3.3
Japan's Raw-Silk Export Growth (£ '000, five-year average)[a]

Years	U.S. raw-silk imports			Japanese raw-silk export growth			Japan's share in U.S. imports (%)		
	Total	Hand filature	Steam filature	Total	Hand filature	Steam filature	Total	Hand filature	Steam filature
1876–80	1,874 (12.5)	1,607	267	547 (19.0)	450	97	29.2	28.0	36.3
1881–85	3,507 (7.9)	2,198	1,309	1,418 (14.4)	991	427	40.4	45.1	32.6
1886–90	5,193 (6.5)	2,324	2,869	2,918 (4.4)	1,310	1,608	56.2	56.4	56.1
1891–95	7,175 (5.4)	2,368	4,807	3,628 (4.5)	814	2,814	50.6	34.4	58.6
1896–1900	9,383 (8.3)	2,590	6,793	4,541 (8.9)	831	3,710	48.4	32.1	54.6
1901–05	14,241	2,831	11,410	7,089	1,003	6,086	49.8	35.4	53.3
1906–10	19,645	2,644	17,000	10,906	564	10,342	55.5	21.3	60.8

Note:
a. Figures in parentheses show percentage rate of increase to the next five-year period.
Source: Niyomka (1975: table A-8).

when only steam-filature exports showed an increase, the commodity-composition effect again showed a positive contribution to the growth of Japan's exports.

Interpretation of the competition effect, however, poses some problems. Although largely positive in most periods, this effect was negative from the second half of the 1880s to the beginning of the twentieth century. In the 1880s, productivity and quality improvements were realized particularly in the hand-filature industry, whereas technological progress and productivity increases were realized in steam filature in the first decade of the 1900s. How then could the competition effect be negative during these periods? One possible explanation is that Japan's filature exports might have been put at a relatively disadvantageous position vis-à-vis China's filature exports as a result of Japan's adoption of the gold standard in 1897. However, it can also be argued that during the preceding decade the silver depreciation that took place made Japan's exports more competitive. The effect of this depreciation on Japan's export growth performance in the United States is discussed in the next section.

Table 3.4
Constant Market Share Analysis of Japan's Silk Exports to the United States (£ '000)[a]

Periods	Increase in Japan's silk exports to the United States (1)	Demand-growth effect (2)	Commodity-composition effect (3)	Competition effect (4)	Interaction effect (5)
1876–80 to 1881–85	871	477 (54.8)	67 (7.7)	265 (30.4)	62 (7.1)
1881–85 to 1886–90	1,500	681 (45.4)	–116 (–7.7)	556 (37.1)	379 (25.2)
1886–90 to 1891–95	710	1,114 (156.9)	–2 (–0.3)	–440 (–62.0)	38 (5.4)
1891–95 to 1896–1900	913	1,117 (122.3)	123 (13.4)	–253 (–27.7)	–74 (–8.0)
1896–1900 to 1901–05	2,548	2,351 (92.3)	247 (9.7)	–3 (–0.1)	–57 (–1.9)
1901–05 to 1906–10	3,817	2,691 (70.5)	222 (5.8)	467 (12.2)	437 (11.5)

Note:
a. Increase of five-year averages in column 1 is decomposed to individual contributions in columns 2 to 5 with percentage shares in parentheses.

Source: Computed by applying equation 3.1 to the figures in Table 3.3.

THE EFFECT OF SILVER DEPRECIATION

Until 1897, when Japan changed to the gold standard, silver was used for all overseas transactions by Japan. When the United States and the major European countries adopted the gold standard in the 1870s (changing from a bimetallic standard in many cases), the value of silver fell relative to gold, as did the Japanese yen. During the decade before the adoption of the gold standard in Japan, the exchange rate of the yen relative to the dollar had declined by 33.2 percent, and this is thought to have encouraged the growth of Japanese exports.[5] As is often observed in contemporary developing countries, an overvalued currency tends to restrain export growth. In the case of Japan prior to 1897, the rapid decline in the value of the yen was the result of changes in the international financial system rather than a planned government policy.

How did the depreciation of the yen affect the growth of Japanese silk exports? Compared to Japan's European competitors in the U.S. market, such as Italy and France, which were already on the gold standard, Japan was in a more favorable position. However, Japan's main competitor, China, remained on the silver standard even after Japan had adopted the gold standard. For this reason, Japan's exports did not gain from the silver depreciation.[6] As was also demonstrated in the earlier CMS analysis, there was no significant increase in Japan's share of the U.S. market at the time of the depreciation of the yen. In order to explain this apparent contradiction, the following hypothesis is presented. The silver depreciation, rather than merely favoring Japan's competitive position through a larger share of the U.S. market, lowered the Japanese and Chinese raw-silk export price (in dollar terms) and hence also the price of raw silk in the U.S. market. This, in turn, reduced the price of silk fabric, encouraged an increase in its demand, and thereby ultimately induced an increase in imports of silk filature. It can therefore be said that the impact of silver depreciation showed up more in the market-demand-growth effect than in the competition or increase-in-share effect. This hypothesis can be verified empirically using import and export functions:

$$M = a_0 + a_1 Y + a_2 (P_s/P) \qquad (3.2)^7$$

$$X = b_0 + b_1 M + b_2 (P_j/P_s) \qquad (3.3)$$

$$X/M = c_0 + c_1 (P_j/P_s) \qquad (3.4)$$

where M refers to the volume of U.S. raw-silk imports; X is the volume of Japan's raw-silk exports to the United States; Y is U.S. income, which is a determinant of the demand for silk fabrics; P_s is the price of raw silk in the

United States; P_j is the price of Japanese raw silk in the United States; and P is the general price level in the United States.

Equation 3.2 shows that U.S. imports of raw silk are determined by the price of raw silk relative to other commodities in the U.S. market and by U.S. income levels. Note that a more accurate formulation would have as the dependent variable silk fabric consumption rather than imports of raw silk. However, the demand for raw-silk imports is a valid proxy since the U.S. processed imported raw silk into silk fabrics. With a statistically significant price coefficient, a_2, the effect of the silver depreciation through the change in P_s can be shown. In addition, it is possible to determine the relative importance of the silver depreciation as a source of growth by computing the income and price effects. Equations 3.3 and 3.4 are Japanese export functions to the United States. Equation 3.3 expresses Japanese raw-silk exports to the United States as a function of the total import volume of raw silk of the United States and Japan's export price relative to the average U.S. price for silk. Equation 3.4 hypothesizes that Japan's share of the U.S. raw-silk import market is a function of Japan's export price of silk relative to its price in the United States.

Table 3.5
Estimates of U.S. Import and Japanese Export Functions of Raw Silk[a]

M	Constant	Y	P_s/P	$\bar{R}^2$	DW
Eq. 3.2	0.9347	0.9268 (20.60)	-1.1445 (3.72)	0.9498	1.49
Eq. 3.2*	11.0703	0.8405 (21.56)	-2.1219 (6.68)	0.9774	0.61

X	Constant	M	P_j/P_s	$\bar{R}^2$	DW
Eq. 3.3	0.0007	1.7003 (11.24)	0.5138 (0.92)	0.8273	0.67

X/M	Constant	P_j/P_s	$\bar{R}^2$	DW
Eq. 3.4	0.3516	1.6467 (2.61)	0.1434	0.76

Note:
a. Equation 3.2 was estimated based on annual data for 1869–1910; equation 3.2* was estimated using the three-year moving average for the same period; and equations 3.3 and 3.4 were estimated using annual data for the period 1875–1910. All equations were estimated using ordinary least squares regression in log-linear form with *t*-values in parentheses.

Table 3.5 shows the results of regression analysis for the parameters of equations 3.2 through 3.4. Equation 3.2 was estimated using annual data from 1869 to 1910 and a three-year moving average of the data over the same period. The results are reported in Table 3.5 as equations 3.2 and 3.2*, respectively. As proxies for Y and P, the volume of U.S. silk fabric production and the U.S. wholesale price index were used. An interesting result of the analysis is that the price elasticities doubled when the three-year moving average data were employed; this implies that the price effect is more pronounced in the long run. On the other hand, the price elasticity in equation 3.3 is positive but not statistically significant, whereas it is both positive and significant in equation 3.4. The incorrect signs of the price elasticities in equations 3.3 and 3.4 may be attributed to the fact that the unit import price used is a weighted average of hand- and steam-filature prices, and therefore the relative price variable may not be directly linked to the changes in shares. While the use of disaggregated hand- and steam-filature price data may have yielded significantly negative price elasticities, the lack of reliable data on a disaggregated basis precludes such reestimation. Furthermore, disaggregation is meaningless in the case of equation 3.2.

However, the significantly negative price effects observed in equation 3.2 support the hypothesis that the silver depreciation ultimately led to an increase in demand for silk fabric and silk filature. Moreover, the differentiation of equation 3.2 with respect to time yields the following relationship between the growth rates of the individual variables:

$$\dot{M} = 0.9268 \ \dot{Y} - 1.145 \ (\dot{P_s}/P).$$

Substitution of the average annual rate of change during the period 1887–97 into $\dot{Y}$ and $\dot{P_s}/P$ (that is, 4.582 and −2.91%, respectively) shows the contribution of the income effect (4.24%) and the price effect (3.33%) in stimulating the increase in total U.S. imports of raw silk during the period.

In addition, during the ten years preceding the adoption of the gold standard, the yen rate declined from 77 to 49 dollars per 100 yen, an average annual decrease of 4.52 percent. Assuming that the Japanese raw-silk export price could be used as a proxy for the U.S. import price, Japan's export price (in yen) would have risen by 1.61 percent relative to the U.S. general price level (in U.S. dollars). Thus, without the silver depreciation the relative price of silk in the U.S. market would have risen by 1.61 percent and would have restrained as much as a third of the actual increase in U.S. imports of Japanese raw silk.

In the foregoing analysis, it was assumed that changes in Japan's raw-silk export price were exogenous. However, since changes in supply conditions also determine prices, it is necessary to employ a demand-supply-equilibrium model to properly evaluate such changes.

Figure 3.1
Mechanism of Silk Export Growth

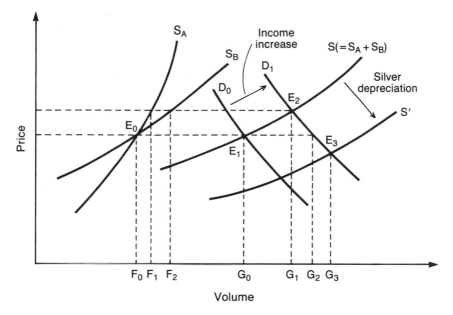

Figure 3.1 illustrates the influence of several factors determining the increase in Japan's silk exports to the United States. On the left-hand side of the figure, S_A and S_B represent the long-run export supply curves of two competing exporter countries, countries A and B, which when summed up horizontally give the total export supply curve S. Given the short-run demand curve D_0, the point of intersection E_1 determines the initial equilibrium in the import market. An increase in income causes D_0 to shift to D_1, moving the equilibrium point to E_2. Both countries' exports increase as a result, but the magnitudes of the increase (F_0F_1, F_0F_2) differ depending on the elasticities of their long-run supply curves. For instance, relative to that of European exporting countries, Japan's long-run supply curve is more elastic, causing its share of the expanding U.S. market to rise. Country A's and B's export supply prices equalize at E_2.

On the right-hand side of Figure 3.1, the effects of the yen depreciation can be examined. Assuming that exporting countries A and B are both on the silver standard while the importing country is on the gold standard, depreciation of silver would tend to lower the exchange rate of the exporting countries and shift the total supply curve to S'. The equilibrium point would then move to E_3. The increase in imports from G_0 to G_3 can be broken down into the income effect $(G_0 \rightarrow G_2)$ and the price effect $(G_2 \rightarrow G_3)$. Given the previous estimate of the import function, in the absence of an exchange depreciation, there would have been no shift in the supply curve, and at the equilibrium point E_2 the negative price effect $(G_2 \rightarrow G_1)$ would have cancelled part of the potential income effect.

To summarize, there were several factors affecting the export growth of Japan's raw silk. Essentially, the increase in U.S. demand for silk fabrics brought about an increase in the demand for raw silk, and hence, for Japanese raw-silk exports. However, compared with other exporting countries, such as China and Italy, the expansion in Japan's share of the U.S. import market for raw silk was due to the high long-run supply price elasticity for Japanese raw silk. This resulted from the growth in raw-silk production capacity brought about by the technological progress that had taken place in the industry. In addition, although the price of raw silk (in terms of yen) rose under the inflationary conditions of the Japanese economy at the time, this potential dampening effect on export growth was more than offset by the fall in market prices for exports caused by the depreciation of the silver-based yen, which followed the fall in the value of silver relative to that of gold. Thus, Japan's competitive position in the U.S. market improved when compared to competing gold-standard countries, such as Italy and France. However, since its major competitor, China, also used a silver-backed currency, the depreciation of silver stimulated Japan's silk export growth not so much in terms of share expansion but more through a lowering of the market price, which prompted an overall increase in import demand for raw silk.

THE CONTRIBUTION OF SILK EXPORTS TO JAPANESE ECONOMIC DEVELOPMENT

This chapter concludes with explanations of five identified effects of the growth of raw-silk exports on Japan's economic development.

Foreign-Exchange-Earnings Effect

The most evident economic contribution of growth in raw-silk exports is its role as a major source of foreign exchange earnings (see Table 3.6). Between 1868 and 1881, raw-silk exports earned approximately 107 million yen, which is about 35 percent of total export earnings. From 1881 to 1893, the value and share of silk exports increased to 253 million yen and 36 percent, respectively. Import demand during the initial period of economic growth was large. During the first period in particular, total Japanese imports reached a value of 473 million yen, and huge deficits were recorded. Although the deficits were fully financed through the outflow of gold and silver coins that had been saved rather than used to pay for imports during the Edo period (1601–1867) when trade was minimal, the government encouraged exports to compensate for the huge current account deficits, and raw silk was always considered an important commercial item to be promoted. Thus, the contribution of raw-silk exports, which represented some 35 percent of total foreign exchange earnings from exports, was substantial.

Income-and-Output-Generation Effect

Although it is impossible to estimate the income generated by raw-silk production and exports, an analysis of the data in Table 3.7 reveals the extent of the industry's contribution to increases in total production in both the agricultural and manufacturing sectors. The growth of raw-silk exports caused a rapid expansion of the sericulture and silk-reeling industries. The share of the sericulture industry in agricultural production was 8 to 9 percent and contributed 11 to 16 percent of the income from agricultural production. However, as noted earlier, sericulture competed with wheat production for available resources so that the more resources devoted to sericulture implied less resources would be devoted to the production of wheat. If the decline in wheat production that results from the growth of sericulture is subtracted, the final contribution of sericulture is 4 percent lower.

In the manufacturing sector, the shares of the silk-reeling and -weaving industries, as well as their rates of contribution to the growth of manufacturing production, were even larger than sericulture's contribution to agricultural production. From the 1880s to the second half of the 1890s, these two industries were responsible for approximately 21 to 25 percent of the increase in total manufacturing output.

It should be noted that the distribution of production from sericulture, silk-reeling, or silk-weaving in the country or even in the cities was not uniform. Producers were unevenly concentrated in certain prefectures such as Nagano,

Table 3.6
Foreign Exchange Earned Through Silk Exports (¥ '000)[a]

Years	Exports (f.o.b.)	Silk exports	Imports (c.i.f.)	Trade balance
1868–81	302,243	107,093 (35.4)	472,927	(170,684)
1882–93	699,006	253,209 (36.2)	721,810	(22,804)

Note:
a. Figures for the trade deficit and silk exports' share of total exports are in parentheses.
Sources: Yamazawa and Yamamoto (1979a: table 2-2); Toyo Keizai Shinposha (1935).

Gifu, and Fukushima. Efforts to introduce sericulture were widespread in mountainous regions that were unsuitable for rice cultivation. For logistical reasons, silk-reeling factories were set up near sericulture areas. Since there was no other major agricultural or industrial production in these regions, the contribution of the sericulture and reeling industries to regional agricultural and industrial production would have greatly exceeded the national statistics cited earlier. The regional economic-development-inducement effect must have been overwhelming.

Employment Effect

In the labor-surplus economies of contemporary developing countries, the labor-absorption effect of the modern industrial sector is one of the considerations in evaluating the effects of industrialization. Since the filature industry is highly labor-intensive, it generated a great deal of employment relative to other industries. In the first decade of the twentieth century, employment

Table 3.7
Production Effects of Silk Exports (%)[a]

Periods	Contribution of sericulture to agricultural production			Contribution of silk reeling to manufacturing production	
	S/A	$S/\Delta A$	$\Delta S'/\Delta A$[b]	R/M	$\Delta R/\Delta M$
1876–80 to 1881–85	7.5	16.6	7.1	9.2	6.0
1881–85 to 1886–90	8.7	—[c]	—[c]	8.5	24.9
1886–90 to 1891–95	8.6	13.6	11.4	11.9	21.6
1891–95 to 1896–1900	9.9	9.7	7.5	15.3	15.9
1896–1900 to 1901–05	9.8	11.4	9.2	15.6	3.6
1901–05 to 1906–10	10.1	15.1	12.3	13.6	13.5
Average	9.1	13.3	9.5	11.5	14.4

Notes:
a. S, A, R, and M denote sericulture, agriculture, silk reeling, and manufacturing, respectively. Δ denotes the increase from the average over the first five years to that over the last five years for individual periods.

b. $\Delta S'$ is ΔS adjusted for the hypothetical decrease of wheat production.

c. — refers to a decrease in both agricultural and sericultural production.

Source: Agricultural production data are from Henmi (1969), and manufacturing production data are from Niyomka (1975).

in this industry made up some 27 to 29 percent of all manufacturing sector employment. In addition, since the filature industries were not normally located in the large cities, their capacity to absorb rural labor, which enjoyed few employment opportunities, was great. Although rural cottage industries did not create many jobs in such prefectures as Gunma and Fukushima, where hand-filature production was concentrated, a significant amount of employment was provided by the steam-filature factòries of Nagano and Gifu prefectures (Kajinishi 1964).

Capital-Accumulation Effect

The mechanism of industrial development depends on capital accumulation for investment, which in turn generates profits for investment in the development of other industries. In the silk-reeling industry, whose exports earned a third of the nation's total export earnings, active and profitable business enterprises were set up. Were these profits reinvested in other industries that in turn contributed to sustained industrialization?

Initially, since steam-filature firms were small enterprises that often lacked funds for both equipment investment and working capital (for example, for the purchase of cocoons), they did not generate surplus capital for investment in other industries. Rather, raw-silk merchants, export traders, and local banks were more likely to provide the working capital for the silk-reeling industry. Regional banks, such as the Fourteenth National Bank in Matsumoto and the First National Bank in Ueda (both of Nagano Prefecture), successfully collected funds from local raw-silk traders. Between these regional banks and the banks in Yokohama, such as the Yokohama Foreign Exchange Company and the Second National Bank, a flow of raw-silk exports was established and was matched by a reverse flow of abundant financing. Thus, although this phenomenon is difficult to demonstrate empirically, raw-silk exports did, in a sense, contribute to the development of modern banking.[8] It can be further inferred that at least some of the funds used to establish new industries became available as an indirect result of these developments.

Linkage Effect

As observed in the foregoing sections, although raw-silk exports had a large foreign-exchange-earnings effect and had contributed greatly to the growth of agricultural and manufacturing production, the linkage effect (in terms of inducing the development of other industries) was limited. Since silk was a luxury item, there was not much room for growth in demand. And, apart from sericulture, there was no need for large investments in a related industry. Moreover, because production was based on traditional production techniques with their limited scale economies, the possibilities for technological progress and productivity improvements were constrained accordingly.

Although government-managed factories introduced steam-filature technology in the early 1870s without much adaptation, its application was not widely used because of the high price of imported machinery. In both the raw-silk and silk-weaving industries, imported machinery and technology began to spread to privately owned firms only when the imports were adapted to Japan's factor endowment conditions in terms of labor intensity, small-scale production, and the already available indigenous technology (Ono 1968). In contrast, it was the cotton industry, which from the start applied modern production techniques and realized scale economies, that would play the key role in Japan's light industrialization.

Four

Catching-Up Product Cycle Development in the Textile Industry

The textile industry is usually the first modern industry to be introduced by late-industrializing countries. In general, domestic demand of a late-industrializing country is initially met by production based on existing indigenous technology. Once quality imported goods made with modern production technology are introduced and gain wide acceptance, demand shifts from traditional to modern goods. Through imitation, domestic production of modern goods begins. In the textile industry, domestic production of modern goods is easily assumed because indigenous technology exists in most late-industrializing countries. Technology absorption is relatively easy, and because the industry is characterized by labor-intensive production, low-wage, late-industrializing countries can easily achieve comparative advantage. The case of Japan was no exception, and after the modern cotton-spinning industry was introduced in the 1860s, the development pattern followed the typical path from import substitution to export expansion.

This chapter analyzes the development of the cotton industry in Japan and explains the role of the catching-up product cycle (CPC) model of development in the textile industry. It includes a discussion of the industry's diversification process from woven fabrics to rayon and synthetic textiles, and the induced development of such related industries as textile machinery and synthetic dyestuffs. It also explains the diversification process. Finally, the CPC theory is considered not only as it applies to commodity trade, but also in explaining the relationship between overseas investment and technology transfer and changes in commodity trade.

THE STRATEGIC ROLE
OF THE COTTON TEXTILE INDUSTRY

The textile industry played a leading role in Japan's industrial growth before the Second World War. Even if raw silk were excluded, textiles made up a third of Japan's total industrial production and half of industrial exports during the period 1890–1930. In addition, raw material imports of the textile industry made up 70 percent of the country's total imports of raw materials (see Table 4.1). Although the textile industry included the wool and rayon industries, its core was the cotton industry; during the entire prewar period before 1940 the woolen fabrics trade showed net imports, and in the 1920s the rayon industry was just beginning to grow.

The cotton industry was the first modern industry based on large-scale production techniques. Although its production technology was perfected around the middle of the nineteenth century, the geographical areas involved in this technological revolution were limited. Nevertheless, with its low-wage, high-quality labor force, Japan was able to achieve comparative advantage in this labor-intensive industry and overtake Great Britain in the 1920s. In the second half of the 1960s, however, when wages rose and a labor shortage set in, Japan lost that comparative advantage to other late-developing countries. As a result, from 1970 onward, imports of textiles exceeded exports of textiles. Thus, the Japanese cotton industry has passed through the complete life cycle of an industry.

Table 4.1
The Textile Industry's Share of Japanese Manufacturing Activity (%)

Period	Share in manufactured exports[a]	Share of textile materials in raw material imports[a]	Share of textile output in manufacturing output[b]
1882–1891	35.2	27.8	42.4
1892–1901	52.0	34.7	78.5
1902–11	50.0	26.8	79.2
1912–21	51.3	30.1	80.8
1922–31	55.5	30.1	71.8
1930–39	43.7	23.7	60.7
1951–55	41.7	18.3	45.5
1966–70	14.0	8.2	12.1

Notes:
a. Raw silk is excluded from both the denominator and numerator.

b. Raw material imports include nonedible agricultural products, forestry products, and minerals.

Sources: Yamazawa and Yamamoto (1979a: tables 1 and 2); Shinohara (1972: table 1).

Figures 4.1 and 4.2 chart the CPC development of cotton yarn and cotton fabrics, using the values of domestic production, exports, and imports in constant 1934–36 prices. Even within the cotton yarn and cotton fabrics groups, there are great differences among products in terms of quality and price per unit (for example, per tonne of cotton yarn or per square meter of cotton fabric). Before the Second World War in particular, the composition of products shifted from low- to high-quality goods. Disregarding such quality and price differentials but still avoiding the simple summation of quantitative data, a composite weighted average index (in 1934–36 prices) based on unit price indices of individual products was constructed and used to deflate the total value. However, for the post–Second World War period, values were obtained by using a simple summation of quantitative data multiplied by 1934–36 prices.

COTTON INDUSTRY DEVELOPMENT

In 1859, with the opening of Japan to foreign trade, cotton yarn and cotton fabrics produced with modern production technology began to be imported. Imports rapidly grew because domestically produced fabrics based on indigenous technology were of inferior quality. By 1870, imported cotton yarn and fabrics constituted 36 percent of Japan's total imports. Because of foreign exchange constraints, rapid import substitution based on modern production technology was encouraged. By 1886, domestic import substitution of cotton yarn was achieved when half of total domestic demand was being met by domestic production (see Figure 4.1). Import substitution of cotton fabrics (1878) preceded that of cotton yarn (1886). In terms of the import/export ratio, however, the opposite was true. Whereas cotton yarn exports matched imports in 1895, this feat was not achieved by cotton fabrics until 1909. The cotton yarn industry reached its mature stage in 1960, and the cotton fabric industry in 1963, as indicated by the slowdown in domestic production growth. The reverse import stage began in 1969 for cotton yarn and in 1972 for cotton fabrics.

As mentioned previously, drastic changes occurred in the product composition of the cotton industry. Cotton yarn production began with the easily absorbed low-count technology and gradually expanded to high-count technology. Similarly, the production of cotton fabrics diversified from gray cotton fabrics to colored and processed cotton fabrics. Export growth, like import substitution, followed the same pattern. Initially, however, the production of cotton yarn and cotton fabric was not integrated and thus the two industries followed separate paths of CPC development. Cotton fabric production in each of the country's traditional weaving areas was easily able to expand as a cottage industry based on traditional technology and imported yarn. Be-

Figure 4.1
Catching-Up Product Cycle Development of Cotton Yarn in Japan

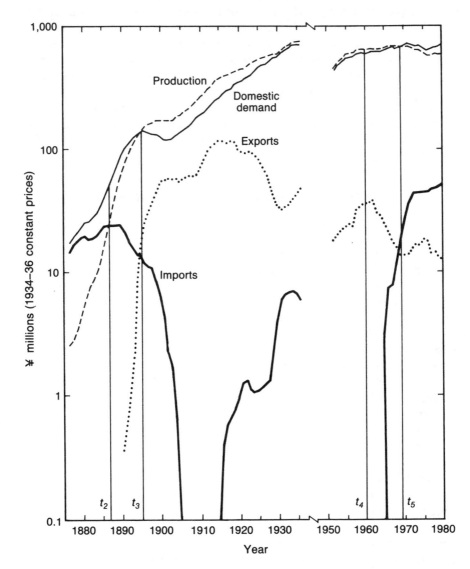

Notes: Seven-year moving averages before the Second World War and five-year moving averages after the Second World War.

Source: Estimated by the author. See Yamazawa (1984) for details of the estimation.

Figure 4.2
Catching-Up Product Cycle Development of the Cotton Textile Industry in Japan

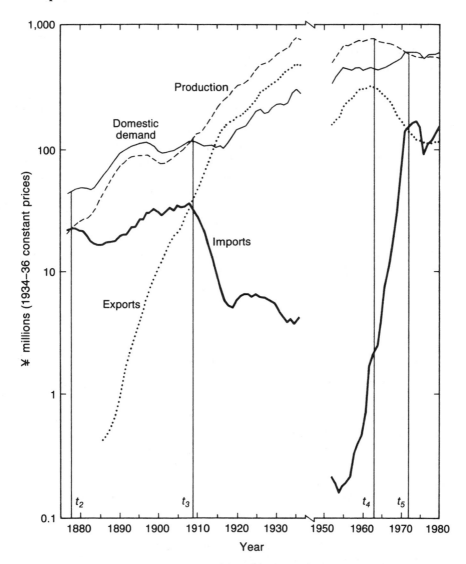

Note: Seven-year moving averages of domestic demand, production, exports and imports of cotton fabrics before the Second World War. Five-year moving averages after the Second World War.

Source: Estimated by the author. See Yamazawa (1984) for details of the estimation.

ginning in 1880, cotton yarn produced in large spinning firms began to compete with imported yarn; these firms were able to rapidly achieve export expansion. The development of Japan's cotton industry is clearly revealed by the changes in the activity of large-scale spinning firms.[1]

From Initial Introduction to Import Substitution in Cotton Yarn: 1883–95

Private firms first began producing cotton yarn in the mid-1870s when the government sold its model factories to the private sector. But because of their small size (2,000 spindles), these firms could not compete with imported cotton yarn. In 1883, Osaka Boseki began spinning production using steam engines and 10,500 spindles. Its success encouraged the entry of an additional 20 large-scale spinning firms into the industry in the following decade. Total spinning capacity rapidly grew from 80,000 spindles in 1886 to 350,000 spindles in 1890, thus achieving import substitution in low-count cotton yarn. Exports to Korea and China, however, met stiff competition from Indian yarn. And since cotton yarn of more than 20-count could not be produced domestically, imports continued. In 1892, imports of better-quality Indian raw cotton began replacing domestic raw cotton as well as raw cotton imported from China. With the decline in domestic cotton cultivation, cotton production based on indigenous technology rapidly disappeared.

Cotton Yarn Export Expansion and Cotton Fabric Import Substitution: 1895–1914

By 1897, domestic spinning capacity reached 1,014,000 spindles. The large spinning mills were able to produce high-count yarn from American raw cotton, and the high-count yarn replaced American and English cotton yarn imports. Most of the spinning mills, however, continued to produce low-count yarn. As much as 80 percent of the cotton yarn produced was low-count yarn, whose exports spread from China to Southeast Asia and directly competed with Indian cotton yarn.

The large spinning firms began to produce fabrics using their own cotton yarn. Such integrated production of yarn and fabrics continued to grow until the 1900s, catering not only to the domestic market but also to China. By 1909, the entire cotton fabric industry had reached the export stage, and in 1913, domestic spinning capacity reached 24 million spindles.

Cotton Fabric Export Expansion: The Interwar Period

Cotton yarn exports began to decline and cotton fabric exports began to expand with the outbreak of the First World War. In 1913, the large spinning mills began to move to China to take advantage of the cheap labor. In many ways, the war favored the development of the Japanese cotton industry and helped the industry reach its mature stage during the two decades after the war. During this period Japanese cotton fabrics replaced English cotton in the Chinese market. The share of Japanese cotton rose from 20.2 percent in 1913 to 66.9 percent in 1926, while the share of English cotton declined from 53.3 percent to 24.0 percent. The war also induced an export boom. Thus small and medium-sized weavers from the traditional weaving regions shifted production from domestic to export markets. In addition, regional production of gray cotton fabrics as well as bleached cotton and colored cotton cloth expanded, and as production expanded, the goods were then exported to China. Because the war halted imports of European dyestuffs and textile machinery, import substitution of synthetic dyes and textile machinery was necessary. Although these import substitutes met stiff competition from imported European goods, complete import substitution was nevertheless achieved in the 1920s and 1930s. By the end of the 1920s, Japan had emerged as the world's major exporter of cheap cotton fabrics and, as a consequence, had to face discriminatory import barriers, particularly in British Commonwealth countries.

Slowdown in Growth and the Reverse Import Stage: The Postwar Period

Cotton fabric production and exports climbed back to their pre–Second World War levels around 1955 and peaked at the start of the 1960s, after which they slowed down. In the 1960s exports to import-substituting countries began to decline, and Japanese imports began to grow. This occurred because the Japanese economy shifted from a labor-surplus economy to a labor-scarcity one. As wages rose, comparative advantage was lost in labor-intensive production. Accordingly, textile production shifted toward more capital-intensive production lines. Concurrently, domestic firms also began to establish subsidiary factories overseas to take advantage of low-wage labor, particularly in Southeast Asia. In turn, this encouraged import substitution and export expansion in the developing countries. Thus Japanese imports expanded in the 1970s as the industry entered the reverse import stage of development, which is the final stage in the life cycle of the Japanese cotton industry.

The Mechanism of CPC Development

What mechanism underlay the successful CPC development of the Japanese textile industry?

First, the existence and growth of sizeable domestic demand certainly contributed to the start and rapid increase of domestic production. It is estimated that domestic consumption was as high as 40,000 tons in 1880 and increased annually by an average of 2.5 percent during the period 1880–1940. Rapid export growth added to domestic consumption. Compositional changes in cotton fabric exports every 10 years (see Table 4.2) illustrate the expansion of the export market, which shifted from Korea and China to Southeast Asia and then to the rest of the world as Nawa (1937) and Kojima (1958) point out.

Second, there was a long-run cost reduction as indicated by the declining prices of domestic products compared to foreign ones, and by product quality improvement and diversification. Because production cost is composed of the costs of raw materials, capital, and labor, Japanese producers were at first handicapped by the high cost of imported raw cotton and machinery. But these costs were offset by the productivity increase realized through improved technology, enabling the mixing of raw cotton imported from various parts of the world and the institution of a 24-hour, two-shift operating schedule. Labor productivity increased faster than wages increased, which implies a reduction in labor costs. Fujino, Fujino, and Ono (1979:10) estimate that labor productivity in cotton textiles increased by an annual average rate of 2.56 percent for the period 1894–97; within cotton textiles the increase was much higher for cotton fabrics than for spinning, reflecting a shift in Japan's comparative advantage from cotton yarn to fabrics. Increased wage costs, however, exceeded productivity increases after the Second World War, which promoted the shift to the mature and reverse import stages.

Third, a group of large private firms played a leading role, while the government's role was quite limited. Large private firms led the development of Japan's cotton textile industry without much support from the government.

Table 4.2
Changes in the Export Market Structure of Japanese Cotton Fabrics (%)

Period	Taiwan and Korea	China[a]	Southeast Asia[b]	Rest of world	Total
1890–1892	14.3	68.9	7.5	9.3	100.0
1900–1902	60.5	37.9	0.8	0.8	100.0
1911–13	33.5	58.4	3.9	4.2	100.0
1924–26	12.6	46.7	26.3	14.4	100.0
1934–36	9.8	15.4	30.8	44.0	100.0

Notes:
a. China includes Hong Kong, Manchuria, and Kwantung provinces.

b. Southeast Asia includes India, the Philippines, and Thailand.

Source: Ministry of Finance (Okurasho), *Dainihon Gaikoku Boeki Nempyo* (Foreign Trade Annual of the Empire of Japan), various years.

Import substitution was achieved under tariffs of 5 percent or less before the recovery of tariff autonomy. Japanese producers were even handicapped by an import duty on raw cotton and an export duty on cotton yarn, though both tariffs were eliminated in 1895. Low conventional tariffs of 7 percent on çotton yarn and 10 percent on cotton fabrics continued to be applied to imports from Great Britain even after the recovery of tariff autonomy in 1899.[2] It was only after the Second World War that Jàpanese cotton textiles received adjustment assistance from the government (see discussion in Chapter 9).

Before the Second World War, the Greater Japanese Association of Spinning Firms (Dainihon Boseki Rengokai) took bold steps to protect the industry's development (Nihon Boseki Kyokai 1982). A typical example was the Indian Cotton Transportation Arrangement in 1891. The association boycotted the English shipping firm Peninsular and Oriental Steam Navigation Company, which had monopolized the market, because of that firm's increase in shipping costs for raw cotton brought to Japan from India. It supported instead the initiation of a Bombay-Yokohama route by the Japanese shipping company Nihon Yusen Kaisha, by assuring that a given minimum amount of raw cotton would be loaded. In this way the association succeeded in stopping the shipping fare increase (Nihon Boseki Kyokai 1982: Pt. 1, chap. 4).

The spinning firm association was also active in arranging production curtailment and export promotion. During the 1890 recession, spinning firms suffered from surplus capacity for the first time, which resulted in a serious management crisis. The association's members all stopped spinning operations for eight full days in June and July in an attempt to maintain market prices of yarn. This production curtailment was repeated ten times before 1937 to secure an orderly expansion of total production. Another initiative of the spinning firm association was the attempt to increase exports by selling products abroad at cheaper prices. The group was also able to have the export duty on cotton yarn and the import duty on raw cotton eliminated (Nihon Boseki Kyokai 1982: Pt. 1, chap. 2).

The organization of cotton fabric production and its export structure merits mentioning. There was an established division of labor in fabric production: small and medium weaving firms produced narrow cotton fabrics for domestic consumption, whereas large spinning firms produced broad cotton fabrics for export using their own yarns. However, due to the wider usage of power looms and the gradual decline in sales of traditional narrow cotton cloth, the small and medium firms began to shift to production of broad cotton fabrics. The production shift began around 1910 and accelerated during the export booms of the First World War and the 1930s. By 1937, small and medium weaving firms were supplying 45.3 percent of the broad fabrics produced for export (Kajinishi 1964: Pt. 4, chaps. 1 and 2).

Unlike the integrated weaving and finishing production of large spinning firms, the small and medium weavers organized cooperative groups in rural cities. Within each group, each firm specialized in a nonintegrated process of weaving, dyeing, and finishing. Through on-the-job experience, firms accumulated technical expertise and developed an efficient group of weavers who could supply a variety of quality fabrics in small lots, a large proportion of which were exported. Big trading companies, as well as their affiliated local wholesalers, provided the weavers with yarns, financing, design, and marketing information and sold their products in Japan and abroad.

Quickly foreseeing a change in the competitiveness of British and American products, Japanese general trading companies promoted the upgrading and standardization of their cotton fabric exports. Unfinished gray fabrics were quickly replaced by finished dyed ones, and cotton weaving firms soon met the higher standards for exports required by trading companies (Kajinishi 1964: Pt. 4, chap. 4). New markets in Southeast Asia, Oceania, Latin America, and Africa were explored, and branch networks were extended. A similar pattern of export development was repeated for rayon fabrics in the 1930s and for synthetic fabrics in the 1960s.

Another export-promotion activity of trading firms was the formation of export cartels. Mitsui Bussan encouraged large spinning firms to organize cartels for the expansion of exports to specific markets. In 1906 Sanei Mempu Yushutsu Kumiai was formed for exports to Korea, and in 1913 the Nihon Mempu Yushutsu Kumiai was formed for exports to Manchuria. At first, Mitsui Bussan provided the cartels with trading services at no charge, but later set low commission rates, with export credit at preferential rates.

The achievements of the cartels were impressive in both the Korean and Manchurian markets. In 1901, British cotton fabrics made up 70 percent of the Korean market, and American cotton fabrics made up 99 percent of the Manchurian market. Because Mitsui supplied Japanese fabrics at prices 20 to 25 percent cheaper than those of its British and American rivals, Japanese fabrics were able to quickly replace the British and American fabrics in both markets. By 1910, Japanese fabrics made up over 90 percent of both markets (MITI 1982). This exemplifies the success of the concerted efforts of manufacturers and distributors in export expansion.

TEXTILE INDUSTRY DIVERSIFICATION

The CPC development of one industry tended to induce CPC development in related industries, thereby causing the diversification in the production and export structures of Japan. Kojima (1958: chap. 10) called this phenomenon the diversification pattern of the CPC and attributed it to a change in the comparative advantage structure of the importing country as a result of capital accumulation. The following section emphasizes two aspects of this diversification development pattern in industries directly related to the textile industry. The diversification development pattern of several industries is discussed in detail in Chapter 5.

Diversification of Textile Raw Materials

Among the raw materials used in textiles—which include natural cotton, chemical yarns (rayon and acetate), and synthetic yarns (nylon, polyester, acrylic)—synthetic yarn is the raw material that is now produced and consumed in the greatest quantity. The shares of raw materials used in textile production (based on yarn tonnage for 1965) are as follows: cotton (36%), chemical fibers (26.1%), and synthetic fibers (24.7%). Chemical fibers were first developed as a substitute for silk and became inexpensive as the use of wider fabrics became popular. Synthetic fibers were also substituted for materials such as silk, cotton, and wool because of their uniform quality, a characteristic not found in natural fibers. Moreover, due to other chemical properties, synthetic fibers were the raw material of choice in the manufacture of fabrics for household and industrial uses other than clothing. Cotton, chemical, and synthetic fibers do not always blend together perfectly, but the technologies used in the weaving through the sewing stages for all three fibers are similar. Because of this similarity, all three fibers have come to be considered substitute raw materials by midstream (e.g., spinning firms) and downstream (e.g., garment manufacturers) firms. This substitutability has led to a drastic change in the industry's production structure.

Figure 4.3 traces the movements of the import/demand ratio (M/D) and the export/production ratio (X/S) for each of the three textile raw materials, following the schema depicted in Figure 2.1. The interrelationships of the ratios depicted in the figure reveal three important findings: (1) the time lag in CPC development for chemical and synthetic fibers reflects the time lag in their technological development; (2) for both cotton and chemical fibers, import substitution (decline in M/D) preceded export expansion (increase in X/S), although in the case of synthetic fibers export expansion commenced without import substitution; (3) in the post–Second World War period the export/production ratio of both cotton and synthetic fibers declined as their import/demand ratios rose. However, net imports of cotton began, whereas for chemical and synthetic fibers large net exports were still evident. The three findings, which provide additional insight into Japanese CPC development, are discussed below in their historical context.

Finding one. The time lag in chemical and synthetic fiber development reflects the time lag in production technology development in the United States and Europe. However, the time interval between technology development and the start of domestic production was reduced in the case of Japan for the

Figure 4.3
Diversification in Textile Industry Development

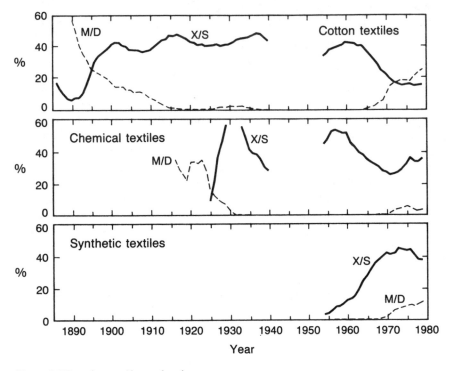

Notes: M/D = import/demand ratio.

    X/S = export/production ratio.

Figures for cotton are smoothed by a seven-year moving average before 1940 and a five-year moving average after 1950.

Source: Estimated by the author. See Yamazawa (1984) for details of the estimation.

following reasons. In 1892, the production technique for viscose rayon was developed in Europe. Although Azuma Kogyo (which became Teijin) succeeded in developing its own technology in 1913, commercial production did not begin until continuous spinning machinery was imported in 1923. Afterward, throughout the rest of the 1920s, Asahi Kenshoku, Toyo Rayon, and the big cotton-spinning firms began production with imported technology and machinery.

The manufacture of synthetic fibers began in 1938 with the acquisition of basic patents for nylon 66 from Dupont. In 1950, Japan developed on its own the technology for nylon 66, and in 1951 the technology for vinylon, and in general made considerable progress in closing the technology gap. Domestic production of polyester and acrylic began in the second half of the 1950s. Although major chemical fiber firms were already actively engaged in autonomous technology development for the preparatory stages, they had to purchase patents from American and European firms that owned the basic patents for production.[3]

Finding two. Although the raw materials for chemical and synthetic fibers were new commodities, it was possible to adapt the technology for cotton and silk weaving (after the yarn-producing stage) to accommodate the shift to the new raw materials relatively easily. Even for chemical fibers, only yarn had to be imported, and thanks to the use of the accumulated technology in silk weaving, the woven fabrics produced were competitive from the beginning. Existing trade channels were used for marketing, and the synthetic textile industry also made use of existing weaving technology and marketing channels (except for yarn). Practically no imports were needed and export expansion was possible. The active shift from silk and cotton to chemical and synthetic fibers took place in every weaving region.

Competition with European imports was severe during the import substitution stage for chemical fibers. From 1919 to 1926, the world price of rayon fell by about 33 percent, and between 1929 and 1931 it dropped further by 50 percent. As a result, the pioneering rayon firms urged the government to raise tariffs by 25 percent. But the increase in tariffs merely induced the entry of other firms, ultimately leading to more severe competition in the domestic market. Although labor productivity rose by 23 percent between 1926 and 1930, most of this was a result of cost reduction from scale expansion (Nihon Kagaku Sen-i Kyokai 1974).

To provide an outlet for surplus production, the spinning firm association resorted to a compulsory export quota of 5 percent in 1929. This generally took the form of rayon fabric exports, which increased rapidly, with Korea, India, Indonesia, Australia, and China as the principal markets. Except in Korea, Japan was able to wrench away a share of the market from Italy, the United Kingdom, France, and the Netherlands by taking advantage of improved production technology, the low prices resulting from economies of scale, and the low wages reinforced by the exchange rate depreciation of 1932. Japan's rayon fabric exports encountered import restrictions in these markets after 1931.

Finding three. After the Second World War there was a marked increase in the production and consumption of chemical and synthetic fabrics as opposed to natural fiber fabrics. The share of chemical and synthetic fibers in total fabric raw materials on a yarn basis rose from 25.4 percent in 1952 to 50.8 percent in 1965. By 1982, the share was 68.7 percent. This was largely due to the rapid rise in usage of synthetic fibers, which were developed after the war. The share of synthetic fibers (excluding chemicals) in total fabric raw materials was 0.5 percent, 24.7 percent, and 57.9 percent for 1952, 1965, and 1982, respectively. Such rapid growth in production was due to the corresponding demand growth that occurred as a result of the wide acceptance of the new synthetic fibers, as well as the price decline that resulted from expansion in the scale of production.

The competitive edge resulted from the shift of traditional cotton- and silk-producing regions to the use of the new synthetic materials. Given such acquired price competitiveness, 45 percent of synthetic textiles were exported in the form of fabrics. About 38 to 39 percent of exports were in the form of yarn, whereas a much smaller percentage, 16 to 17 percent, was accounted for by finished forms of textiles. Although developing countries had caught up with Japan in the production of chemical and synthetic fibers (to the extent that the import/demand ratio had risen in Japan), the increase in imports was concentrated in finished products. Today, by contrast, synthetic textiles as a whole still exhibit large export surpluses. Recently, a few firms in the synthetic fabric industry have begun to use a new type of yarn, and the resulting difference in fabrics has called for a special processing technology. These new fabrics were exported mainly to the American and Middle Eastern markets from 1979 to 1984 in response to the sophisticated demand at higher income levels. This export boom contributed in part to the revitalization of the Japanese textile industry.

Linkage Effects of Cotton Industry Development

CPC development in the textile industry has induced similar growth patterns in its two supplying industries (known as the backward linkage effect): (1) the textile machinery industry (spinning preparation, spinning, weaving, dyeing, and knitting), and (2) the dyestuffs industry (alizarin, aniline, and other dyes). Expansion in the cotton yarn and cotton fabric industries called for increased investments in textile machinery and synthetic dyestuffs; however, since there was no domestic production of these goods at the time, they began to be imported in 1883. With continued growth in domestic demand, domestic production was attempted, but unlike in the textile industry where indigenous technology made absorption of new technologies easier, technology absorption in the machinery and dyestuffs industries was more difficult and came about only after a considerable time lag. Domestic production of textile machinery came before dyestuff production because of the accumulated production technology know-how derived from traditional weaving and spinning machinery. By 1889, there were 100 machines that had been produced domestically compared to 3,386 units that had been imported. By 1897, Sakichi Toyoda had already built the Toyoda weaving loom (made of wood), but due to the large gap between modern and traditional spinning technologies, domestic production of modern spinning machinery did not come about until 1925. Although import substitution occurred continuously, imports reflected the equipment-investment cycle, which peaked in 1920 and rapidly declined thereafter. By 1925, the level of imports was less than domestic production and by 1933 even less than exports.

In contrast, production of synthetic dyestuffs was an entirely new chemical industry. Before the First World War all dyestuffs had to be imported, but in 1912, the government-run industrial laboratory succeeded in synthesizing alizarin. By 1914, commercial production of dyestuffs began in a factory attached to the privately owned mine Mitsui Kozan. With the onset of the First World War, import volume during the period 1915–17 fell to less than one-seventh of the volume during the period 1911–12. In 1915, however, a bill was introduced and enacted to promote the production of dyestuffs and medical goods (Senryo-Iyakuhin-Seizo-Shorei-ho). As a result, a dyestuff manufacturing firm (Nippon Senryo Kaisha) was set up and by 1918 domestic production had caught up with import volume. Although imports recovered during the period 1922–24 due to dumping, they later declined and fell below exports in 1930. Steady export expansion of both textile machinery and dyestuffs to China and Korea began only in the 1930s.

It is difficult to empirically measure the magnitude of the backward linkage effects. The relationship between textile machinery and synthetic dyestuffs (domestic demand in volume terms) and cotton production is estimated using ordinary least squares method techniques as follows:

Textile machinery (1883–1936)

$$\ln D_2 = 1.5575 + 0.8294 \ln S_1 - 0.0011t$$
$$ (0.08) \quad\ \ (7.33) \qquad\qquad (0.10)$$
$$\bar{R}^2 = 0.8262, \ DW = 1.0212$$

Synthetic dyestuffs (1883–1937)

$$\ln D_3 = -96.2934 + 0.4810 \ln S_1 + 0.0515t$$
$$ (6.31) \qquad\ \ (5.72) \qquad\qquad (6.09)$$
$$\bar{R}^2 = 0.9233, \ DW = 0.5826$$

where D_2 and D_3 are domestic demand for textile machinery and synthetic dyestuffs, respectively; S_1 refers to production volume of cotton textiles; t is the time-trend variable; and the figures in parentheses are the t-values. In both equations, statistically significant, positive coefficients for cotton production endorse the backward linkage effects on supplying industries over the whole period of the latter group's CPC development. However, such factors as technology gaps and the occurrence of wars exert their influences on domestic demand expansion (which is the basis for the CPC development), so that it is not possible to specify exactly the scale of domestic demand needed in order for domestic production to begin.

FOREIGN INVESTMENT AND TRADE CHANGES

As discussed in Chapter 2, foreign investment plays an important role in the last stage of CPC development. It hastens the "catching-up" process of host (late-developing) countries and the decrease in production growth of investing (developed) countries, leading to the latter's reverse import stage. In fact, direct foreign investment (DFI) was undertaken by the Japanese textile industry during the period of export expansion and the subsequent slowdown in production. In turn, this contributed to the textile industry's development in East Asia and the ASEAN member countries, while encouraging the growth of reverse imports in Japan.

Direct foreign investment by the Japanese textile industry had been undertaken by spinning firms during the First World War in the Shanghai, Qingdao, and Tian Jing districts of the Chinese mainland. After the Second World War, Toyo Boseki set up a spinning mill in Brazil. Table 4.3 shows the amount of DFI by the Japanese textile industry after the Second World War and plots its structure. Between 1955 and 1976 there were a total of 377 DFI projects. The 317 DFI projects during the two periods 1965–69 and 1970–74 represent a concentration of some 84 percent of total DFI. Before 1964, Japan suffered from a scarcity of funds to invest overseas, and since 1975 DFI activity has virtually come to a standstill. The large amount of overseas investment in the period 1965–74 is characteristic of the Japanese textile industry when compared with the relatively small amount of DFI by American and European textile firms (OECD 1981:64). Since DFI implies the transfer of a package of managerial skills, capital, and technology, the active DFI undertaken by the Japanese textile firms reflects the industry's abundance of human resources possessing such skills and technology.

Table 4.3 also shows that DFI by the Japanese textile industry in developed countries was rare; about 92 percent of the industry's total DFI was in developing countries. Of this, East Asia and the ASEAN member countries had shares of 40 and 28 percent of Japan's total DFI, respectively, and became the principal host countries for Japanese investment.

Of the 258 DFI projects in East Asia and the ASEAN member countries, 238 are almost equally divided between the midstream and downstream stages of production. Investments have been concentrated in the downstream stage (clothing and other finished products) in East Asia, whereas in ASEAN, investments in the midstream stage (spinning, weaving, dyeing, finishing) are almost double those in the downstream stage. The upstream stage, which supplies raw materials to the midstream and downstream stages of production, consists wholly of chemical and synthetic fiber making. But in both East Asia and ASEAN, however, investments in this stage are small.

Much of the DFI undertaken by the Japanese textile industry has been in chemical and synthetic textiles. In contrast to the cotton textile industry, which had generally been established by local firms, the chemical and synthetic textile industry, being a new industry, was often encouraged by host countries through promotion policies, including high import tariffs and exemption from corporate and business taxes. A number of investments took the form of joint ventures with local entrepreneurs, and the share of wholly owned Japanese firms ranged from 62 to 100 percent in the upstream stage in each country except Taiwan. In contrast, at the midstream stage, majority-owned Japanese firms constituted a smaller share; for Malaysia's spinning industry the share was 45 to 57 percent, for Thailand's spinning industry the share was 20 percent, and for Indonesia's spinning industry it was 15 percent (all in 1978 values). At the downstream stage, Japanese firms represented an even smaller share (Tran 1985).

The motives for DFI by Japan's textile industry include: (1) DFI has allowed the industry to preserve its market in the host country by circumvent-

Table 4.3
Direct Foreign Investment by the Japanese Textile Industry (number of projects)

Period	Production stage	East Asia	ASEAN	Other developing countries	Developed countries	Total
1955–64	U	0	1			
	M	4	4	20	1	38
	D	2	6			
1965–69	U	5	2			
	M	17	18	24	4	106
	D	31	5			
1970–74	U	3	9			
	M	29	38	29	23	211
	D	51	19			
1975–78	U	0	0			
	M	2	5	5	3	22
	D	7	0			
Total upstream		8	12			
Total midstream		52	65			
Total downstream		91	30			
Total		151	107	88	31	377

Note: U, M, and D denote the upstream, midstream, and downstream stages of synthetic fiber textile production.

Source: Tran (1985).

ing the import barriers set up to encourage domestic production of the import substitute, and (2) DFI has allowed the industry to avoid the rising trend in wages in Japan by transferring production to low-wage developing countries. While Japan's DFI has helped Japanese industry, it has also promoted the growth of the East Asian and ASEAN textile industries. This has resulted in a drastic change in the direction of the textile goods trade in the region. In the early 1950s, Japan was virtually the only country with a modern textile industry in the East and Southeast Asian regions and was competitive in exports. Cotton textile production began in the early 1950s in Taiwan and Hong Kong and in the mid-1950s in Korea. However, until the 1960s only Hong Kong was competitive in export markets. Since the ASEAN member countries had just begun cotton production, Southeast Asia was Japan's major export market for cotton products in the 1950s. In the 1960s, however, import substitution in cotton products grew rapidly in the ASEAN member countries. During this period, East Asian exports of cotton products to the United States swelled and displaced Japanese exports. It was thus in the U.S. market that trade competition between Japanese and late-developing East Asian countries began.

Chemical and synthetic yarn production began in the second half of the 1960s in both the East Asian and the ASEAN member countries. By the early 1970s, Taiwan and Korea had rapidly achieved import substitution and exports were growing. The ASEAN member countries reached the export stage in the second half of the 1970s. As discussed earlier, Japan's DFI played a leading role in the industrialization of the chemical and synthetic textile industries in these countries. Rapid localization of production was achieved in the East Asian countries that had already reached the export stage in cotton textile manufacturing, and in the ASEAN member countries in which import substitution in cotton and synthetic textiles had taken place. Japanese firms made significant contributions even in the development of the midstream stages of these countries' textile industries. Today, even in ASEAN's slowest-developing country (Indonesia), cotton and synthetic textile exports have begun to expand. As a whole, the East and Southeast Asian region has had great capacity to supply textile exports. Indeed, in the 1970s, East Asian export goods began leading the penetration of the Japanese market. This "boomerang effect," as Shinohara (1982: chap. 9) calls it, is the major cause of the Japanese textile industry's entering the reverse import stage. Chapter 9 discusses in greater detail the corresponding structural adjustment in Japan's domestic market.

Five

CPC Development
of the Iron and Steel Industry

The development of the iron and steel industry followed a pattern similar to that advanced in the previous chapter. Here, however, a simulation analysis is conducted using a simple econometric model based on the hypothesized development pattern. The summary that follows outlines the CPC development for the chemicals and other heavy industries and attempts to identify the mechanisms behind the diversification of Japan's industrial structure.

DEVELOPMENT OF THE IRON AND STEEL INDUSTRY

The iron and steel industry has three production processes: the iron-making process in which pig iron is refined from iron ore in a blast furnace fired by coking coal; the steel-making process through which pig iron is changed into steel ingots in open-hearth furnaces or converters; and finally, the milling and casting processes in which ingots are fabricated into various types of steel products such as bars, rods, plates, pipes, and rails. The output of ingots in the steel-making process is often used to measure the growth of the industry in international comparisons. But the output of ingots is not a good measure of the impact of the Japanese steel industry in the international market because Japan's ingot trade has been almost negligible relative to its ingot production. Industry trade has been in pig iron and steel products, and domestic ingot output by and large goes into the domestic production of steel products.

This situation can be partly accounted for by technical explanations, but it also reflects unbalanced growth between the iron-making process on the one hand, and the steel-making and milling processes on the other. This imbalance is partly explained by the historical development of the industry. Before the Second World War, the integrated operation of the three processes occurred only in the government-owned Yawata Iron Works and one private firm; the remaining firms in the industry, including major *zaibatsu* firms, were steel-making and milling firms that were dependent on imported pig iron.[1] Because production of iron was handicapped by high-cost imports of iron ore, and because large investments of capital were necessary to reach optimum-scale production, the private firms were forced to specialize in the steel-making and milling processes. Therefore, in the following analysis, steel products represent the industry as a whole. For comparison, however, frequent reference will be made to the growth pattern of pig iron production.

CPC Development of the Steel Industry

Figure 5.1 shows the growth of domestic production (S), imports (M), exports (X), and (apparent) domestic demand (D) for steel products over the past one hundred years. Domestic demand for steel products is defined as $D = S + M - X$ and represents the demand by the Japanese for steel products, both domestic and imported. Seven-year moving average values are plotted to show the relationships between the growth trends of the four variables. Figure 5.1 exhibits the typical pattern of growth, with successful import substitution followed by export expansion. The industry's steady growth began in 1901 when the government-owned Yawata Iron Works commenced operations. At that time, there already existed a fairly large domestic market for imported steel products. Yawata was equipped with integrated facilities for iron and steel making at the time of its establishment, but nine years passed before the firm was able to operate at a profit. Both the deficits and capacity expansion over this period were financed by the government. Until 1910, the major *zaibatsu* firms followed Yawata's lead, but they were equipped with only open-hearth furnaces and milling facilities and were dependent on either Yawata or foreign suppliers for their pig iron inputs. Domestic steel production expanded rapidly during this period.

The First World War spurred the industry to expand rapidly once again. Price hikes due to the stoppage of imports from Europe and tax exemptions under the Iron-Manufacturing Encouragement Act (1917) increased profits and encouraged the entry of small and medium-scale firms into the industry. Production grew rapidly and exceeded imports in 1923; imports then decreased and by 1934, exports exceeded imports. Rapid growth in both production and exports resumed following the recovery from the destruction of the Second World War and even accelerated in the postwar period of heavy investment and technology transfer. Exports of steel products in the early years of the interwar period seem to have been mainly reexports, and before the Second

Figure 5.1
CPC Development of Steel Products

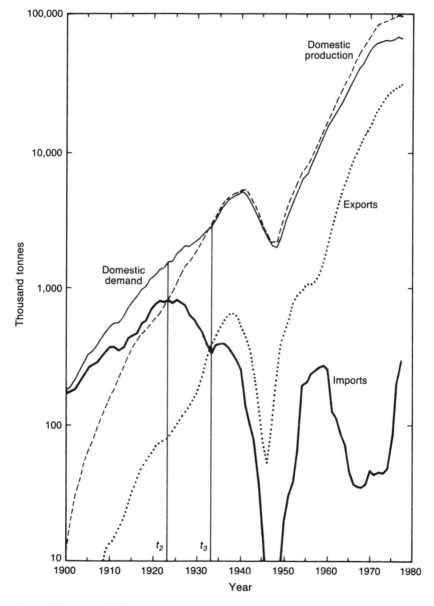

World War exports were mostly to Japan's colonies (Korea, Taiwan, Manchuria, and the rest of China). Only after the Second World War were Japan's steel products sold in the world market at competitive prices. Table 5.1 shows the average annual growth rates of domestic demand, production, imports, and exports for the periods 1900–1914 to 1952–66.

It is interesting to view the interwar period from the perspective of industry growth. Having suffered both from overcapacity and severe competition from cheap imports after the First World War, the industry undertook rationalization and cost reduction and achieved complete import substitution. The industry also benefited from government support, which included tariff hikes (1921, 1926, 1932), tax exemptions to steel-making firms, subsidization of steel production for shipbuilding (1921), the formation of cartels, and finally the establishment of the Nippon Steel Company (1934) (see Table 5.2). In addition, a 43 percent depreciation in the exchange rate in early 1932 was effectively equivalent to a rise in tariffs on imports and a subsidy to exports.

Cartels were formed according to categories of steel products; in each category, Yawata and the major private firms collaborated to maintain prices of domestic products as low as those of imports. Price-reducing competition could thus be avoided and the combined share of Japanese firms in the domestic market increased, although some inefficient firms had to sell at a loss at cartel prices, but the cartels themselves were eventually terminated. In 1934, Yawata and six *zaibatsu* steel mills merged to form Nippon Steel Company, which produced 95.2 percent of the pig iron and 43.9 percent of all steel products in Japan. Elimination of duplicate capacity, rationalization through economies of scale, and the strengthening of international competitiveness were put forward as reasons for the merger, but the merger also helped some inefficient private mills. Import dependence (M/D) declined rapidly from 60 percent to less than 10 percent in the interwar period.

Table 5.1
Average Annual Growth Rates of Steel Products (%)

	1900–14	1914–23	1923–38	1952–66
Domestic demand	10.1	8.9	7.6	15.9
Production	26.3	11.0	12.9	16.5
Imports	6.5	7.6	−5.7	−0.3
Exports	23.7	13.4	15.1	18.9

Note: Rates are calculated from the seven-year moving averages for each of the four variables in 1900, 1914, 1923, 1938, 1952, and 1966.

Source: Nihon Tekko Renmei, *Tekko Tokei Yoran* (Iron and Steel Statistics Annual) (1970).

Unbalanced Growth between Iron and Steel

The growth of pig iron production was much slower than that of steel. The first success in the production of pig iron in a blast furnace came in 1887, and almost half of Japan's needs were supplied domestically by 1900. But

Table 5.2
Government Policies Protecting the Iron and Steel Industry

Period	Policy
Before 1900	Experimental operations in government-owned small-scale foundries
1901	Yawata (government-owned) Iron Works commenced operations
1907–09	First expansion plan for Yawata
1911	General Revision of Customs Tariff Act (1.67 yen per tonne of pig iron and 15% ad valorem equivalent rate on steel products)
1911–16	Second expansion plan for Yawata
1917	Iron-Manufacturing Encouragement Act (tax exemption for iron-making firms)
1921	First amendment to Iron-Manufacturing Encouragement Act (enlarged tax exemption). Change in tariffs on steel products from specific duties to ad valorem ones (15% ad valorem rate).
1926	Second amendment to Iron-Manufacturing Encouragement Act (subsidy to pig iron production; 3 to 6 yen per tonne). Rise in customs tariff on steel products (18% ad valorem rate).
1926–31	Formation of cartels by category of steel products with government support
1932	Rise in customs tariff on pig iron (6 yen per tonne)
1934	Establishment of the Nippon Steel Company (the merger of Yawata with six *zaibatsu* firms. Eighty-two percent of its shares were held by the finance minister. It produced 96 percent of the pig iron and 44 percent of the steel products in Japan).
1937	Iron-Manufacturing Enterprise Act (support for integrated iron- and steel-making firms; a change to production expansion policy for wartime economy)
1937–41	Five-year expansion plan for steel production
1947–50	Reconstruction of steel production under Priority Production Project
1951–55	First rationalization project for steel
1956–60	Second rationalization project for steel

pig iron imports increased at a pace that almost equalled growth of domestic production, and as a result, import dependence declined by only 10 percent during the interwar period. During the period 1900–1936, domestic demand for pig iron increased at an average annual rate of 9.7 percent, the same rate as the demand for steel products, whereas imports and production of pig iron increased by 8.6 and 10.7 percent, respectively. Exports of pig iron remained negligible, even in recent years. Figure 5.2 illustrates the decreasing dependence on imports of both pig iron and steel products, and clearly contrasts the import-substitution process occurring in both. The dependence on steel imports declined rapidly from 94 percent in 1900 to 9 percent in 1936, except for the slack period during the First World War. The dependence on pig iron imports, however, declined slowly from 55 percent to 30 percent during the same period. The differing patterns of growth between the pig iron and steel products industries can be partly explained by the fact that during the First World War, *zaibatsu* firms began producing pig iron near deposits of iron ore and coke in Manchuria and Korea, and the pig iron was imported to Japan for further fabrication. Dependence on pig iron produced in Manchuria and Korea amounted to 18–20 percent of domestic demand during the First World War and in the 1930s. Slow import substitution of pig iron is also explained by Japan's lack of iron ore and coke, the continued competition from cheap Indian imports during the 1920s, and the existence in Japan of a large group of steel-making firms largely dependent on imported pig iron. These firms resisted an increase in the tariff on pig iron until 1932.

Throughout the 1930s, national security arguments promoted self-sufficiency in pig iron and further expansion of integrated iron and steel production. The rise in pig iron tariffs (1932), the dominance of pig iron production by Nippon Steel (1934), and the Iron-Manufacturing Enterprise Act (1937) were all in accordance with the promotion of integrated iron and steel production. A five-year expansion plan for steel production (1937–41) was designed to increase Japan's self-sufficiency in pig iron to 89 percent. In addition, the substitution of Manchurian pig iron for Indian pig iron was further encouraged. With the help of such government policies, 80.5 percent self-sufficiency in pig iron was achieved in 1940; in addition, two-thirds of all imported pig iron came from Manchuria. The substitution of integrated iron and steel production for imports was thus accomplished immediately before the Second World War.

AN ECONOMETRIC MODEL OF CPC DEVELOPMENT

Mechanism of CPC Development

The review of the steel industry's development in the previous section gives a clue as to the mechanism behind the successful import substitution and

Figure 5.2
Dependence on Pig Iron and Steel Product Imports

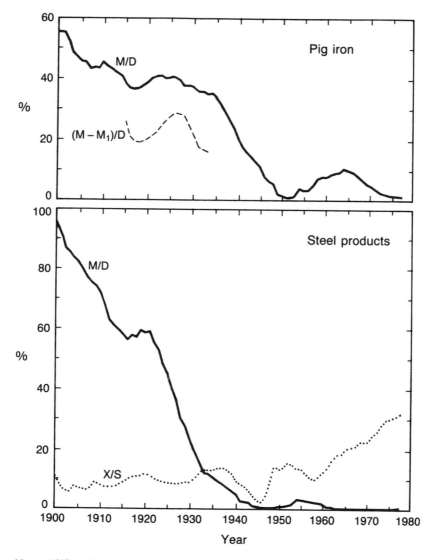

Notes: M/D = import/demand, *X/S* = export/production, and *M*₁ = imports from Korea and Manchuria, all calculated from the seven-year moving average series.

Source: Yamazawa (1984).

export expansion of an industry. The factors behind this mechanism may be summarized as follows:

- Steady reduction in production costs as the industry's production expands is required. Reduction in costs tends to lower the price of the domestic product relative to import and world prices, thereby making possible import substitution and export expansion.

- Growth of domestic demand is also required to induce investment and output expansion in the industry. Foreign trade is also important as export expansion occurs and as domestic demand increases through import substitution.

- Government protection accelerates the growth of demand, which leads to output expansion, cost reduction, and finally import substitution and export expansion for the industry. Industry protection may include such policies as tariffs and subsidies, and more direct but less apparent instruments such as tax exemptions and preferential purchasing policies. Furthermore, in the case of the steel industry, the government-owned Yawata Iron Works initiated and led the growth of the industry.

For Japan, both cost reduction and increased domestic demand were indispensable factors behind the successful import substitution and export expansion strategies; government protection was also important for most of Japan's heavy manufacturing industries. The following econometric model traces both the long-run growth trend of the industry and its short-term fluctuations.[2]

Four behavioral equations and an equilibrium condition are needed to determine the equilibrium values of five endogenous variables for a given set of values of exogenous variables in each year (see Table 5.3). The level of domestic demand for steel is a function of domestic income and the demonstration effect (equation 1, Table 5.3). Domestic income is represented by the total output of industries using steel products as inputs. This is different than the indicator used for income in the case of consumer goods, which is represented by per capita gross domestic expenditure or consumption expenditure, because demand for steel, an intermediate good, will be determined by the income of steel-using firms. The demonstration effect reflects the changing pattern of demand over time for a new product in the domestic market. It can be formulated as a monotonically increasing function of time beginning from the introduction of the product to the domestic market. The function can be represented by a growth curve that rises first at an increasing rate, then at a decreasing rate, and finally approaches a fixed level. The time necessary for the demonstration effect to reach this fixed level differs from one commodity to the next. It will be shorter, for example, for synthetic products, as a domestic market has already been developed for their natural substitutes.

The level of imports is determined in equation 2 in Table 5.3 by the ratio of the import price and the domestic price for a given level of domestic demand. Steady reduction of the domestic price relative to the import price promotes import substitution, and imports will decline in absolute volume when the price effect more than offsets the income effect (that is, the increase in domestic demand).

When the domestic price of a product declines significantly relative to the world price, export of the domestic product begins. The growth of exports will depend on both the growth of foreign income and the decline in the domestic price relative to the world price (equation 3, Table 5.3).

The price equation, equation 4 in Table 5.3, represents the relationship between the domestic price (cost) and the total production of an industry, and, therefore, the basic relationship of the model. Equation 4 hypothesizes a negative correlation between the domestic price and the total production of the industry. This correlation has been widely observed in the growth processes

Table 5.3
Model of CPC Development

Domestic demand	$D = D(Y, L)$	(1)
	$D_Y' > 0, D_L' > 0$	
Imports	$M = M(D, P, PM)$	(2)
	$M_D' > 0, M_P' > 0, M_{PM}' < 0$	
Exports	$X = X(Z, P, PZ)$	(3)
	$X_Z' > 0, X_P' < 0, X_{PZ}' > 0$	
Price	$P = P(S, PO, W)$	(4)
	$P_S' < 0, P_{PO}' > 0, P_W' > 0$	
Equilibrium condition	$D = S + M - X$	(5)

Note:
Symbols
- D: Domestic demand
- S: Production
- X: Exports
- M: Imports
- Y: Domestic income variable
- Z: Foreign income variable
- L: Demonstration effect (monotonically increasing function of time)
- P: Price of steel products
- PM: Import price of steel products (including tariff)
- PZ: World price of steel products
- PO: Import price of iron ore
- W: Wage rate of metal workers

of principal industries in Japan and implies long-run decreasing costs in these industries. As one example, except during the First World War and the late 1930s, there was a negative correlation between price and total production of steel products.[3] Because this relationship has been observed in the development of several industries, it was introduced into the model. A theoretical explanation is, however, also needed and is given below.

Long-run Decreasing Costs in an Industry

Long-run decreasing costs in an industry seem to stem from the complex interaction of various factors. Among these various factors, the following seem most significant:

(1) The expansion of an industry's total production is generally accompanied by an enlarged scale of production (as measured by productive capacity). In the process of industry expansion, new firms enter the industry and new plants are established by existing firms, thus increasing the total number of plants. But more important is the fact that the newer the plant, the larger is its optimum scale of production, and the larger the optimum scale, the lower the unit cost of production.

It may be that new small or medium-scale plants are established during the years of persistent excess demand and price increase. But as the excess demand slackens and the price decreases to its previous level, the inefficient plants are eliminated through competition. This is in fact what happened in the steel industry during and after the First World War. If the market is competitive enough, the unit production cost in the most efficient new plant tends to dominate the market price in the long run, and inefficient old plants are scrapped and replaced by more efficient and larger plants. Cost reduction due to large-scale production seems to be one of the main factors for an industry's decreasing costs over the long run. A new large-scale plant makes it possible to reduce production costs in various ways. Although there is little room for saving on material costs, since raw materials are used in proportion to the level of output, a large-scale plant reduces the costs of construction, energy, and labor per unit of production. Production capacity of blast furnaces increased steadily from 160 tonnes per day in 1901 to 500 tonnes in 1930 and 1,000 tonnes in 1937, and to more than 3,000 tonnes in 1965. This is also the case for the production capacity of open-hearth furnaces in steel manufacturing. Larger-scale production also makes possible the automatic and continuous operation of production processes, thereby leading to reduction of costs per unit of production. A good example is the "hot strip" mill process in steel making, which has replaced the old-fashioned "pull-over" mill process because of its profitability in larger-scale production.

(2) Long-run decreasing costs can be partly explained by improvements in the production process—including improvements in production equipment

and in management systems—that are a result of the accumulation of production experiences and improvement in skills of production workers. In order to expand a newly introduced industry, foreign technology must be quickly learned, and the cost reduction that occurs with the learning effect is important in the early stages of industry growth. This learning effect may not necessarily increase in proportion to the level of production but may rise in proportion to the accumulated total output. For example, it took several years for Japanese iron- and steel-making firms to adapt foreign technology to the types of iron ore and coke that were available in Japan.

(3) Cost reduction is also accelerated by external economies, that is, by the effect of one industry on related industries. Machinery production in Japan benefited a great deal from the growth of the steel industry, which in turn gained from successful domestic production of steel-making machinery in the 1930s. The steel industry has also benefited from the development of the automatic control system in the post–Second World War years.

The relative contributions of these three factors, which seem to have brought about a steady cost reduction in the case of steel products, differ considerably in different industries and at different stages of industry growth. In the case of the steel industry, the learning effect was most important in the industry's early years, and economies of scale and external effects gained importance in the 1920s and the post–Second World War years.

It is not easy to quantitatively analyze long-run decreasing costs because of the unavailability of reliable data on capacities and input-output relationships in steel making. It is possible, however, to introduce this observed relationship as the combined effect of various factors. Increases in costs of materials and labor (equation 4) tend to offset the reduction in costs mentioned earlier.

The dynamics of the model can be demonstrated. Industry growth is first generated on the demand side, primarily with the growth of domestic income and assisted by the learning effect in the domestic market and the growth of foreign income. Steady growth of domestic demand induces output expansion, which is accompanied by the reduction in unit cost and market price. This, in turn, leads to import substitution and export promotion for a given level of import prices, world price of the product, and input prices, thereby adding to the growth of domestic demand.[4] Exogenous changes in these prices can affect this process. Government protection of an industry can lead to a change in prices. Tariffs on imports, for example, raise import prices and accelerate import substitution of the product.

One theoretical question remains. What assurance is there that the industry always moves along the long-run decreasing cost curve? Movement down the curve depends on two conditions being met. The first condition is that firms accurately forecast any increase in demand and then expand production accordingly without a time lag. The second condition is that the productive capacity be divisible so that firms can produce any level of production at minimum cost. The actual growth process of steel products is characterized by cyclical fluctuations along a steady growth trend; this observation appears to attest to the accuracy of the assumptions underlying the model. However, except for the First World War years and the late 1930s, which were unusual periods for Japan because of persistent excess demand for steel products, it may be assumed that the industry moved along the curve with only some random divergences. Government support for the industry through government-owned firms and preferential purchasing policies helped the industry meet the first condition.

ECONOMETRIC ANALYSIS
OF PRE–SECOND WORLD WAR DEVELOPMENT

The hypothesis and model put forward in the previous section need to be tested by empirical data. Thus far, the model has been applied to actual data for the pre–Second World War period excluding the years of persistent excess demand, namely 1900–1914 and 1921–36, and for the post–Second World War period (1952–68). Simulations of the growth process under counter-factual policy assumptions were done for each period. The results are described in this and the following section.

Four behavioral equations were estimated in log-linear form by the two-stage least squares method for the periods 1900–1914 and 1921–36. The results are summarized in Table 5.4.

The growth of domestic demand is explained fairly well by the domestic income variable and the demonstration effect. Several alternative indicators for income were used, including manufacturing production and the sum of the net products of mining, manufacturing, and construction. However, the production index of machinery gives a better estimate than either of the alternatives. The machinery and metal goods industries make up the bulk of the demand for steel products, and the sum of the two would improve the estimates, but no data are available for this alternative. The demonstration effect is estimated by a truncated exponential function of time. Alternative values are applied to the time coefficient, and the value 0.1 gives the best estimate.

The import function seems to capture fluctuations completely. The elasticity of domestic demand for imports is estimated to be .45, and the domestic and import price elasticities are 1.4 and -1.4, respectively. The low value of the elasticity of domestic demand for imports is worth noting. This means that when domestic demand for steel products increases by 1 percent, demand for imported steel products increases by less than .5 percent. This low elasticity of demand can be explained in part by the fact that a large part of domestic

Table 5.4
CPC Development of Steel Products: 1900–14, 1921–36

Estimates[a]

Domestic demand (1)

$$\log D = 6.6967 + .8511 \log Y + 1.0804 \log L$$
$$(12.02)(1.72)$$

$$s = .1610 \quad \bar{R}2 = .9741 \quad DW = 1.57$$

Imports (2)

$$\log M = 4.4806 + .4494 \log D + 1.3779 \log PP - 1.4317 \log PPM$$
$$(3.37)(2.30)(5.87)$$

$$s = .2936 \quad \bar{R}^2 = .7152 \quad DW = 1.80$$

Exports (3)

$$\log X = -1.0181 + 1.7015 \log Z - 6.4112 \log PP + 2.0700 \log PPZ$$
$$(3.47)(6.29)(3.36)$$

$$s = .6904 \quad \bar{R}^2 = .8701 \quad DW = 1.12$$

Price (4)

$$\log PP = 1.1994 - .0910 \log S + .1800 \log PPO$$
$$(4.79)(1.23)$$

$$s = .1332 \quad \bar{R}^2 = .7011 \quad DW = .96$$

Final Tests	*D*	*M*	*X*	*S*	*PP*
Root Mean Square	3729.5	2317.75	576.41	3070.90	0.11
Von-Neuman Square	0.45	0.57	1.10	0.34	0.87

Notes:
Symbols
- *D:* Domestic demand ⎤
- *S:* Production   ⎬ of steel products (hundred tonnes)
- *X:* Export   ⎪
- *M:* Import   ⎦
- *Y:* Production index of machinery
- *Z:* World production of steel ingots
- *L:* Demonstration effect $(= 1 - \exp[-0.1(t - 1890)])$; *t:* year, $t = 1$ for 1900
- *PP:* Price of steel products ⎤
- *PPM:* Import price of steel production including tariff ⎬ deflated by GDE deflator
- *PPZ:* World price of steel products ⎪
- *PPO:* Import price of iron ore ⎦

a. Figures in parentheses show *t*-values of estimates.

demand for steel products came from the government for military production and railroad construction. Therefore, there existed a strong preferential
purchasing policy by the government for domestically produced steel products.

This explanation is supported when the elasticity of domestic demand for
imports of steel is compared with that for pig iron (1900–1936).

$$\log M = -.09 + .9093 \log D + .1800 \log PM/P$$
$$(45.54) (1.11)$$

$$\bar{R}^2 = .9836 \quad DW = 1.68$$

Domestic demand elasticity for pig iron imports is twice as large as that for
steel products. As mentioned previously, a large group of steel-making firms
depended on imported pig iron, and the import demand for pig iron increased
almost in proportion to the growth of domestic demand.

The export function explains the rapid growth of steel exports before the
Second World War. World production of steel ingots, a proxy variable for
world consumption of steel products, grew annually at 2.9 percent for the
period 1900–1936, and it induced a 4.9 (= 2.9 × 1.7) percent growth rate
in Japan's exports. The rest of export growth is attributed to price effects,
that is, the decline in the domestic price and the rise in the world price. Of
course, it cannot be denied that other factors not included in the export equation, such as preferential purchasing in Japan's domain, contributed to some
part of this export growth.

The price equation gives a statistically significant negative relationship between price and production, but the estimated coefficient for material cost
is less significant. The wage variable has been eliminated since its coefficient
is statistically insignificant and has the wrong sign.

A partial test of the estimation (standard error of residual (s), coefficient
of determination ($\bar{R}^2$), and Durbin-Watson ratio (DW)) shows a relatively good
fit of the model to actual data. But it may be worthwhile to see whether the
model generates the process of import substitution and export expansion over
the whole period when only exogenous variables and initial values of endogenous variables are given. The results can be seen in the final tests in Table 5.4. The final tests do not follow every fluctuation in the observed data,
but they do trace the rapid growth of domestic production, import substitution and export expansion, and the steady decline in the domestic price.[5]

The effect of government policy on the process of industry growth and trade
has already been mentioned. But which policy had a greater effect on import
substitution of steel products in Japan: import tariffs or the preferential purchasing policy? Simulation 1 traces the values of imports and production in
the case where import tariffs are not levied over the whole period. Simulation 2 traces those values in the absence of a preferential purchasing policy.

In simulation 1, the import price is lowered by the absence of tariffs; thus imports shift upward and domestic production downward over the whole period. In simulation 2, imports increase in proportion to domestic demand, and domestic production shifts downward by the corresponding amounts. Thus the effect of a preferential purchasing policy is almost three times as large as that of import tariffs. In either case, however, the value of imports follows a pattern similar to that in the estimations; growing slowly at first, then turning downward in the mid-1920s, which demonstrates import substitution through price effects. Thus the production values in both cases approach those of the estimations because of the rapid decline of imports.

DEVELOPMENT OF THE POSTWAR IRON AND STEEL INDUSTRY

By the end of the Second World War, production in the iron and steel industry had fallen to 1.5 million tonnes, or one-fourth of the production level of 1939. The industry's postwar development led initially to a recovery to the prewar production level, followed by industry reorganization and increased international competitiveness through technological innovation. This postwar period was characterized by the expansion of domestic production based on domestic- and export-oriented growth. Since the industry's integrated production base had already been established, imports of both pig iron and steel products during periods of domestic supply imbalances played only a supplementary role. The following section reviews a number of phases in the industry's pattern of production expansion.

Overview of Postwar Development[6]

The first phase of postwar development consisted of the recovery of the iron and steel industries under the Priority Production Policy (*Keisha Seisan Hoshiki*) during the period 1947–50. Three major industries—coal, iron and steel, and electric power—were given priority access to scarce raw materials through the government's fiscal, financial, and foreign exchange control policies. The government's intent was for the development of these key industries to spur the overall development of the Japanese economy.

In order to reactivate the iron and steel industry's production equipment, investment funds were made available through the Reconstruction Finance Corporation (Fukko Kinyu Koko). The industry was also given priority access to the supply of domestically produced coal, as well as to scarce foreign exchange for imports of iron ore, coal, pig iron, and other raw materials and equipment. Moreover, in order to be able to provide low-priced steel products to other industries, the difference between the production cost and the product price was subsidized by the government. As a result, by 1953, pig iron and steel production had reached their prewar levels, and the industry was able to supply other industries with steel products at low prices.

The heavy government subsidization of these industries contributed to inflation. Moreover, the concentration on the reactivation of machinery and equipment whose use dated to before the Second World War did not necessarily lead to a sound remodeling of the industry.

The second phase of postwar development consisted of the adoption of an industry rationalization policy. Between 1951 and 1955 under the first reorganization program (*Gorika Keikaku*), the price control and subsidization systems were dismantled.[7] Instead, low-interest financing as well as accelerated depreciation policies were adopted to encourage the modernization of equipment, particularly in the rolling-mill sector. To this end, the foreign exchange rationing mechanism was used to give the industry priority in importing American and European technology and equipment that were also exempted from import tariffs. This was followed by the second rationalization program (1956–60), which concentrated on the construction of the most modern integrated mills and the modernization of cargo-handling and transport equipment for the industry's raw materials and products. During this period (1951–60), more than half of the needed investment funds were financed internally, although loans from the World Bank were also used.

In the process of industry rationalization, there was an increasing concentration of production within the integrated firms. The affiliation of the semi-integrated and nonintegrated firms with the large integrated firms was strengthened, and the present industrial structure, which is dominated by six large-scale firms, was firmly established. The modernization of production equipment reduced raw material utilization per unit of production, leading to cost reductions and the strengthening of international competitiveness. The volume of steel production doubled during the first reorganization period and grew 240 percent during the second period. During this period, the relationship between production expansion and price decline is clear.

From 1951 to 1960, domestic demand (including indirect export demand in the form of machinery and ships) exceeded prewar levels by 16.3 percent. This high level of domestic demand led to an expansion of domestic production, since pig iron and steel product imports were controlled by the government's foreign exchange allocation policy. As the prices of domestic steel products were higher than those of imports from the United States and Europe in the early years of the rationalization program, the import control system effectively restricted steel imports. Except for the 9 percent increase in imports during the severe supply scarcity of 1957, imports represented only 1 to 2 percent of the domestic demand for steel products. In 1960, pig iron imports were fully liberalized, and in 1961 steel product imports were liberalized. During the period 1956–69, Japan registered a 6 to 12 percent dependence on imports of iron and steel (Tecson 1985).

Boosted by the growth of world demand and the special demand conditions of the Korean War, exports began to expand in the early 1950s mainly to the Southeast Asian countries. In order to maintain the rate of capacity utilization during periods of domestic slowdown, each firm endeavored to sharpen its export competitiveness. With export expansion further cost reductions were achieved, leading to intensified export competition among domestic firms. Firms were thus driven to diversify their export markets, and the American market became Japan's largest market for steel exports. From an average export volume of 840,000 tonnes from 1950 to 1952, exports rapidly grew to 2.2 million tonnes from 1960 to 1962, and to 18.9 million tonnes from 1970 to 1972. The process of export expansion was actively supported by the government through various export promotion policies, such as exemption from the export income tax (1953–64) and special accelerated depreciation of the fixed assets of overseas branches (1953–58). The contribution of Japan's general trading companies to foreign market development and export expansion must also be acknowledged (cf. Chapter 6, pp. 132–136).

Econometric Analysis of Postwar Development

The equations for domestic demand, exports, and prices in Table 5.5 are estimated using the same method as the estimates in Table 5.3 and cover the years 1952–68, a period of rapid export growth. Import equation 4 was omitted in this case since imports were negligible during the period. Estimates of the domestic demand function closely resemble those of the prewar period. The learning effect can be excluded from the estimates because the value of log L is close to zero. The income elasticities and constant terms hardly differ from those of the prewar estimates. This implies that the domestic demand function during the two time periods remained stable.

Different estimates were obtained for the export function between the prewar and postwar periods. Income elasticity increased and price elasticity decreased in the latter period. World consumption of steel products grew faster in the postwar period, and Japan's exports grew more than twice as fast, without even considering the favorable price effect. The markets for Japan's steel products changed, however, a great deal after the war. Southeast Asia and North America became Japan's principal markets, replacing East Asia. Exports were concentrated in steel products such as plates and sheets, for which world demand was rapidly increasing, while the supply capacities of European and American competitors were limited. These factors seem to explain the high income elasticity previously mentioned.

Japan's steel industry also gained a share in the world market in this period as a result of a decline in cost (price) relative to its European and American competitors. This is tested in the simulation based on the model of Table 5.5.

The price equation is less successful because of volatile price fluctuations in the mid-1950s, but price elasticity with respect to production is four times higher than before the war. This reflects the heavy investment since the late 1950s in large-scale plants equipped with newly developed technology. Additionally, the coefficient of the price of materials turned out to be insignificant and of the wrong sign, whereas the wage level coefficient has the correct sign but is also statistically insignificant.

Table 5.5
CPC Development of Steel Products: 1952–68

Estimates[a]

Domestic Demand (1)

$$\log D = 6.2531 + .8137 \log Y$$
$$(40.19)$$

$$s = .0755 \quad \bar{R}^2 = .9902 \quad DW = 1.97$$

Exports (2)

$$\log X = .0289 + 2.2711 \log X - 1.4337 \log PP/PPZ$$
$$(3.68) \qquad\qquad (1.64)$$

$$s = .4070 \quad \bar{R}^2 = .8376 \quad DW = .69$$

Price (3)

$$\log PP = 5.9651 - .4043 \log S + .3437 \log PW$$
$$(1.43) \qquad\qquad (.38)$$

$$s = .1731 \quad \bar{R}^2 = .6298 \quad DW = 1.86$$

Final Tests	D	X	S	PP
Root Mean Square	19051.01	16518.72	18044.54	0.22
Von-Neuman Square	1.72	0.48	1.00	1.25

Note:
Symbols

D: Domestic demand ⎤
S: Production   ⎬ of steel products (hundred tonnes)
X: Export   ⎦
Y: Production index of machinery
PP: Price of steel products ⎤
PPZ: World price of steel products ⎬ deflated by GDE deflator
PW: Wage rate of metal workers ⎦

a. Figures in parentheses show *t*-values of estimates.

Final tests show that, apart from fluctuations, the model succeeded in tracing the growth trends for the major variables of steel products during the postwar period. A simulation was attempted for the mechanism of export growth in the postwar development of the steel industry. As mentioned previously, rapid export growth is one of the main features of the industry's postwar development and is partly explained by high income elasticity and partly by relative price decline. Simulations are computed on the assumption that the world price fell to a level comparable with that of Japan so that the relative price remained constant. Simulations trace export and production values in the absence of relative price declines. Although the growth of exports slows to 11.0 percent, the strong growth trend of production continues.

The growth of Japan's iron and steel industry continued after 1968, reaching a production level of 100 million tonnes in 1973–74, after which the rapid growth in domestic demand and exports decelerated. However, even before this took place, toward the end of the 1960s, voluntary export restraints had begun to be imposed on Japanese steel exports to the United States, so that Japanese exporters were overtaken by new steel-producing countries such as South Korea and Brazil. This period's export mechanism thus differs from that of the high-growth period and is discussed in greater detail in Chapter 9.

DIVERSIFICATION OF THE INDUSTRIAL STRUCTURE

In the foregoing sections, CPC development in the textile and steel industries was analyzed. Japan's other manufacturing industries also followed a similar pattern of development though with varying time lags, leading to a diversification of the entire industrial structure as well as an upgrading of the industries as they became more capital- and technology-intensive.

Sequence of CPC Development

In order to compare the development of several industries, graphs employing the S/D curve of Figure 2.1 are used. Since exports and imports of homogeneous products can be netted, it is possible to show each industry's CPC development by the movements in the curve denoting the ratio of domestic production to domestic demand (also referred to as the self-sufficiency ratio when production falls short of demand). The process begins in the year domestic production begins. Import substitution takes place as domestic production overtakes imports and S/D equals 0.5. The export stage begins in the year S/D equals 1.0. In the stages of export growth and export deceleration, S/D is greater than 1.0, and the stage of reverse imports sets in when S/D becomes less than 1.0.

Figure 5.3 shows the S/D curve of four industries—textiles, steel products,

Figure 5.3
CPC Development of Major Industries

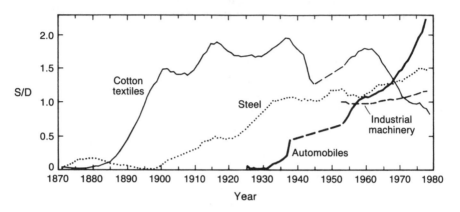

Note: Dashed lines in cotton textiles and automobiles indicate figures are not available.
Source: Yamazawa (1984).

automobiles, and industrial machinery. The development process of textile products is representative of labor-intensive light industries, whereas the development pattern of steel products is similar to that of artificial dyestuffs, chemical fertilizers, and textile industry machinery. Automobiles and industrial machinery are representative of postwar export-oriented industries. By looking at Figure 5.3 from left to right, it is possible to see which industries have reached the export stage and which industries are in the import substitution stage at any point in time. The industrial and export structures become diversified. Moreover, as some industries reach the export stage, a highly self-sufficient industrial structure is created when reverse imports do not take place.

At this point, some explanation for the growth processes in the automobile and the industrial machinery industries is needed. Although domestic production of passenger cars was begun in 1914 by Kaishin-sha, *S/D* began to rise in 1924–25 when Ford and General Motors started production in wholly owned subsidiary firms. In the 1920s, the government's subsidization policy encouraged production in domestic firms, while a rise in tariff rates on imports of parts for knock-down production promoted import substitution. Unassembled imports were banned in 1939, and imports of finished cars ended in 1941. Domestically owned firms achieved complete import substitution under the strong quantitative controls on imports, high tariffs, and foreign exchange controls of the postwar period (cf. Chapter 7, pages 159–164). Expansion in production volume led to cost reductions, and ultimately to export growth and export market diversification.

Industrial machinery includes machinery and tools, excluding electrical machinery and transportation equipment, and thus represents all types of industrial and precision machinery. Many of these industries began production even before the war. Cameras and watches had reached the export stage by the early postwar years, whereas machine tools and industrial robots only began to be exported in recent years. Disregarding the many different product types at every development stage of the industry, production value in 1980 was 17.6 trillion yen. The ratio of imports to domestic demand was 4.7 percent, and the export/production ratio reached 19.1 percent.

The time span from the start of production to import substitution and then exports (depicted by the slope of the S/D curve) differs from industry to industry and depends on the influence of many factors. The faster the growth of domestic demand and the greater the possibility for the achievement of economies of scale, the shorter is the time lag involved. The more difficult the technology to be absorbed is, however, the longer the process will take to reach its final stage (Yamazawa 1972). These observations conform with the basic mechanism of CPC development presented in Figure 4.1.

Mechanism of Industrial Diversification

What patterns can be discerned in the CPC development of different industries? Within a given industry, there is a tendency for cruder manufactured products to develop earlier than the more sophisticated ones (for example, low-count as opposed to high-count cotton yarn or black-and-white television sets as opposed to color televisions). As discussed earlier, however, such a pattern also depends on the degree of ease with which the technology is absorbed as well as on the relative speed of domestic demand growth.

The second pattern is that of backward and forward linkage effects. Since import substitution in consumer goods and finished products requires intermediate goods, parts, and capital goods inputs, it initially induces imports of these goods. Later, the demand for these goods leads to the start of new industries and is known as the backward linkage effect. Examples are the development of the chemical dyestuffs and textile machinery industries, which was induced by the growth of the textile industry (cf. Chapter 4). The forward linkage effect consists of the development of industries supplying the intermediate goods or raw materials at low prices, such as the development of a cotton yarn industry for cloth production or the development of the iron and steel industry for the production of automobiles and ships.

The diversification of CPC development into new industries depends on the relative factor endowments of the country, particularly on its capital accumulation and the scale of its domestic market. Due to constraints in the degree of capital accumulation, labor-intensive industries such as the textile industry are introduced in the early stages of industrialization. Where the size of the domestic market is small, however, it is difficult to achieve economies of scale. Even more important than these conditions is the ability of entrepreneurs to correctly identify the possibility of domestic demand growth as well as the existence of potential comparative advantage so as to begin the process of import substitution production (this topic is covered in Chapter 6, which focuses on entrepreneurial ability, as exemplified by trading companies, and its relationship to the opening of trade and new industries).

Finally, there should be some mention of the development of construction industries and public utility industries such as communications and electric power. Since these industries produce nontradable goods (services), the CPC development process is not evident. However, they have greatly contributed to the development of other manufacturing industries. Excluding the 1920s, the growth of the public utility industries during the pre–Second World War period occurred at the high annual rate of 9 percent, while that of the construction industry grew at 8.5 percent and included the construction of the transport-communications and electric power service network. It would be interesting to see how the CPC development in Figure 5.3 corresponds to the development of the construction and public utility industries, with the period when each of these industries achieved its nationwide organization denoted (that is, 1873–83 for railways, 1873–83 for the postal service system, 1896–1900 for the telephone system).

The proportion of factories equipped with electric motors was 28.2 percent in 1909. By 1929 the proportion had risen to 87.0 percent. This infrastructure was an important factor favoring the effective development of modern manufacturing industries. Thus, although the government's protective and industrial nurturing policy certainly contributed to the promotion of CPC development, except in the case of strategic industries such as iron and steel and automobiles, a high-handed nurturing policy was rare. Rather, the Japanese government offered indirect support, including the development of necessary infrastructure.

Six

Trading Companies and
the Expansion of Foreign Trade

This chapter analyzes the role of trading companies in the expansion of Japan's foreign trade before the Second World War. Only a few articles have been devoted to this subject. The theoretical literature on foreign trade has concentrated on such aspects as income growth, capital accumulation, and technical progress, and the players involved in Japanese foreign trade transactions have seldom been mentioned.

Recently, however, there has been increasing interest in trading companies, especially general trading companies (GTCs), which are peculiar to Japan. Several articles on these companies have been published by business historians. Nakagawa (1967) and Yamamura (1976), for example, examine the origin of GTCs and try to explain why they developed. Because trading companies were one of the forces promoting the CPC development of Japanese industries, this chapter concentrates on the interrelationship between the development of trading companies and Japan's foreign trade expansion.

FOREIGN TRADE TRANSACTIONS IN THE MEIJI PERIOD

Merchant House Trade and Direct Trade Policy

Japan's foreign trade began at merchant houses in foreign settlements that were established at major port cities in Japan.[1] Japanese sellers brought such products as raw silk, tea, crafts, and artifacts from inland areas to these merchant houses while Japanese buyers bought cotton cloth and sundry Western goods to be sold in domestic markets. Western merchants and their Chinese interpreters set the prices and typically dictated the terms of the transactions. Japanese merchants knew neither how much would be paid for their products nor how much their purchases cost abroad.

Initially, the Japanese merchants could not compete on an equal footing with foreign merchants. After 250 years of seclusion, the Japanese had no experience in the business of foreign trade and no knowledge of currency exchange, marine insurance, and ocean shipping. Furthermore, they were poorly equipped financially, and some Japanese sellers were paid by foreign merchants in advance for their commodities.

In 1875, after a futile attempt to foster semiofficial trading companies, the government announced it would subsidize private trading companies in order to promote direct exports.[2] A score of small trading companies (including Mitsui) responded and attempted the direct export of raw silk, tea, and other Japanese specialties. They were also encouraged by the nationwide movement demanding the abolition of extraterritoriality.[3] Mitsui and Company opened five branches in Europe and the United States (London, Paris, Lyons, Milan, and New York), and by 1878 more than 70 merchants had gone to Europe and North America with samples in an attempt to establish direct contacts with customers.

Most Japanese efforts failed due to the lack of experience of the Japanese in foreign trade and their lack of access to trade-promoting services. By 1882, Mitsui and Company had closed all overseas branches, except one branch in London, and the raw-silk trade continued to be dominated by foreign merchants. Japanese merchants received unfavorable treatment from foreign banks, marine insurance companies, and shipping companies.[4] Direct trade began to expand steadily only after the establishment of trade-promoting service agencies such as the Yokohama Specie Bank in 1880, the Tokyo Marine Insurance Company in 1879, and Nihon Yusen Kaisha for ocean shipping in 1885, which were either financed or heavily subsidized by the government.

Expansion of Direct Trade

The expansion of direct exports and imports is shown in Figure 6.1. Statistics for Japan Proper are not available for the years 1901-36, but the trend during these years can be estimated from statistics on record at the ports of Kobe and Yokohama. The direct export ratio rose to between 13 and 15 percent after the government's promotional policy began. It remained stagnant until 1892, when it again began to rise, reaching 35 percent by 1900. The direct import ratio, which began to rise after the early 1880s, lagged behind the direct export ratio but reached 40 percent by 1900 and 90 percent by 1920.

The period 1884-1920 is characterized by rapid expansion of the total volume of foreign trade. In the first 16 years of this period, from 1885 to 1900, both exports and imports expanded rapidly (7.7% and 8.9%, respectively, in terms of the annual compound rate). Exports and imports continued to expand during the rest of the period, albeit at slightly lower rates (by 6.2% and 4.3%, respectively).

Figure 6.1
Japan's Direct Export and Import Ratios: 1874–1960

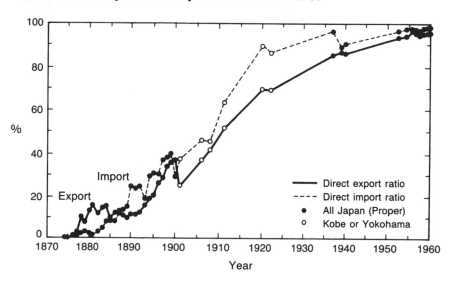

Note: All Japan (Proper), and Yokohama or Kobe indicate ratios are calculated from figures covering all of Japan (excluding colonies) and figures covering only the Ports of Yokohama and Kobe.

Sources: Ministry of Finance (1882–1943); MITI (1952–60); Asahi Shinbunsha (1930).

During this period, Japan's export and import structures changed dramatically. Raw silk and tea, which comprised 80 percent of total exports in the early 1880s, were rapidly replaced by light manufactures, whose market share increased from 13 percent in the 1880s to 43 percent by the early 1900s. Imports of light manufactures, on the other hand, had a market share of 68 percent in the 1880s, but by the early 1900s their share had fallen to 24 percent. By this time, imports of heavy manufactures and raw materials exceeded imports of light manufactures with shares at 33 percent and 29 percent, respectively.

The regional composition of Japan's foreign trade changed markedly from 1880 to 1990; Europe's share of exports and imports declined from 38 to 21 percent and 63 to 37 percent, respectively, while East Asia and North America became Japan's major trading partners. This reflects the evolution of Japan's foreign trade, which began with Japan as a producer of primary goods immediately after the opening-up of trade to Japan becoming an industrial exporter.

From 1900 to 1920, the changes in Japan's foreign trade structure were strengthened. Japan's export share of light manufactures continued to expand and reached 49 percent by 1920, and the share of light manufactures in total imports contracted to 15 percent. Exports of a few heavy manufactures also began at this time, but the share of imports of raw materials and heavy manufactures in Japan's total imports reached 31 and 38 percent, respectively. Whereas East Asia and North America continued to be major trading partners, Europe's share of exports to Japan declined to 8 percent and imports from Japan decreased to 14 percent due to the diversification of both export destinations and import sources.

The expansion of direct trade—that is, the replacement of foreign merchants with Japanese merchants in Japan's foreign trade—was closely associated with the rapid change in both the commodity and regional trade structures. The values of individual commodities that were traded by foreign and Japanese merchants as recorded in the customs statistics for the years 1884–1900 are the source for the data used to support this assertion below.

A sample of 110 export and 231 import commodities was selected; the total value and percentage share of Japanese merchants are calculated for each commodity in three sets of three-year averages: 1884–86, 1891–93, and 1898–1900. The sample covers between 87 and 89 percent of total exports, and between 88 and 94 percent of total imports throughout the three periods. Exports are classified as follows:

- indigenous (traditional Japanese manufactures) versus modern goods (goods produced by introduced technology)
- old versus new exports (exports that took place before or after 1868)
- exports primarily to Europe and North America (Europe-North America) East Asia, and the rest of the world.

Imports are classified as follows:

- by end use
- old versus new imports
- imports primarily from Europe-North America, East Asia, and the rest of the world.[5]

Changes in the shares of major export and import groups are shown in Tables 6.1 and 6.2. As Table 6.1 shows, distinct shifts in exports occurred from old to new exports, from indigenous goods to modern goods, and from Europe-North America to East Asia. To highlight the importance of the East Asian market, Europe and North America are grouped together. It should be noted, however, that exports of new indigenous products contributed to export expansion in later years. The export and import shares for the group Indigenous, Old, and Europe-North America declined markedly and contrast

Table 6.1

Shares in Total Exports, Direct Export Ratios, and Rates of Increase in Exports by Major Commodity Groups

Commodity group	Shares in total exports[a]		Direct export ratios[a]			Rates of increase in exports[a]		
	1[b]	3	1	2	3	2/1[c]	3/2	3/1
All sample commodities	100.0	100.0	19.2	19.4	32.0	13.72	12.39	64.42
Old exports (Old)	93.4	72.3	15.7	16.6	29.6	4.08	2.12	11.82
New exports (New)	6.6	27.8	22.6	21.9	33.7	22.85	21.95	114.22
Indigenous goods (Indigenous)	99.1	80.7	16.0	18.2	29.9	11.95	3.77	40.32
Modern goods (Modern)	0.9	19.3	38.3	25.9	43.4	24.05	59.58	204.58
Europe-North America	72.2	57.0	15.3	14.0	26.7	22.91	3.92	72.21
East Asia	21.6	38.3	19.9	20.7	32.3	9.19	19.49	67.76
Indigenous and New	5.9	8.5	16.1	20.7	30.5	21.84	5.86	76.21
Indigenous and Old	93.2	72.2	15.8	16.1	29.4	4.15	2.13	12.01
Modern and New	0.7	19.2	40.1	25.0	41.7	25.61	63.21	218.14
Indigenous, Old, and Europe-North America	68.4	50.0	12.9	10.3	22.9	6.67	1.52	22.69
Modern, New, and East Asia	0.7	19.1	43.9	27.4	41.9	28.43	71.90	248.87

Notes:

a. Arithmetic means for major commodity groups.

b. Year 1, 1884–86; year 2, 1891–93; year 3, 1898–1900.

c. The ratio of export value in year 2 to that in year 1. See note 5 for commodity classifications.

Source: Ministry of Finance, *Dainihon Gaikoku Boeki Nempyo* (Foreign Trade Annual of the Empire of Japan), 1884–86, 1891–93, 1898–190C.

Table 6.2
Shares in Total Imports, Direct Import Ratios, and Rates of Increase in Imports by Major Commodity Groups

Commodity group	Shares in total imports[a]		Direct import ratios[a]			Rates of increase in imports[a]		
	1[b]	3	1	2	3	2/1[c]	3/2	3/1
All sample commodities	100.0	100.0	13.9	19.9	32.6	4.88	4.78	30.20
Old imports (Old)	63.7	39.1	12.3	17.2	29.6	3.17	.85	22.20
New imports (New)	36.3	60.9	16.0	23.3	36.6	7.13	4.68	40.69
Europe-North America	72.3	44.9	13.1	21.2	34.9	4.48	4.63	23.79
East Asia	4.8	18.4	18.9	20.9	25.7	7.18	7.07	74.10
Group A: Unprocessed foodstuffs, raw materials, and investment goods	20.2	57.5	19.4	26.8	38.4	8.66	5.72	71.08
Group B: Processed foodstuffs, intermediate goods, and consumption goods	79.8	42.6	11.5	16.8	30.0	3.21	4.36	12.07
New and Group A	6.0	45.0	24.2	34.7	44.1	13.18	4.67	86.25
Old and Group B	49.6	26.8	11.3	16.4	28.2	2.64	4.12	8.45
New and Group B	30.0	15.8	11.9	17.5	32.7	4.02	4.69	17.22
Old and consumption goods and Europe-North America	22.4	11.1	15.4	22.1	33.3	2.46	3.50	7.74
New and investment goods and Europe-North America	1.0	3.0	21.6	49.8	59.9	18.57	4.99	136.07

Notes:
a. Arithmetic means for major commodity groups.
b. Year 1, 1884–86; year 2, 1891–93; year 3, 1898–1900.
c. The ratio of import values in year 2 to that in year 1. See note 5 for commodity classification.
Source: Ministry of Finance, Dainihon Gaikoku Boeki Nempyo (Foreign Trade Annual of the Empire of Japan), 1884–86, 1891–93, 1898–1900.

with the shares of the group Modern, New, and East Asia, which increased rapidly and significantly.

As Table 6.2 shows, the share of imports of processed foodstuffs, intermediate goods, and consumption goods declined, whereas the share of unprocessed foodstuffs, raw materials, and investment goods increased. Old imports were replaced by new imports far more rapidly than occurred among exports, indicating rapid import substitution of modern manufactures. The source of imports shifted from Europe-North America to East Asia and to other areas. These structural changes in imports and exports, and their association with increasing direct trade ratios, are discussed in the next section.

THE EXPANSION ROLE
PLAYED BY JAPANESE TRADING COMPANIES

The simple association between direct trade ratios and trade expansion in aggregate terms does not reveal much about the causal relationship between the two. The contribution of Japanese merchants to the expansion of Japan's foreign trade is best determined by a theoretical consideration of both the function of trading companies and the changes in economic conditions affecting them. In this section, a proposition on the difference between Japanese and foreign merchants regarding business conduct is presented. As well, two hypotheses are presented and tested using individual commodity data to derive direct trade ratios and rates of trade expansion.

The Function of a Trading Company

The primary function of a trading company is to link sellers with buyers across national borders and carry out transactions between the two groups. A trading company's income is generated primarily from the commissions the company receives upon the successful completion of transactions.

Foreign trade transactions require service inputs of various types:

- The trading company must acquire both demand and supply information (an accumulated managerial asset) so that it can connect the buyer that is paying the highest price with the producer showing the lowest cost.

- The trading company must acquire enough skills in order to conduct the complicated procedures of foreign transactions (an accumulated managerial asset), and must also have the trust of both the buyer and the seller to act as an intermediary.

- The trading company must be able to provide the seller (or buyer) with trade credit until the transaction is completed.

- The trading company must be able to arrange services such as ocean transportation and marine insurance.

In terms of the production function, a trading company's output is the conducting of foreign trade transactions, whereas its inputs are information, skill in conducting foreign trade transactions, and such services as obtaining trade credit, marine insurance, and ocean transportation. The first two inputs are provided by the trading company. Other services, which may be called *trade-promoting services*, are provided through outside firms that specialize in these services, but the trading company must procure and combine them at the right time and place.

In conventional economic analysis, the growth of trade is attributed to such factors as the reduction of production costs, increases in productive capacity, and demand growth. In reality, however, a trading company's services are required for these factors to be realized in the actual growth of trade. In this sense, these factors may be called *factors of trade potential*. Since every trading company that can realize this trade potential would face similar profit opportunities, the incentives for both Japanese and foreign merchants would be equal, provided that other incentives are not at work. It appears that in the early stages of Japan's trade expansion Japanese merchants had additional nonprofit incentives as well. They were either driven by economic nationalism or assisted by any advantage they might have had over foreign competitors.[6]

Although Japanese merchants were eager to expand their business, they were at first greatly hampered by foreign merchants. When Japan was opened to foreign trade in 1859, Japanese merchants were inexperienced in foreign transactions, lacking both knowledge and skill, and they had little information about the foreign markets for their products. No trade-promoting services were available from a Japanese source even at the end of the 1870s. Moreover, before the establishment of the Yokohama Specie Bank in 1880 no Japanese bank provided trade credit. Japanese merchants had no choice but to seek funds on unfavorable terms from Yokohama branches of foreign banks such as the Oriental Banking Corporation and the Hong Kong and Shanghai Banking Corporation.[7] It was a matter of course that almost all Japanese foreign trade was conducted by European and American merchants, who were equipped with the necessary managerial assets and access to trade-promoting services.

Gradually, information and skill in foreign transactions were accumulated by Japanese trading companies through on-the-job training and formal education in commerce. Japanese merchants acquired the necessary knowledge and trading skills through their contacts with foreign merchants. Some Japanese, after working at foreign merchant houses and acquiring the necessary skills, started their own businesses. Takashi Masuda, the first general manager of Mitsui and Company, is an example. The first school of commerce, Shōhō Kōshūjo (which later became Hitotsubashi University), was established in 1876 and began supplying graduates equipped with an education in commerce and with knowledge of foreign languages to Mitsui and other Japanese trading companies. The companies, in turn, sent their new employees abroad to begin overseas branches. The new corps of specially trained personnel, the accumulation of trade skills, and an improved supply of Japanese trade-promoting services tended to lessen the disadvantages experienced by Japanese merchants.

In several respects, however, Japanese merchants had an advantage over their European and American competitors. First, European and American merchants charged a much higher commission than did Japanese merchants, partly because of the high cost of living and partly because of the commissions they in turn had to pay to Chinese or Japanese employees. Second, Japanese merchants had an advantage both in exploiting new demand within Japan for imported products and in organizing new Japanese supply sources of Japanese products for export. Without these advantages, the increase in the direct export ratio would have been much slower. It is true, however, that these advantages tended to be offset by the disadvantage of Japan's lack of knowledge of and access to foreign markets. Nevertheless, the advantages of Japanese merchants at home tended to more than offset their disadvantages abroad, which is discussed in more detail in the following section.[8] Because Japan, as a small, new entrant to the world trade arena, could not offer either new products or a large, new market, new opportunities for trade between Japan and the rest of the world were found mainly in Japan.

The Treaty of Amity and Commerce in 1858 restricted foreign merchants in their business activities outside foreign settlements. In exchange for extraterritoriality in foreign settlements, foreign merchants could not travel freely beyond a 40-kilometer radius outside their settlements. This regulation restricted direct contact of foreign merchants with local customers or producers and tended to strengthen the Japanese advantages mentioned above.[9] However, since foreign merchants relied heavily on their Japanese employees in transactions with the Japanese, it seems likely that the travel regulation did not give Japanese merchants enough of an advantage to offset any disadvantage.

Comparative Advantage of Japanese Trading Companies

The direct trade ratio did not increase uniformly across all commodities but increased early on for some commodities and for trade with some regions. Two testable hypotheses regarding this situation are advanced below to prove the proposition that Japanese merchants had greater incentive to expand their businesses than did their foreign competitors.

Hypothesis 1 concerns the differences in the increase in direct trade in various commodities and with different regions. Compared with their foreign competitors, Japanese merchants were at first at a disadvantage in all commodities, but the degree of disadvantage differed from one commodity to the next. It seems plausible that Japanese merchants tended to increase their shares in those commodities in which they had comparative advantage. Hypothesis 1 may, therefore, be stated as follows: direct trade ratios tended to increase each year (1) in new exports (or imports) rather than in old ones; (2) in exports of modern goods rather than in exports of indigenous ones, and in imports of such commodity categories as unprocessed foodstuffs, raw materials, and investment goods rather than in imports of other categories; and (3) in export and import trading with East Asia rather than with Europe and North America.

There are several reasons behind hypothesis 1 which suggest that Japanese merchants had comparative advantage in trade of various commodities and with specific regions. First, trade in old exports such as raw silk and tea and old imports such as cotton cloth and sundry Western goods began immediately after the opening of trade. European and American merchants had long-exploited supply sources and established marketing channels for those commodities. When Japanese merchants entered the foreign trade market, they found it easier to begin to export and import new commodities or to enter areas where markets were not fully established.

Second, modern goods such as matches and cotton yarn were initially imported from Europe. But they were soon produced domestically, and these domestically produced goods eventually replaced imports (import substitution). These goods were then exported, primarily to Asian countries. Japanese merchants often worked closely with new industries and were eager to sell their products abroad, whereas foreign merchants, who had initially brought the product to Japan, tended to underestimate the quality of Japanese products and did not want to risk trading them.

Moreover, the advantage of having close ties to the market helped Japanese merchants enter the import trade in such commodities as unprocessed foodstuffs, raw materials, and investment goods. The demand for imported rice and agricultural products was greatly affected by each year's domestic yields, and because of their long experience in the domestic trade of these products, Japanese merchants held an absolute advantage. Cotton and other raw materials, as well as industrial machinery, were in demand by the new industries, such as those producing yarn and matches, to which Mitsui and other Japanese trading companies were closely tied from the start.

Third, European and American merchants exploited the trade between Japan and their own countries and maintained a strong advantage over the Japanese. However, when trade between Japan and East Asia later expanded,

Japanese merchants were at less of a disadvantage in the region vis-à-vis their European and American competitors. In their business with China, European and American merchants had typically relied on Chinese *compradors*, to whom they paid a 1 percent commission. Mitsui, however, avoided this custom by introducing instead a program of Chinese language instruction for its Japanese employees when it attempted export expansion into the Chinese market in the late 1890s.[10] Here, however, Japanese merchants had another foreign competitor: Chinese merchants who had long dominated trade within this region.

Hypothesis 2 is also based on the proposition that the Japanese merchants' incentive to expand foreign trade was stronger than that of their foreign competitors: For a given commodity, the higher the direct trade ratio or the more rapid its increase, the higher the rate of trade expansion will be in that commodity.

Tables 6.1 and 6.2 show average direct export and import ratios for three periods, 1884–86 (period 1), 1891–93 (period 2) and 1898-1900 (period 3) and average rates of export and import expansion between these periods (i.e., 2/1 refers to the ratio of export [import] value in period 2 over the export [import] value in period 1) for major commodity categories. A simple comparison of averages between the ratios for the different categories supports hypothesis 1—that is, direct trade ratios of new exports and imports (group A, Table 6.2) exceed those of old exports (group B, Table 6.2) each year. Similar differences are found between the export of modern goods and indigenous goods, and between import groups A and B. The differences by export destination are also consistent with hypothesis 1 (part 3), but those by import source turned out to be obscure. All differences between pairs of combined categories such as Indigenous, Old, and Europe-North America and Modern, New, and East Asia are consistent with the hypothesis.[11]

Comparing the rate of trade expansion between the categories yields differences that parallel the differences between direct trade ratios, which implies a positive association between direct trade ratios and trade expansion. However, this relationship between averages of individual categories is insufficient to support hypotheses 1 and 2: a rigorous test of the two hypotheses by regression analysis based on individual commodity data is needed.

Regression Analysis
of Direct Trade Ratios and Trade Expansion

The following set of regression equations is given for exports (a set of regression equations for imports can be derived by substituting *DIR* and *GI* for *DER* and *GE,* respectively):

$$\ln DER_t = a_0 + a_1N + a_2M + a_3R_1 + a_4R_2 + a_5NR_1 \\ + a_6MR_1 + a_7NM \tag{1}$$

$$\ln GE_{t/s} = b_0 + b_1N + b_2M + b_3R_1 + b_4R_2 + b_5NR_1 \\ + b_6MR_1 + b_7NM + b_8\ln DER_s \\ + b_9\ln GDER_{t/s} \tag{2}$$

where $DER_t(DIR_t)$ is the direct export (import) ratio at period t ($t = 1, 2,$ 3); $GE_{t/s}(GI_{t/s})$ is the ratio of the export (import) value in period t to the export (import) value in period s; $GDER_{t/s}(GDIR_{t/s})$ is the ratio of the direct export (import) value in period t to the direct export (import) value in period s; N and M are dummy variables for new exports (imports) and exports of modern goods (imports of unprocessed foodstuffs, raw materials, and investment goods), respectively; R_1 and R_2 are regional dummies; and NR_1, MR_1, and NM are interaction terms between N, M, and R_1.[12]

The first equation is formulated to test hypothesis 1 (parts 1, 2, and 3) by individual commodity data: that is, the equation examines how the DER(DIR) of individual commodities is affected by commodity categories such as Old or New. The second equation is formulated to test hypothesis 2 by estimating the effect on the GE(GI) during a particular period of both the DER(DIR) at the beginning of the period and the GDER(GDIR) during the same period as well as the effect of commodity categories mentioned above.

The log-linear formulation of the two equations implies a multiplicative relationship between variables.[13] Interaction terms are included in order to explain high DERs or DIRs in the combined categories such as the category New, Modern, and East Asia in Table 6.1 and the category New and Group A in Table 6.2. The two equations are estimated using data for 109 export and 231 import commodities for the three periods (1884–86, 1891–93, and 1898–1900). Alternative specification sets of interaction terms are estimated, and the results from one of the regressions with the best fit are listed in Tables 6.3 and 6.4. Coefficients of determination are generally low. This is because these equations are estimated from cross-commodity data of large sample size and because the specification does not include such powerful explanatory variables as income and relative prices, which are used in conventional export and import analysis. However, significant F and t-values support the relevance of the specification in spite of low $\bar{R}^2$s.

This detailed examination of the individual equations allows the following interpretation. As shown in regression equation 1E in Table 6.3, the introduction of NR_1 produced significant and positive coefficients but resulted in the coefficients for N and M becoming nonsignificant and of an indeterminate sign.[14] The coefficient for R_1 is significant and is negative (this was true in an alternative specification of the interaction terms). These results imply that

Table 6.3
Regression of Direct Export Ratio and Export Expansion

	CONSTANT	N	M	R_1	R_2	NR_1	$\ln DER_s$	$\ln DGER_{t/s}$	$\bar{R}^2$	F
(1E) $\ln DER_t$										
(a) $t = 1$	-2.7025	-0.2535 (0.44)	0.8848 (0.74)	-1.3026 (2.24)	0.7177 (1.00)	1.7673 (2.26)			0.0650	2.50
(b) $t = 2$	-2.4902	-0.1741 (0.33)	0.6738 (0.63)	-1.2765 (2.44)c	0.8516 (1.32)a	1.5469 (2.20)b			0.0848	3.00
(c) $t = 3$	-1.5699	-0.0766 (0.19)	0.8735 (1.06)	-0.6131 (1.52)	0.5146 (1.03)	0.5369 (0.99)			0.0193	1.43
(2E) $\ln GE_{t/s}$										
(a) $t/s = 2/1$	1.2316	0.4599 (1.80)b	-0.0674 (0.09)	0.1531 (0.58)	0.2438 (0.52)		0.1858 (2.49)c	-0.1053 (1.18)	0.1241	3.55
(b) $t/s = 3/2$	0.8655	0.7053 (4.36)	-0.5510 (1.13)	0.0864 (0.51)	0.33368 (1.13)		0.2464 (4.19)c	0.2346 (2.86)c	0.2511	7.04
(c) $t/s = 3/1$	2.2212	1.1199 (3.73)	-0.5737 (0.63)	0.2524 (0.80)	0.5304 (0.96)		0.4368 (3.90)c	0.1446 (1.16)	0.2643	7.47

Notes: Estimated by ordinary least squares method. Numbers in parentheses show *t*-values. See text for the explanation of symbols.

a. Significant at the 90 percent level.
b. Significant at the 95 percent level.
c. Significant at the 99 percent level.

Table 6.4
Regression of Direct Import Ratio and Import Expansion

	CONSTANT	N	M	R_1	R_2	MR_1	$\ln DIR_s$	$\ln GDIR_{t/s}$	$\bar{R}^2$	F
(1I) $\ln DIR_t$										
(a) $t = 1$	3.2339	-0.2682 (0.85)	0.3277 (0.79)	-0.5130 (1.30)[a]	-1.0842 (2.44)[c]	0.6102 (1.08)			0.0161	1.75
(b) $t = 2$	2.5526	-0.0636 (0.21)	0.1557 (0.40)	-1.1814 (3.18)[c]	-1.5900 (3.80)[c]	1.0650 (1.98)[b]			0.0874	5.41[c]
(c) $t = 3$	1.6858	0.3452 (1.89)[b]	0.5167 (2.12)[b]	-1.0432 (4.52)[c]	-0.4838 (1.86)[b]	-0.2597 (0.01)			0.0968	5.93[c]
(2I) $\ln GI_{t/s}$										
(a) $t/s = 2/1$	0.6566	0.5618 (3.52)[c]	0.2538 (1.21)	-0.0797 (0.39)	0.0096 (0.04)	0.4586 (1.60)[a]	0.0681 (1.77)[b]	0.0249 (0.55)	0.1571	7.13[c]
(b) $t/s = 3/2$	1.3491	0.1242 (0.88)	0.3779 (2.05)[b]	0.0775 (0.43)	-0.5090 (2.53)[c]	-0.2643 (1.05)	0.1757 (3.51)[c]	0.1558 (2.59)[c]	0.0797	3.85[c]
(c) $t/s = 3/1$	2.0123	0.6812 (3.27)[c]	0.6173 (2.27)[b]	-0.0166 (0.06)	-0.5320 (1.83)[b]	0.2268 (0.62)	0.2482 (3.35)	0.1806 (2.13)[b]	0.1852	8.47[c]

Notes: Estimated by ordinary least squares method. Numbers in parentheses show *t*-values. See text for the explanation of symbols.

a. Significant at the 90 percent level.
b. Significant at the 95 percent level.
c. Significant at the 99 percent level.

the DER is raised significantly when commodities N and M are sent to region R_1.

The effect of $N \times M \times R_1$ is illustrated in equation 1E by comparing the constant term (that is, the DER) when $N = M = R_1 = R_2 = 0$ with the DER when $N = M = R_1 = 1$. Converted into percentages, the DERs for the category Modern, New, and East Asia in the periods 1, 2, and 3 turn out to be 20.6 percent, 17.9 percent, and 42.8 percent, which are two or three times as high as the DERs for the category Indigenous, Old, and Europe-North America (6.7%, 8.3%, and 20.8%, in the respective periods). This result is roughly consistent with the data in Table 6.1 and supports hypothesis 1.[15] The coefficients of R_2 are stable and positive, which may be attributed to special circumstances, such as the fact that the R_2 category includes only a small number of foodstuffs (rice, peas, rice wine, soy sauce, Japanese noodles) in the category Old and Indigenous regardless of destination.

Regression equation 1I in Table 6.4 was also estimated including the variable *NM,* though this is not shown in the table. The interaction NM has the best fit, but it affects the coefficients of N and M. Positive and significant NM produces nonsignificant N and M with a positive or negative sign in periods 1 and 2, while in period 3 positive and significant M and N are accompanied by nonsignificant NM. In the absence of an interaction term, both M and N turn out to be positive and M is significant in the three periods. In contrast, the negative and significant coefficients of both R_1 and R_2 are not affected by the interaction between M and N.

To conclude, both N and M, or their interaction NM, tend to raise the DIR, whereas R_1 and R_2 tend to lower the DIR. This is not inconsistent with hypothesis 1, parts 1 and 2, but it does refute part 3 of hypothesis 1. The negative effect of R_1 on both the DER and DIR suggests that it was never easier for Japanese merchants to enter the export or import trade with neighboring countries than it was to enter trade with Europe and North America. Both the DER and DIR tended to be lower instead of higher in trade with neighboring countries, which is contrary to hypothesis 1, part 3. This may be partly attributed to competition from Chinese and Indian merchants and to the fact that many European and American merchants had a firm foothold in East Asia.

In Table 6.3, regression equation 2E suggests that N and the DER tend to significantly accelerate GE. Both R_1 and R_2 are positively correlated with DER, but neither is significant. NR_1 is omitted from equation 2E since it neither produces a significant coefficient with a stable sign nor significantly effects the coefficients of other variables. An ambiguous effect of M is attributed to the interdependence of the M and N categories. The DER turns out to be positively related with export expansion, which supports hypothesis 2. However, the acceleration of the GE by the GDER is significant only for the period 3/2 and ambiguous for the period 2/1. For imports, both *M* and *N* (and *NM* in period 2) have positive and significant correlation with GI, but the effects of R_1 and R_2 are ambiguous. Both the DIR and the GDIR tend to accelerate GI significantly, which is consistent with hypothesis 2.

Negative and nonsignificant coefficients for GDER and a nonsignificant coefficient for GDIR for the period 2/1 (Tables 6.3 and 6.4) are inconsistent with hypothesis 2. A more careful examination of GE and GDER for major individual commodities may help to resolve this contradiction (Table 6.5). Export data for silk fabric, umbrellas, cotton flannel, and cotton yarn in period 1 illustrate that high direct export ratios (period 2 in the case of cotton yarn) are associated with high rates of export expansion during the period 2/1 (period 3/2 in the case of cotton yarn). All of the goods were new exports, and Japanese merchants exploited their trade potential by expanding exports. However, Japanese shares declined and foreign competitors' shares increased in all cases in the following period. This seems to imply that foreign merchants were not passive; rather than stay on the sidelines, they would enter into trading those new goods that showed good prospects for expansion. This competition between Japanese and foreign merchants was vigorous, and the replacement of foreign merchants by Japanese merchants did not take place smoothly or amicably.

Table 6.5
Direct Trade Ratios and Rates of Increase of Selected Commodities

	Direct Trade Ratios			Rates of Increase	
	$t=1$	$t=2$	$t=3$	$t/s=2/1$	$t/s=3/2$
Exports					
Raw silk	15.6	9.0	29.2	2.3	1.6
Habutae (silk fabric)	61.9	16.0	19.9	73.5	4.8
Umbrellas (Western)	48.9	4.3	12.0	64.1	2.2
Cotton flannel	84.4	30.7	21.4	122.6	4.2
Cotton yarn	—	80.9	59.6	—	926.0
Imports					
Raw cotton	7.8	44.8	57.0	18.7	5.0
Rice	12.7	46.2	27.3	13.1	6.9
Indigo	92.4	10.1	13.7	10.9	8.9
Spinning machinery	78.8	65.1	74.3	13.7	1.7
Locomotives	6.3	52.8	80.6	4.7	6.4

Note: — = Periods when there were no exports.

Source: Ministry of Finance, *Dainihon Gaikoku Boeki Nempyo* (Foreign Trade Annual of the Empire of Japan), 1884–86, 1891–93, 1898–1900.

Evidence similar to that in the export analysis is found for imports of indigo and spinning machinery. In this case, however, the high rate of import expansion was accompanied by an increasing Japanese share in such major commodities as raw cotton, rice, and locomotives. This may explain the ambiguous effect of the GDIR for the period 2/1 in Table 6.5.

The preceding analysis supports the proposition presented above. Japanese merchants had comparative advantage in new exports and imports, exports of modern goods, and imports closely related to modern industries, as reflected by the higher DERs and DIRs for the commodities in those categories. The higher ratios indicate that Japanese merchants were active in exploiting the trade potential of those commodities. The expansion of exports and imports also tended to be greater in commodities with higher and increasing direct trade ratios. Thus Japanese merchants contributed to the expansion of Japan's foreign trade.

The rapid development of Japanese trading companies did not, however, occur independently, but was in fact strongly based on Japan's industrialization. This analysis does not refute the role of domestic industrialization in the expansion of both exports and imports of N and M commodities, which increased the share of Japanese merchants. This argument of a causal relationship is consistent with the previous finding that Japanese merchants were relatively more involved in production and trade of commodities N and M than their foreign competitors and took advantage of business opportunities in these commodities to further increase their shares. It may be concluded that there existed a strong interaction between the Japanese merchants' increase in shares and the M- and N-biased expansion of Japan's foreign trade.

INTENSIFICATION OF TRADING COMPANY ACTIVITY BEFORE THE SECOND WORLD WAR

The rapid expansion of direct trade from 1900 to 1920 is attributed to the increase in activity of Japanese trading companies, which evolved from the earlier general trading companies. By 1910 Mitsui and Company had already succeeded in diversifying its business in commodities and expanding to other regions, and had become the premier foreign trading company in Japan. Mitsubishi and Suzuki followed Mitsui's lead between 1910 and 1920, and by 1920 the three companies had established worldwide branch networks and were trading in a wide variety of commodities.

Smaller trading companies generally specialized in exports such as textiles and sundry goods and imports such as iron and machinery. These smaller trading companies all contributed to domestic industrial development. Two companies were established jointly by domestic cotton traders and spinning firms to import raw cotton from India and the United States. Beginning in the 1890s, their business expanded rapidly to meet the increasing demands of the developing cotton textile industry. Foreign merchants, meanwhile, watched their shares in Japan's foreign trade diminish steadily. They were forced either to withdraw from Japan or take advantage of the few remaining opportunities such as handling such commodities as fuels and chemicals.

During the interwar period, Japanese trading companies developed their capacity far beyond the mere handling of transactions. They expanded their operations by:

- diversifying commodities to include promising new products
- exploring new, growing markets
- and acting as brokers and organizing producers and consumers.

EMERGENCE OF GENERAL TRADING COMPANIES

Mitsui and Company led all of the general trading companies (GTCs) in every area of activity described above. Between 1900 and 1910, Mitsui expanded its share of coal exports from 45.8 to 82.5 percent, of machinery imports from 12.1 to 42.6 percent, and of raw-silk exports from 14.0 to 23.7 percent. Its share for all commodities increased by 21 percent from 11.5 to 24 percent during the same period and remained at that level thereafter. Its transactions were diversified to include a wide variety of commodities, especially those associated with both the export and import needs of growing industries. For example, Mitsui imported raw cotton and spinning machinery and exported cotton yarn and cloth—goods that were needed for the development of the cotton textile industry. In 1910, its shares of raw-cotton imports and cotton yarn and cloth exports reached 25.2, 33.0, and 51.0 percent, respectively.

Mitsui aggressively pursued new products that were projected to have high domestic marketability and maintained its share of the new product market through sole agent contracts. Exports of coal from the Miike mine in Japan to other parts of Asia and imports of spinning machinery from Platt and Company illustrate this practice. In 1908, Mitsui had 80 sole agent contracts, and by the late 1920s, the number had grown to 152, consisting mainly of textile and electrical machinery contracts. The sole agent practice sometimes led Mitsui to establish domestic firms for import-substituting production, as was done for electrical machinery (Nihon Denki) in 1899 and rayon (Toyo Rayon) in 1926.

Table 6.6 details Mitsui's regional expansion. The number of branches and staff, as well as the value of sales, increased greatly from 1893 to 1910 and expanded further by 1919. The percentage shares of both staff and sales declined in Europe, Taiwan and Korea, and Manchuria, but increased in such new areas as Southeast Asia, North America, and Oceania. In China, Mit-

Table 6.6
Features of Mitsui Branches by Region

Region	Number of branches			Number of employees (% of total)			Sales in thousands of yen (% of total sales)		
	1893	1910	1919	1893	1910	1919	1893	1910	1919
Taiwan and Korea	0	5	8	0 (0.0)	69 (19.9)	186 (13.2)	0	15,511 (10.4)	67,869 (6.2)
Manchuria and Kwantung Province	0	8	8	0 (0.0)	67 (19.3)	210 (14.9)	0	13,906 (9.3)	76,100 (6.9)
China	3	9	18	26 (74.3)	106 (30.5)	521 (37.5)	4,790 (48.2)	42,871 (28.7)	217,855 (19.8)
Southeast Asia	2	6	12	4 (11.4)	42 (12.1)	238 (16.9)	603 (6.1)	8,173 (5.5)	229,113 (20.3)
Oceania	0	1	2	0 (0.0)	2 (0.6)	25 (1.8)	0	108 (0.9)	14,756 (1.3)
Europe	1	3	3	5 (14.3)	28 (8.1)	61 (4.3)	4,554 (45.7)	31,911 (21.3)	103,151 (9.4)
North America	0	3	6	0 (0.0)	33 (9.5)	168 (11.9)	0	37,045 (24.8)	390,130 (35.5)
Total	6	35	57	35 (100)	347 (100)	1,409 (100)	9,947 (100)	149,525 (100)	1,098,954 (100)

Note: Percentage shares are shown in parentheses.
Source: Yamaguchi et al., eds. (1974).

sui's share of staff increased, but its share of sales fell. In general, the changes in shares show general expansion.

A similar trend of diversification was observed in the activities of Mitsubishi and Suzuki. Initially, Mitsubishi was only a trading department within a larger firm, Mitsubishi and Company, and specialized in the export of Japanese coal to East and Southeast Asia. Eventually, Mitsubishi became a separate corporate entity and established many branches in Asia, Europe, and North America during the First World War. The firm also expanded the variety of commodities traded. Suzuki, a trading company that was started in the late 1890s, exported specialty commodities from Japan and Taiwan such as peppermint, camphor, and sugar. After establishing branches in Europe, it rapidly expanded and by the early 1920 had established a branch network.

Although not reflected in the increase in direct trade ratios in Figure 6.1, the expansion of offshore trade between countries other than Japan with Japanese traders as intermediaries merits brief mention. The first large-scale trade of this type was conducted by Mitsui and Company in 1908, when it sold soybeans from Manchuria to Europe. Mitsui conducted similar transactions involving products such as raw cotton, sugar, and hemp bags. Mitsubishi and Suzuki followed Mitsui's lead with similar moves. This implies that Japanese trading companies had by that time progressed beyond simple competition with Japan-based foreign merchants and had started competing for shares in the world market.

The exporters' unions, organizations of domestic producers promoting cotton-cloth exports, also deserve mention. Sanei and Nippon-Menpu, both established in 1906, are well known. The former was established jointly by three cotton weavers to promote exports to Korea, and the latter by five cotton weavers for exports to Manchuria. However, they were actually led by Mitsui and Company who conducted the export business for both unions. Mitsui was the principal player in the efforts to expand these exports, and Mitsui received little or no commission and provided the unions with trade credits on very favorable terms.

Mitsui's success in expanding exports was remarkable in both the Korean and Manchurian markets. In 1901, British cotton cloth had more than a 70 percent share of the Korean market and American cotton cloth almost 99 percent of the Manchurian market. But Mitsui succeeded in greatly reducing prices (to 20–25% lower than American cotton cloth in Manchuria) and quickly replaced the British and American products. By 1910, Mitsui had captured more than a 90 percent share of the market.[16]

Trade-Promoting Services

The improved implementation of trade-promoting services should not be overlooked. During the early 1880s, the government started to promote agents specializing in trade-promoting activities to supplement its direct trade policy, but this only came to fruition in the late 1890s and its effect in supporting the expansion of direct trade could only be felt after 1900. Marine transportation, faced with severe competition from foreign shipping companies, had been heavily protected since the early Meiji period. In 1893, Japanese ships entered the ocean transportation business with the introduction of ships on the Indian route. This was followed by the introduction of ships to the European, North American, and Australian routes in 1896. Japan's share of the world's total freight tonnage rose from 22 percent in 1890 to 35 percent in 1900, further increasing to 46 percent in 1910 and 64 percent in 1920.[17]

The first Japanese marine insurance company, Tokyo Marine Insurance Company, was established in 1879 with government support, but Japanese traders had to continue to depend on foreign insurance companies. The foreign companies initially discriminated against Japanese traders by refusing to insure ships that were steered by Japanese captains. In 1896, the second marine insurance company, Nippon Kaijo, was established. It was followed by a few others but these had not fully developed before the First World War.[18]

By around 1890 the Yokohama Specie Bank had expanded its foreign exchange business, with substantial government support, to handle the transactions of a large proportion of Japanese traders. But foreign banks continued to dominate the Japanese market and colluded to set the market rate of the yen around its gold par value. It was only after the First World War that Japanese trading companies were free of the disadvantages resulting from the dominance of these foreign banks.

POSTWAR EVOLUTION OF JAPANESE GTCs

After the Second World War, Japan experienced rapid economic growth and dramatic change in its industrial and trade structure. In the 1960s, this growth centered on heavy industries. The share of the metals, machinery, and chemicals industries increased from 49 percent of manufacturing in 1950 to 61 percent in 1960 and reached 72 percent by 1970. The export structure also changed. The shares of heavy industrial goods in total manufacturing exports in 1951, 1960, and 1970 were 36, 44, and 78 percent, respectively.

Following the Second World War, ten major GTCs were established.[19] Of these ten, Mitsubishi and Mitsui are of *zaibatsu* origin and had already diversified in the prewar period. Although these two companies were divided into more than a hundred companies by the Occupation authorities in 1947, they were later reunited—Mitsubishi in 1954 and Mitsui in 1959. Export substitution of heavy industrial goods was common for individual GTCs and was most evident in the case of the Kansai Gomen, the five big trading companies in the Kansai (Osaka) area that specialized in textiles before the war. They took over some domestic steel distributors to promote steel exports. At the

Table 6.7
Export Structure of Japanese GTCs: 1960 and 1970

Company	Year	Foodstuffs	Textiles	Chemical products	Metals	Machinery	Others	Total
Mitsui	1960	20.2	22.5	13.4[a]	28.6[a]	18.2[b]	14.4	117.4[a]
	1970	30.2	62.9	78.6	246.3	255.2	49.7	722.9
Mitsubishi	1960	24.6	20.2	0.7[b]	20.1[a]	29.9[a]	16.5	111.9[a]
	1970	39.4	51.4	55.8	197.8	259.5	43.2	657.2
Marubeni	1960	8.1	46.6	2.5[b]	11.4[b]	18.5[b]	10.2	97.3[a]
	1970	13.3	75.9	26.1	121.0	249.7	36.1	522.2
C. Itoh	1960	5.0	56.5	1.0[b]	8.3[b]	5.7[b]	7.6	84.1
	1970	14.5	101.6	21.3	94.3	132.9	21.1	385.7
Sumitomo	1960	0.7[a]	0.6[b]	3.2[b]	16.1[a]	4.1[b]	2.6	27.4[b]
	1970	6.0	7.6	34.5	150.8	115.2	11.6	325.6
Nissho-Iwai	1960[c]	1.4[b]	11.9	—	14.5[a]	2.8[b]	4.2[a]	36.7[a]
	1970	8.6	40.6	—	110.7	100.5	31.9	292.3
Toyo Menka	1960	2.5[b]	31.7	0.8[b]	5.1[a]	3.8[b]	7.7	51.6
	1970	25.4	60.6	11.8	32.0	65.3	2.4	197.4
Nichimen	1960	1.6[a]	40.6	1.6[b]	8.0	14.4	6.2	72.3
	1970	10.1	38.7	18.6	39.9	54.5	8.5	170.4

Company	Year	Foodstuffs	Textiles	Chemical products	Metals	Machinery	Others	Total
Kanematsu-Gosho	1960[d]	3.4	25.6	—	9.3	11.1	12.1	61.6
	1970	10.7	34.8	—	28.6	28.4	20.4	122.9
Ataka	1960	0.2[b]	4.6	1.2[b]	8.4[a]	3.0[a]	4.7	22.1
	1970	3.9	23.4	12.5	44.3	19.6	8.2	111.8
GTCs total[e]	1960	67.7	260.8	24.4[b]	129.8[a]	111.5[b]	86.2	582.4
		(70.3)	(59.6)	(27.0)	(58.9)	(30.3)	(33.8)	(46.8)
	1970	162.1	497.5	259.2	1,065.7	1,280.8	243.1	3,508.4
		(69.5)	(62.6)	(58.3)	(77.8)	(39.8)	(36.9)	(50.4)
Japan's total[f]	1960	96.3	430.5	90.4[a]	220.3[a]	367.4[a]	254.7	1,459.6

Notes: All figures, except those in parentheses, are in billions of yen. Fiscal years except as noted. Export price indices in 1970 are (1960 = 100): food-stuffs, 129; textiles, 103; chemical products, 77; metals, 103; machinery, 94; all commodities, 106.

a. The ratio of the 1970 to 1960 exports for this company is above the 5.14 ratio of total 1970 GTC exports to total 1960 GTC exports.

b. The ratio of the 1970 to 1960 exports for this company is over 10.

c. The total of Nissho and Iwai, which were separate companies in 1961.

d. The total of Kanematsu and Gosho, which were separate companies in 1961.

e. Figures in parentheses are GTCs' percentage share of the total for Japan.

f. Calendar year.

Sources: Financial statements of the companies and Yamazawa and Yamamoto (1979a).

same time, Nissho, Iwai, and Ataka, which were originally steel and machinery trading companies, became more diversified.

Diversification of Transactions

Diversification of product and geographic markets and types of transaction characterized the strategy of the postwar GTCs and mirrored the general move towards diversification of the economy. From 39 percent of the total exports of Japan's GTCs in 1960, exports of heavy industrial goods such as metals, machinery, and chemicals expanded to make up 74 percent of the total exports of GTCs in 1970. Although this pace of change in export structure was common to every GTC, it was especially remarkable for companies that had begun as textile trading companies. For example, the share of heavy industrial goods exported by the Kansai Gomen increased from a range of 18 to 33 percent in 1960 to a range of 54 to 76 percent in 1970; textiles fell from 50 to 66 percent to 15 to 31 percent in the same period. Such a sharp decline in the textile share of total exports is comparable to what occurred at Mitsui in the prewar period.

The rate of increase for total exports of Mitsui, Mitsubishi, Marubeni, Sumitomo, and Nissho-Iwai is close to or above the average rate of increase of the ten GTCs (see Table 6.7). This indicates that the greater the scale of the company's initial export level, the greater the rate of increase for exports in the 1960s. The rate of increase for heavy industrial goods is much higher than the rate of increase for all commodities. As Table 6.7 shows, the share of chemical products, metals, and machinery are 10.6, 8.2, and 11.5 times higher, respectively, in 1970 than in 1960. Although the ten GTCs exported over three-fourths of Japan's total metal exports in 1970, their share of machinery is much lower (about two-fifths) because of the prevalance of manufacturers to directly export electrical machinery and motor vehicles. As the firms sought to expand into new markets, the number of overseas branches increased 150 percent between 1961 and 1970, primarily in Europe, Africa, and Australia. Mitsui and Sumitomo were the most aggressive in opening new offices (see Table 6.8).

There was also diversification in the type of transaction. Offshore trade (involving non-Japanese buyers and sellers) became more important, although it comprised only 3 to 8 percent of the activity of individual GTCs in the 1960s. Exports from Japan provided 14 to 19 percent of total offshore trade volume, while imports to Japan provided 16 to 26 percent.

Less than half of all the GTCs' volume involved foreign trade. Domestic transactions accounted for 50 to 62 percent. The GTCs were thus in a good position to hedge between domestic and foreign markets. Although exact figures are unavailable, it is widely agreed that domestic transactions have the highest profit margin, followed by imports and exports. Offshore trading is the least profitable because of high operating costs and greater risks.

Organizing Capability of GTCs

Expansion of heavy industries in the 1960s provided GTCs with ample opportunity to demonstrate their organizing capability:

- Increasing demand for energy and raw materials led GTCs to explore import sources in such unfamiliar areas as Australia, Latin America, and Africa, where they risked investment in new mines and related infrastructure.
- GTCs utilized their information networks to investigate American and European suppliers of technology and equipment, and joined domestic manufacturers in new import-substitution production.
- GTCs promoted joint ventures in import-substitution production in Asian and Latin American developing countries, and the shift in Japanese export structure from final goods to intermediate goods and machinery. This contributed significantly to the resumption and further expansion of trade by Japanese GTCs in Southeast Asia. Equity investments by the GTCs were aimed not so much at earning direct returns on the investments as obtaining commitments from the new ventures to give the GTCs exclusive rights to handle their trade.
- GTCs also participated as prime contractors or consultants in the export of plant and equipment, and in aid programs.

Trading companies specializing in promoting products frequently merged with like companies to expand business activity. In the late 1950s Japanese steel firms actively invested in new manufacturing plants and equipment to expand capacity. At the same time, trading companies took over the steel export business from domestic steel distributors through a series of mergers. Although knowledgeable in the steel business and long affiliated with the large steel mills, the domestic steel distributors were inexperienced in conducting foreign transactions. Thus, to expand exports they sought partners with overseas experience and pursued the diversification strategy of the large textile trading companies to meet their needs. In 1955 Marubeni absorbed Takashimaya-Iida, which specialized in machines and steel, and in February 1960, Marubeni absorbed Daiichi Kozai. C. Itoh took over Morioka Company in October 1961, and Toyo Menka merged with Nankai Company in October 1963.

The success in diversifying the activities of the GTCs was largely due to the organizing capability of the GTCs' top and middle management. To achieve this level of skilled personnel, the GTCs attracted competent university gradu-

Table 6.8
Overseas Branches of Japanese GTCs: 1961 and 1970

Company	Year	Asia	North America	Latin America	Europe	Middle East	Africa	Oceania	Total
Mitsui	1961	23[a]	14	13[a]	6[b]	3[a]	5[a]	3[b]	67[a]
	1970	39	18	26	25	8	14	10	140
Mitsubishi	1961	18	10[a]	10	5	5	4[a]	3[a]	55
	1970	23	17	11	6	7	11	7	82
Marubeni	1961	21	8[a]	9	5[a]	4	5[a]	4	56[a]
	1970	27	15	10	14	6	9	6	87
C. Itoh	1961	15	9	12	5[a]	4	5[a]	3[a]	53
	1970	17	13	12	14	6	8	8	78
Sumitomo	1961	16	7	4[a]	4[a]	1[b]	1[b]	1[b]	34[a]
	1970	20	10	11	11	6	6	6	70
Nissho-Iwai	1961[c]	25	9	9	10	4	5[a]	6	68
	1970	21	12	5	14	6	9	8	75
Toyo Menka	1961	12	7	8	2[b]	3	1[b]	3	36[a]
	1970	17	10	9	8	3	4	4	55

Company	Year	Asia	North America	Latin America	Europe	Middle East	Africa	Oceania	Total
Nichimen	1961	23	12	6	4[a]	3[a]	6	2	56
	1970	20	10	8	9	5	7	3	62
Kanematsu-Gosho	1961[d]	20	9	3	4[a]	3	2	2[b]	43
	1970	15	11	4	7	1	3	6	47
Ataka	1961	12	5[a]	2[a]	4	1[a]	0	3[a]	27[a]
	1970	14	10	5	6	2	2	7	46
Total	1961	185	90	76	49[a]	31[a]	34[a]	30[a]	495
	1970	213	126	101	114	50	73	65	742

Notes:

a. The total of Nissho and Iwai, which were separate companies in 1961.

b. The total of Kanematsu and Gosho, which were separate companies in 1961.

c. The ratio of the number of overseas branches in 1970 to the number in 1961 is greater than 1.5, which is the ratio of total GTC branches in 1970 to the total in 1961.

d. The ratio of 1970 branches to 1961 branches is over 3.

Sources: Company financial statements.

ates and trained them on the job to be business experts. In addition, GTCs frequently sent their staff, a major supply source for entrepreneurship in Japan's private companies, to affiliated companies to perform functions that otherwise could not be handled by the respective companies.

Direct Export by Manufacturers

Not all manufacturers in Japan left overseas marketing to the GTCs; producers of electrical machinery and motor vehicles exported most of their products directly or via their own subsidiary trading companies. By the late 1960s, the value of exports by Matsushita, Toyota, and Nissan was almost at the same level as the major GTCs.

Some common reasons for manufacturers relying on their own sales efforts rather than use the established channels of the GTCs were the technical sophistication of the products and the timing of export expansion. For automobiles and electrical goods, for example, significant technical skills and knowledge were required and after-sale service had to be provided. Thus, it was not considered profitable for GTC branches to market these goods, especially since the volume was small at the start. Moreover, when exports began to expand in the early 1970s, the big manufacturers were prepared to do their own marketing overseas. However, the technical skill requirement does not completely explain the lack of involvement by GTCs in these products. It is more likely that the GTCs simply failed to see the rapid growth potential of these exports and allowed the manufacturers to rely on their own sales efforts.

CONCLUSION

The existence of a number of profit-making opportunities and a shortage of entrepreneurial and managerial skills (a typical characteristic of backward economies) in Japan before the Second World War induced the evolution of GTCs. But the GTC was not invented by the Japanese. Diversification of commodities and markets was a natural extension of trading company activities, as was the case for Jardine, Matheson and Company and East Asiatic Company in East and Southeast Asia during the late nineteenth century. The Japanese developed this institutional device so fully that Japan's industrialization and foreign trade expansion were promoted considerably by the GTCs despite the various handicaps they had to overcome when they started. In this sense, the GTC in Japan exemplifies Gerschenkron's (1966) institutional devices of late-starting countries to overcome barriers in their industrialization process.

Such business historians as Nakagawa (1967) and Morikawa (1976) dispute whether the GTC served as the core of *zaibatsu,* financially backed by a bank affiliated with the company and the sending of personnel to new industrial undertakings, as well as serving as a powerful marketing arm for the affiliated firms. Despite Nakagawa's and Morikawa's reservations, the argument does, however, apply quite well to prewar Mitsui and Mitsubishi, the two major firms of the period. But after the Second World War, control by *zaibatsu* families was eliminated. Today, both financial and personal relationships are a less significant element in transactions between the GTCs and their affiliated banks and manufacturers.

Part III

The Role of Government
in Industrial Growth

Seven

Japan's Industrialization and Protection Policy Before the Second World War

Although many free-trade advocates attribute Japan's industrial success to its free trade policy at the beginning of its industrialization, Japan's heavy industrialization was actually achieved under tariff and nontariff protection. Japan's industrialization began under the low tariff protections agreed upon with the Western industrialized nations in 1866. But Japanese tariffs gradually rose until the early 1930s when Japan promoted heavy industrialization through import substitution. Because tariffs were a major policy instrument of governments around the world before the Second World War, this chapter analyzes Japan's tariff structure in the context of its trade policy during its prewar industrialization.

HISTORY OF TARIFF PROTECTION

The tariff treaty with foreign powers in 1866 (Kaizei Yakusho) established the initial conditions for the development of Japan's industry and trade. Under the terms of the treaty, Japanese import and export duties were limited to unilateral rates as low as 5 percent (ad valorem equivalent) on most commodities. Except for foodstuffs, grains, and coal, these duties were levied on most raw materials used in industrial production. Due to inflation, the equivalent ad valorem rate of these duties declined to between 2.0 and 2.5 percent in the first two decades of the Meiji period. These conventional tariffs were levied on 40 percent of all dutiable imports and were maintained until complete tariff autonomy was achieved in 1911.

After continued efforts to revise the tariff treaty of 1866, Japan partially restored tariff autonomy in 1899, and the Tariff Law that was enacted in March

1897 took effect in January 1899. Subsequently, general revisions of the Tariff Law were made in 1906, 1911, 1926, and 1932, and partial revisions were made almost every year. Meanwhile, the tariff treaty with the United Kingdom and other nations in 1866 continued to restrict tariffs on the products from these countries to levels as low as 5 to 15 percent.

In addition to the Tariff Law and conventional tariffs, a third category—special tariffs—was created for all imports including rice and other essential foodstuffs. Under the First and Second Emergency Special Tariffs laws that were enacted in 1904 and 1905 to finance the Russo-Japanese War, surcharges from 5 to 20 percent were levied on most imports except those under conventional tariffs.[1] Although intended to be temporary at the outset, these special tariffs were maintained for some time and were eventually incorporated into the tariff schedule. For example, the 100 percent duty on luxury merchandise, consisting of 147 items in 1924, was initially levied primarily for balance-of-payment purposes; but after meeting its intended objective the duty was incorporated into the tariff schedule in 1926 and remained in effect until the Second World War.

Industrial Protection

Raising revenue was the main purpose of tariff imposition in Japan before the First World War. During the early Meiji period (1868–1912), Japan imposed a duty of 5 percent on most exports. The revenue from these export duties was on average two-thirds the revenues obtained from import duties. Because the senselessness of export duties was well known, a movement for their elimination spread nationwide in the early 1890s. Duties on such major exports as raw silk and tea were, however, maintained until 1899, when, under partial tariff autonomy, import duties were raised to yield a greater portion of tariff revenue. The main source of government revenue in the Meiji period, however, was land taxes, and tariff revenue constituted at most between 5 and 10 percent of total government revenue.

As industry grew, however, industrial protection became the main reason for tariff imposition. Beginning in the late 1890s, tariffs were used selectively to protect domestic industries. Figure 7.1 shows changes in the average tariff rates, which are defined as the ratio of total tariff revenues to either the value of total imports or the value of dutiable imports.

Average tariffs on manufactures followed a pattern similar to that of dutiable imports (see Figure 7.1); these are analyzed in greater detail in the following sections. Raw material imports were initially subject to the same tariffs as manufactures but were exempted from duty by the late 1890s. For example, ginned cotton was exempted from import tariffs in 1896 and iron ore was exempted in 1901. Furthermore, the number of duty-free raw material items

Figure 7.1
Average Tariffs of Japan: 1868-1980

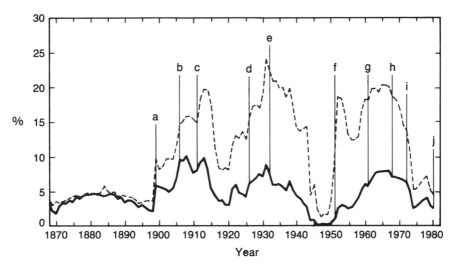

Notes: Solid line = average tariff rates calculated for total imports; dotted line = average tariff rates calculated for dutiable imports.

a. Tariff act, recovery of tariff autonomy (1899)
b. Tariff revision (1905)
c. General tariff revision (1911)
d. General tariff revision (1926)
e. Surcharge of 35 percent on specific duty items (1932)
f. General revision (1951)
g. General revision and shift to BTN (1961)
h. Kennedy Round reduction started (1968)
i. Unilateral reduction by 20 percent (1972)
j. Tokyo Round reduction started (1980)

Sources: Yamazawa and Yamamoto (1979a: table 22) for the years 1868-1970; Ministry of Finance (1982) for the years 1970-80.

increased from 49 to 89 in the general revision of 1906. This, in effect, was tariff differentiation, which implies a deliberate policy of industrial protection. If policy makers had been seeking complete self-sufficiency in the Japanese economy, they would have levied high tariffs uniformly on all imports. But protection of a given industry can only be undertaken at a cost to all other manufacturing and nonmanufacturing industries.

Japan's import dependence on raw materials began with the elimination of import duties on raw cotton. Initially, as part of its import substitution policy, the Meiji government encouraged domestic cultivation of cotton, but

Japanese raw cotton was unsuitable for spinning fine quality yarn. In the early 1890s, while domestic production of cotton textiles was growing, and because of the lack of domestic raw cotton of fine quality to produce cotton yarn, imports of cotton yarn were increasing. Thus, to achieve import substitution of cotton yarn, imports of fine quality raw cotton were necessary and import duties on raw cotton were eliminated. The elimination of the import duties resulted in an increase in domestic spinning of imported, higher-quality raw cotton. At the same time, export duties on cotton yarn were also eliminated, although Japan's export market at the time was small. In a few years, however, exports of the higher-quality cotton yarn exceeded imports. Domestic cultivation of raw cotton for both the export market and domestic consumption decreased rapidly after 1896.

Start of Agricultural Protection

Tariffs on agricultural products were originally intended to supplement emergency surcharges on the land tax during the Russo-Japanese War. Tariffs on cereals set the precedent for agricultural protection in Japan. Rice, which had been exempted from duty, became subject to a duty of 15 percent in 1905. In the same year, duties on wheat and barley were raised from 5 to 15 percent. These agricultural tariffs remained in effect even after the emergency surcharges were eliminated, and were incorporated into the tariff schedule in 1906.

In 1911, the duty on wheat was raised further to 20 percent. The duty on rice, on the other hand, provoked a public controversy between landowners and manufacturers over agricultural protection. The controversy was finally resolved in the Japanese Diet in 1913 when compromise tariffs were agreed upon. Under the agreement, a specific duty of one yen per 60 kilograms (the ad valorem equivalent was 23% of average import prices in 1910–12) was levied on imports of rice from outside the Japanese empire, but imports of rice from Taiwan and Korea were exempted. Unlike the effect of the British Corn Laws in the United Kingdom, which led to the expansion of grain imports, the tariff policy for rice in Japan resulted in self-sufficiency in rice throughout the Japanese empire. Tariffs on refined sugar continued to be as low as 10 percent under the tariff treaty of 1866 until 1911, when they were raised to an ad valorem equivalent of between 50 and 60 percent. Since these higher tariffs were imposed on sugar imports from outside the empire, they tended to encourage colonial agriculture in Taiwan and Korea, which expanded production of sugar and rice for export to Japan (see Table 7.1).

It should be emphasized that Japan's tariff policy did not remain unaffected by the alternating worldwide waves of free trade and protectionism (Haberler 1964). Initially, free trade was forced on Japan during the free-trade move-

Table 7.1
Rice and Sugar Imports of Japan Proper: 1898–1933 (%)

Product and origin	1898	1903	1908	1913	1918	1924	1928	1933
Rice and paddy								
from outside the empire	97.7	91.4	69.1	63.3	52.4	25.1	16.9	5.0
from Korea[a]	14.9	33.1	57.8	56.4	66.7			
from Taiwan	2.3	8.6	30.9	21.8	14.5	17.1	26.7	28.3
Sugar[b]								
from outside the empire	94.7	87.2	67.5	70.4	38.0	34.1	34.7	9.7
from Taiwan	5.3	12.8	32.5	29.6	62.0	65.9	65.3	90.3

Notes:
a. Korea was not part of the Japanese empire during the first three periods and is therefore treated separately.
b. Imports of sugar from Korea were negligible.
Source: Toyo Keizai Shinposha (1935).

ment that was initiated by the 1860 Cobden-Chevalier Treaty between Great Britain and France. But Japan's initial period of free trade was followed by a period of protectionism that extended from the late 1870s until the First World War. During this protectionist period, Japan resumed tariff autonomy and began to raise tariff barriers. After the First World War, protectionism was further strengthened, escalating to autarky within each trade bloc in the worldwide tariff war of the 1930s. By this time Japan had the highest level of tariff protection in the world.

ANALYSIS OF INSTITUTIONAL INDUSTRIAL TARIFF PROTECTION

In the preceding section it was suggested that Japan's imposition of tariffs became selective, and that the main objective was to protect industry. To further support this assertion, more evidence is presented in the following sections. The structure of tariff protection for manufactures during the period 1890–1940 is analyzed in detail, and special attention is given to changes in the tariff structure in response to the progress of industrialization. Two complementary approaches are used in the analysis. The first examines the principles that justify tariff imposition and the structure of the nominal tariff schedule. The second compiles tariff data on individual principal commodities and quantitatively analyzes the changes in tariff protection for manufactures over time.

Principles of Tariff Policy

Evidence of industrial protection by selective tariffs can be found in tariff reports that were made at each general tariff revision (Ministry of Finance 1938). The tariff report for the general tariff revision in 1911 proposed that tariffs be levied principally to raise revenue and that industrial protection be given secondary consideration. But this proposition merely indicates that the government did not want to appear protectionist. In fact, industrial protection dominated the structure of the tariff schedule. Even the two special tariffs—one that allowed emergency surcharges in 1904–05 and one that imposed luxury duties in 1924—eventually ended up protecting domestic industries even though they were initially motivated by the necessity to increase revenue. The emergency surcharges began the move toward agricultural protection, and the luxury duties were incorporated into the general tariff schedule as prohibitive tariffs on imported consumer goods.

After the First World War and during the early 1920s, special tariffs were occasionally levied to protect particular industries. Manufacturers of iron and steel products, and synthetic dyestuffs and other chemical products had been established or had developed rapidly during the First World War. After the war, enthusiasm to industrialize was still strong, and the strong desire for autarky was rooted in the belief that all existing manufacturing industries should be maintained at any cost. Thus, when these industries were confronted with reorganized foreign competition after the war, the domestic producers demanded and received tariff protection.

While explaining the general tariff revision of 1926 in a speech to the Japanese Diet, Prime Minister Osachi Hamaguchi explicitly proposed that Japan's tariff policy be based on the concept of industrial protection. His general criteria for tariff imposition are as follows:[2]

- Raw materials for industrial production that are either not produced domestically or only produced in small quantities should be exempt from duties or have low duties.

- Important industries not yet fully developed but with prospects for further development should be given enough protection to enable them to compete with foreign industries.

- Tariffs for important industries that are already fully developed and that compete with foreign products should be lowered or kept at the present level.

- Daily necessities should either be exempted from tariffs or have the lowest possible tariffs.

- Luxury consumer goods should have the highest tariffs in order to discourage their consumption domestically.

The criteria were reasonable and could easily have been expanded to be even more protectionist. Further protection was in fact realized with the adoption of a series of tariff revisions in the 1920s and early 1930s. Newly developed heavy manufactures were given higher tariff protection under the general tariff revision of 1926. This was followed by tariffs on sugar and starch in 1927, lumber in 1929, artificial silk in 1931, and tariff increases on pig iron and other heavy manufactures in 1932. Another general tariff revision that was planned in 1936 to add protection to new industries resulted in increased protection for several manufacturing sectors including automobile production and petroleum refining in 1937.

Strong objections to this increasing tendency toward protectionism were raised by free-trade advocates. They argued against fully embracing protectionism and contended that protection should be confined to a few promising industries whose progress could be regularly reviewed. They also demanded the elimination of tariff protection for fully developed industries. In most cases their advice went unheeded. One example of this is the movement to eliminate the duty on cotton yarn. Cotton yarn was subject to a duty of 5 percent (although it was not being imported at the time). In 1925 cotton weavers and hosiers, which were typically small and medium-sized firms, pleaded publicly and in the Diet for the elimination of the duty on cotton yarn to increase their competitiveness with large firms. The 5 percent duty on Chinese cotton yarn, which because of the depreciation of silver had become more competitive, was an added cost to small and medium-sized firms trying to compete with large firms. Large firms could offset the higher cost resulting from the duty by dealing in large volumes. But several big cotton-spinning firms were able to exert their influence in maintaining the tariff until 1930, when it was finally lowered to 3.3 percent.

Disaggregation in the General Tariff Schedule

The degree of detail in the commodity classification of the general tariff schedule provides more evidence for tariff differentiation. The tariff schedule that was in effect in 1899 included only 532 classes. However, with the general tariff revision of 1906, the tariff schedule was broken down into a standard commodity classification consisting of 19 categories, 538 classes, and 819 items. In 1911, the tariff schedule was disaggregated further into 1,599 items and in 1926 to 1,699 items. This system was used until the Brussels Tariff Nomenclature (BTN) system was adopted in 1961. The disaggregation of the commodity classification reflected not only the emergence of new industries and commodities in foreign trade but also the need for deliberate protection of domestic industries.

Escalated Tariff Structure

The first tariff schedule of 1899 set up nine classes of tariff rates between 0 and 40 percent at intervals of 5 percent. Rates were assigned to the various stages of processing or type of good. Individual commodities were then assigned one of these rates. For example, a rate between 0 and 5 percent was levied on raw materials, a rate of 10 percent was levied on semimanufactures, a rate between 15 to 20 percent was levied on finished manufactures, and a rate of more than 25 percent was levied on luxury goods.

The differential between tariffs increased with the degree of processing (tariff escalation) and the passage of time. In the tariff schedule of 1906, raw materials were assigned tariffs from 0 to 5 percent, finished manufactures had tariffs from 30 to 40 percent, and luxury goods were subject to tariffs of 50 to 60 percent. In the tariff schedules of 1911 and 1926, commodities were differentiated within the same escalated structure by such factors as the need for protection for import-competing production, the future prospects for domestic production, and the effects on export competitiveness (in the case of materials used in export industries). The effective rates of protection produced by this escalated structure differed from the nominal tariffs; in fact, nominal tariffs gave higher effective protection to manufacturing than implied by their levels because of this escalated structure of protection.

Ad Valorem Versus Specific Duties

The Tariff Law of 1899 mandated the adoption of ad valorem duties but permitted, for administrative convenience, specific duty rates (that is, a set amount per piece or per ton) using average import prices for the preceding six months. The Tariff Law of 1906 increased the role of specific rates by commodity, and the number of imports subject to specific duties was expanded. The ad valorem equivalent rates of the specific duties declined prior to 1920 when import prices were rising, but they were later revised upward several times. For example, during the First World War, rapidly rising import prices had lowered ad valorem equivalents to levels as low as 1–2 percent. In 1921, however, tariffs were raised back to their former levels by changing many specific duties to ad valorem rates (but most of these were changed back to specific duties in the general revision of 1926).

In the 1920s, the ad valorem equivalent of specific duties increased as import prices decreased, but specific duties were seldom revised downward. In June 1932, specific duties were raised uniformly by 35 percent to adjust to the devaluation of the yen. The adjustment was needed to maintain the ad valorem equivalent of specific duties vis-à-vis the higher prices of imports resulting from the decrease in the value of the yen relative to the dollar. However, since prices for many imports were raised by less than 35 percent and since currency depreciation by itself produces the same effect as a uniform schedule of import tariffs and export subsidies, this uniform adjustment of specific duties effectively doubled protection for domestic producers.[3]

Other Tariffs

Although tariffs had increased industrial protection by 1906, supplementary tariffs to protect domestic producers against "unfair foreign competition" were also established that year under new tariff laws. Specifically, three special-purpose tariffs—the countervailing, retaliatory, and antidumping duties—were created, although they were seldom enforced before the 1930s. In keeping with the worldwide trend toward industrial protection in the 1930s, the special-purpose tariffs were strengthened and enacted into the Trade Protection Law of 1934. Under the new law, a 50 percent surcharge was imposed on all imports from Canada and Australia in retaliation for the discriminatory tariffs those nations imposed on Japanese goods. However, after six months, new trade agreements between Japan and the two nations eliminated these tariffs but established exemption and payback rules for materials used in export industries.

Another set of tariff laws was adopted in 1900 under the Temporary Storage Yard Law. The laws exempted imported materials from duties provided the imported materials were simply processed for export in special areas known as temporary storage yards, which, in effect, were the first free port (or export-processing) zones. In order to further promote exports, domestically produced materials were permitted to be similarly processed in 1912. By the early 1920s, the concept of free ports was openly discussed in business circles and the debate moved to the Diet in 1925. In 1927, the government responded by enacting the Tariff Factory Law, which changed the temporary storage yards into "tariff factories." Under the new law, improvements such as the simplification of procedures and extension of the storage period from six months to one year were made. Owing to these changes, by the late 1920s, the number of tariff factories had increased.

INDUSTRIAL PROTECTION BY TARIFF: A QUANTITATIVE ANALYSIS

Thus far, the history of tariffs in Japan has been discussed in terms of the average tariffs on total imports or on large commodity groups such as manufactures, foodstuffs, and raw materials. But in order to establish a pattern of industrial protection through the imposition of tariffs, analyzing the average level of tariffs is not as important as analyzing the upward or downward deviations from the average—that is, analyzing the structure of individual tariffs. To this end, data on individual tariffs have been compiled for 61 principal commodities at five-year intervals from 1893 to 1938. The 61 commodities under consideration do not correspond to the original commodity classification in Ministry of Finance statistics (1882–1943). The 61 commodities make up 60–70 percent of the value of total imports. Based on this data, a quantitative analysis of the tariff structure is presented in the following sections.

Tariffs on Individual Commodities

The value of every commodity imported into each of Japan's main ports from outside the Japanese empire was recorded along with the tariff revenues collected on the commodity. The tariff rate was estimated by dividing tariff revenues by the value of the imported commodity for each of the 61 individual commodities.[4] The commodities were then divided into six to eight groups by industry and by economic use (or stages of processing), and the average tariff rates of individual groups are compared to identify the structure of tariff protection.

The tariff rates collected were used in the analysis rather than the nominal tariff rates listed in the tariff schedule. While this ratio tends to underestimate the restrictive effect of tariffs on imports,[5] it is used here nevertheless because of the following difficulties pertaining to nominal tariffs:

• In addition to general tariff revisions, nominal tariffs were revised almost every year (including special tariffs) and were subject to conventional tariffs or complete or partial exemptions. Thus, the actual nominal tariff rate on each of the 61 commodities throughout the period 1893–1936 would be difficult to determine.

• Many commodities were subject to specific duties. Aggregating these commodities into larger categories requires calculations of the ad valorem equivalents of the specific tariffs. Determining reliable levels of import prices to derive ad valorem equivalents is beyond the scope of this analysis.

The tariff rates that were calculated for the groups that are classified by industry and by economic use are summarized in Tables 7.2 and 7.3. The tariff rates are calculated approximately every five years: 1893, 1898, 1903, 1908, 1913, 1918, 1924, 1928, 1933, and 1938. Rates for a few of the selected years were affected by several events. For example, because of the Great Earthquake of 1923, original data on goods imported through the Port of Yokohama in 1922 and 1923 are not complete; the year 1924 was therefore selected instead of 1923. In addition, the rates for 1924 were lower since daily necessities were exempt from import duty in March of that year. In 1937, the publication of statistics on important imported commodities was discontinued for security purposes, and in 1938, data were available for only 30 percent of the commodities covered in the sample.

Table 7.2 and Figure 7.1 summarize changes in average tariffs (simple and weighted arithmetic means, respectively) for the 61 commodities. The simple mean (last row, Table 7.2) increased after 1898 and, except for the decreases in 1918 and 1924, continued to increase until the Second World War. The arithmetic mean weighted by import values of individual commodities (solid line, Figure 7.1), however, increased until 1913 and tended to decline in the 1920s and 1930s. This occurred in part because the share of duty-free or low-duty items (such as raw materials) increased, but it also reflects underestimation of the restricting effect of higher tariffs. The standard deviation of tariffs of the 61 commodities increased from 1900 until the First World War, and, despite the decreases in 1918 and 1924, continued to increase until the Second World War. This evidence supports the discussion above on the selective imposition of tariffs.

Table 7.2
Simple Average Tariffs on Individual Commodity Groups by Industry (%)

Classification by industry	1893	1898	1903	1908	1913	1918	1924	1928	1933	1938
A Agricultural products	2.52	2.49	8.57	20.61	19.99	14.39	8.63	14.37	23.08	24.24
C Raw materials	3.96	2.79	5.66	8.73	6.42	3.34	1.77	4.01	7.63	4.16
S Primary products (A+C)	3.43	2.68	6.63	12.69	10.94	7.02	4.06	7.46	12.78	12.19
B Manufactured foodstuffs	3.22	3.36	12.61	35.89	42.67	24.44	19.02	47.37	50.55	58.31
D Textile manufactures	3.20	2.84	12.43	14.86	20.68	9.55	11.85	26.31	25.54	39.17
E Other light manufactures	4.71	4.62	11.86	16.21	21.11	11.71	10.33	20.97	19.15	18.00
Q Light manufactures (B+D+E)	3.78	3.69	12.24	20.87	26.13	13.99	13.07	29.35	29.13	34.96
F Chemical products	4.63	4.75	6.29	6.51	13.50	4.13	17.15	32.63	28.43	47.15
G Metals and metal products	4.17	3.83	9.83	12.06	15.31	6.30	3.74	17.19	17.99	21.45
H Machinery	4.20	4.24	12.59	24.33	25.45	18.25	17.34	22.38	26.94	19.46
R Heavy manufactures (F+G+H)	4.32	4.24	9.32	13.33	17.66	9.06	12.34	23.47	23.89	31.75
Total	3.91	3.71	9.88	16.19	19.81	10.68	10.93	22.60	23.76	29.16

Note: Percentages represent simple arithmetic means of individual tariffs belonging to each group. Commodities not imported are excluded from calculation.
Source: Yamazawa and Yamamoto (1979a).

Table 7.3
Simple Average Tariffs on Individual Commodity Groups by Economic Use (%)

Classification by economic use	1893	1898	1903	1908	1913	1918	1924	1928	1933	1938
A + B Foodstuffs	2.91	2.97	10.81	29.78	33.60	20.42	14.86	34.17	39.56	44.69
C Raw materials	3.96	2.79	5.66	8.73	6.42	3.34	1.77	4.01	7.63	4.16
I Intermediate goods 1-L[a]	4.04	3.45	6.60	4.07	12.25	5.74	6.80	13.60	16.48	9.54
J Intermediate goods 1-H[a]	4.84	4.44	3.72	3.84	6.41	2.84	13.92	14.68	15.02	13.99
O Intermediate goods 1 (I + J)	4.49	3.95	5.16	3.96	9.60	4.42	10.04	14.09	15.82	10.65
K Intermediate goods 2-L[a]	4.24	4.17	10.59	8.10	18.11	7.67	6.14	15.27	11.05	6.75
L Intermediate goods 2-H[a]	4.04	4.03	8.88	9.42	16.21	3.44	7.08	19.88	17.29	15.97
P Intermediate goods 2 (K + L)	4.14	4.09	9.56	8.89	16.97	5.13	6.67	17.90	14.61	10.85
M Capital goods	3.67	3.86	8.75	13.75	17.33	6.98	10.60	14.27	16.89	7.27
N Consumer goods	4.04	4.12	17.31	31.21	30.12	20.55	20.43	41.23	41.59	63.10
Total	3.91	3.71	9.88	16.19	19.81	10.68	10.93	22.60	23.76	29.16

Notes: Percentages represent simple arithmetic means of individual tariffs belonging to each group. Commodities not imported are excluded from calculation.

a. Intermediate goods are divided into four groups, cross-classified by stages (1 and 2) and factor intensity (light (L) and heavy (H) manufacture).

Source: Yamazawa and Yamamoto (1979a).

Escalated Tariff Structure

The tariff structure continued to be differentiated by degree of processing throughout the period. The sample commodities are classified into groups by industry and by economic use, thus facilitating comparisons of changes in average tariffs (see Tables 7.2 and 7.3). The average tariffs for four broad groups—agricultural products, raw materials, light manufactures, and heavy manufactures—remained at about the same level until 1898, but tended to diverge after 1903. The infant industry argument leads to the hypothesis that tariffs on heavy manufactures exceeded those of light manufactures at the early stage of heavy industrialization; but this was not the case. The tariff rates for both light and heavy manufactures followed a pattern similar to that of the total average tariff (see Table 7.2), but the rate for light manufactures exceeded that for heavy manufactures from 1903 onwards. The rate for agricultural products increased and kept pace with that of light manufactures until 1913 when its rate of increase slowed, and eventually fell below that of heavy manufactures after the 1920s. The rate for raw materials fluctuated between 2 and 8 percent from 1893 through 1938 (the fluctuation of average rates of raw materials seems to be the result of changes in tariffs on fuels).

The disaggregation of light and heavy manufactures shows that the tariff rates on manufactured foodstuffs increased earlier and remained at a level higher than those of any other group. The tariff rate for textiles kept pace with that of other light manufactures until 1924 but exceeded the tariff rate on other light manufactures after 1928. The tariff rates for heavy metals and chemicals lagged behind that of the other groups, but after 1924 they rose rapidly and exceeded those for textiles. Average tariffs on machinery were raised earlier and remained between 20 and 25 percent, but they were surpassed by the rates for metals in the 1930s. From the data, no clear principle of tariff differentiation is discernible.

When classified by economic use, the average tariffs of the groups show an escalated structure of tariffs and a pattern of tariff differentiation that is clearer than when the groups are classified by industry (see Table 7.3 and Figure 7.2). Average tariffs for both consumer goods and foodstuffs increased earlier than any other group and remained at a level higher than any other group throughout the period. Intermediate goods 1 and 2 and capital goods had average tariffs that showed no rapid increases and remained at about 15 percent. Raw materials had the lowest average tariffs—between 2 and 8 percent.

As Table 7.2 shows, there is no relationship between tariff rates for light and heavy manufactures. The rapid increase in average tariffs on chemicals and textiles after the late 1920s was largely the result of the increase in tariffs on individual commodities in the consumer goods category within the two groups. This leads to the conclusion that classification by economic use (or

Figure 7.2
Average Tariffs on Commodity Groups Classified by Economic Use

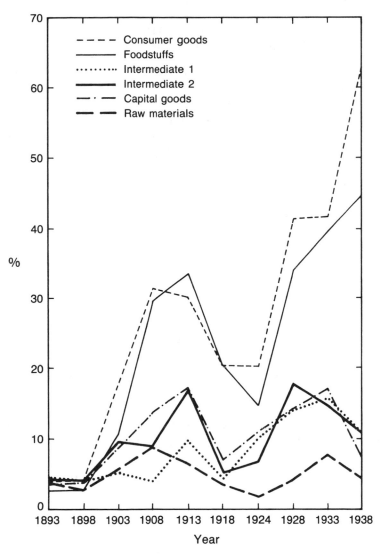

Source: Calculated from Yamazawa and Yamamoto (1979a: table 21).

stages of processing) of individual commodities was the main criterion relied upon to determine tariff levels.

OTHER NONTARIFF
INDUSTRIAL PROTECTION POLICIES

While the Japanese government used tariffs as a principal policy instrument for industrial protection before the Second World War, especially after tariff autonomy had been fully restored, it also resorted to the use of other policy instruments such as quantitative import restrictions, production subsidies, and other direct and indirect government assistance to affect the course of industrial development. Although it is difficult to measure the impact these instruments had on industrial protection, they are discussed briefly in the sections that follow.

Quantitative Restrictions on Imports

The import-approval system, which was first introduced for rice with the enactment of the Rice Law in 1921, empowered the government to intervene in the market to adjust the supply of rice. The system was extended in 1924 to include synthetic dyestuffs to confront German dumping, and in 1931 to ammonium sulfate after the breakdown of the international ammonium sulfate cartel. But it was not until 1937 that the Japanese government resorted to general quantitative restrictions on imports.[6]

In January 1937, Japan's quantitative restrictions began with the establishment of an exchange control system, which was introduced with the aim of stabilizing yen exchange rates. To this end, trading licenses were issued to importers based on their past performance. But in September 1937 the Adjustment Law introduced a stricter import quota system that was devised to improve the persistent deficit in the balance of payments and to secure supplies of commodities for military purposes. Except for a few industries, such as automobiles and machine tools, quantitative import restrictions had little effect on industrial development before the Second World War.

Production Subsidies

Production subsidies were used by the Japanese government to promote the modernization of the Japanese economy, especially during the 1880s, the 1890s, and the interwar period. This is reflected in the ratio of industry subsidies to government expenditure, which, for the period 1880–90, was between 4 and 5 percent. This ratio declined to 1 to 2 percent between 1900 and the First World War and increased again to 8 percent during the interwar period.

The distribution of subsidies changed over time. In the 1880s, construction firms were the main recipients of subsidies. Between 1890 and 1910, subsidies went mainly to transportation and communications firms, and after the late 1920s subsidies were used mainly to support agriculture. Production subsidies for mining and manufacturing were relatively small (ranging from 3.6 to 5.4% during the period 1925–38). The ratio of subsidies to manufacturing income was less than 1 percent from 1880 to 1938. However, it is not so much the quantitative magnitude but the qualitative impact that should be considered, since subsidies were directed at building infrastructure and at fostering strategic industries such as shipbuilding (under the Shipbuilding Encouragement Act of 1896), steel, and automobile production.

The exemption from corporate and other taxes had the same effect as a production subsidy. For example, although the impact was not incorporated in the calculation of subsidies mentioned above, steel-producing firms with more than a predetermined production capacity were exempted from all domestic taxes under the Steel-Manufacturing Encouragement Act of 1917.

Direct Government Aid

Direct government aid to initiate and develop new industries can also be viewed as a form of protection. One example is government financing, which lessened the risks entailed in the start-up of new industries. In the initial stages of the industry's development, the government established experimental plants for the silk, cotton, and woolen industries. These plants were then turned over to private firms after it was apparent that they could be operated as independent, viable entities. The early development of the chemicals, metals, and machinery industries also benefited greatly from the activities of government-owned foundries, research institutes, and national universities. These governmental institutions played an important role in introducing new techniques, and in training and supplying engineers for employment in private firms.

For two decades, private firms had failed to establish a viable steel production industry. It was only after the government exercised strong leadership in developing steel production did the integrated production of iron and steel succeed for the first time in Japan. The government's efforts were directed toward the creation and development of the Yawata Iron Works. During the start-up period, the losses of Yawata and the subsequent expansion of investment in the firm were financed by the government. After nine years of operation, Yawata began to show a profit. Yawata played a central role in the expansion of steel production in Japan throughout the period before the Second World War (see Chapter 5).

Government Purchases

The pace of an industry's development depends largely on the scale and growth of its potential domestic market. In the process of import substitution, which is achieved by lowering the costs and improving the quality of domestically produced goods, domestic producers have to compete with foreign producers for a share of the domestic market. If, however, part of domestic demand is reserved for domestically produced goods regardless of the cost and quality differences between domestically produced and imported goods, the pace of import substitution will be considerably accelerated.

Recognizing this, the Kokusanshōreikai (the Association to Encourage Domestic Manufacturing) initiated a semiofficial "buy-Japanese" movement at the end of 1914. The aim of this movement was not only to work toward the substitution of domestic for imported goods but also to increase the use of domestic goods. Led by Baron Eiichi Shibusawa, one of the most eminent business leaders in the Meiji and Taishō periods (1868–1926), the association "pledged itself to conduct the following program: survey home industries; hold fairs and exhibitions to display domestic products; give public lectures; answer inquiries on home manufactures; collect and display samples and catalogues; publish a review, etc." (Kobayashi 1930:238–39). The government appropriated 3,000 yen for the association's maintenance in 1914 and increased the appropriation to 5,000 yen a year from 1915 onwards.

The imported goods that were targetted in the buy-Japanese movement included drugs and chemicals, iron and steel, machinery, glass, paper, and woolen fabrics. These goods had been mostly imported in the past. With the outbreak of the First World War in 1914, the volume of these imports decreased and their prices rapidly rose. Domestic products in these commodity groups were, however, widely perceived to be inferior to imports, and foreign products such as heavy electrical machinery were considered a necessity in government factory work (Takeuchi 1972).

In the 1920s, the buy-Japanese movement was given further impetus by domestic industries seeking further protection against renewed competition from foreign competitors and by the need for improvement in the balance of payments. The British consulate in Tokyo reported on the buy-Japanese movement as follows:

> Though it is not strictly within the category of legislation, mention should be made of an extremely strong official campaign to encourage the use of domestic products. This has ramifications in all quarters, such as, for example, the issue of instructions by the Railway department laying down what domestic goods must be used and what imported goods may be used. It is understood that certain government departments when calling for tenders now specify in many cases articles of Japanese manufactures irrespective of quality.[7]

It is difficult to make a quantitative appraisal of the effect of the buy-Japanese movement on import substitution. Before the First World War, a large part of domestic demand for such manufactures as steel, ships, and automobiles came from the Japanese government, which needed these items in areas such as railroad construction and the military. For example, in 1903 two-thirds of Yawata's sales of steel products were to the government. In 1921 only one-half of Yawata's sales were to the government, and by the late 1920s the share of Yawata's sales to the government had declined to less than one-fourth. But such data are misleading since domestic demand would be much higher if the indirect demand by private producers of machinery and metal manufactures that was induced by government demand is included. There is no doubt that the government pursued a policy of preferential purchasing of domestic goods, weighing the differences in price and quality between domestically produced and imported goods.

At the same time, domestic producers tried to match imports both in quality and cost. In the mid-1920s, in industries in which a wide technological gap existed between domestic and foreign goods (such as in the electrical machinery industry), major Japanese manufacturers rushed to introduce advanced technology into their manufacturing processes under license contracts from European and American manufacturers.

Export Promotion

As European competition revived in the world market after the First World War, Japan's exports fell and the government was prompted to make export promotion a more important part of trade policy. Various export promotion measures were pursued and enacted in the 1920s. These measures, which included the establishment of a quality control system for traditional Japanese exports such as silk, cotton textiles, and celluloid, were strengthened in the 1930s. In addition, new markets for these exports in Latin America, the Middle East, and Australia were encouraged, sometimes through the use of government guarantees that supported bank acceptance of export bills.

The government's policies toward its colonial possessions allowed for the development of markets for the export of emerging manufactures such as metals, chemicals, and machinery. Exports of these commodities expanded steadily to Manchuria and Kwantung Province in the 1930s, but they were tied to the growth of Japanese investment in these areas.

FOREIGN INVESTMENT POLICY

The discussion of foreign investment policy in this section is limited primarily to commodity trade policy. However, since government policy toward direct foreign investment (DFI) by foreign firms and toward imports played an important role in the introduction of a part of the heavy industrial sector from abroad, this policy is also discussed.

Japan adopted three methods to establish new industries. The first was to produce by imitation, that is, importing the necessary machinery and employing foreign technicians in the process. This method was principally employed in light industrialization, a good example of which is the cotton-spinning industry. The second method was to purchase patents and expertise from firms in developed countries, which is similar to the first method in that it also involved machinery and technicians being introduced from abroad. This second method was used in a number of heavy industries, including the iron and steel and ammonium sulfate industries. The third method was to allow stock ownership of patented supplies, skills, and machinery. This method allowed joint ventures to be established.

Direct Foreign Investment

From the 1900s onwards, especially before the First World War and in the 1920s, Japan was a host country for DFI.[8] As was shown in Chapter 2 (see Table 2.2), the value of DFI was low, at 70–100 million yen from 1904 to 1913 and only 145 million yen from 1920 to 1931. Examination of its composition, however, shows that its role in heavy industrialization in Japan was significant.

Two characteristics of DFI in Japan should be noted (see Table 7.4). First, DFI in Japan was concentrated in heavy industry. Because of the industrialization taking place during the period 1900–1940, domestic demand for heavy industrial goods and imports grew. The gradual rise in the tariff rates for industrial goods that occurred following the recovery of partial tariff autonomy in 1899 further induced growth of domestic heavy industries. In some cases, DFI was used to jump the tariff barrier in these industries.

Second, DFI in Japan generally took the form of joint ventures (with the exception of 100 percent foreign ownership in the automobile assembly and rubber manufacturing industries), with management in the hands of the Japanese partner. The foreign partner was limited to capital participation and supplying technology and machinery. In this way, the main objective of technology borrowing—the establishment of import-substituting firms—was most easily achieved.

Although certain firms (Teijin for rayon and Hitachi for electrical machinery) developed technology independently, many firms relied on technology borrowing through DFI to shorten the time needed for technological development.[9] The end result was not, however, the mere copying of technology; rather, in adapting such technologies to domestic conditions, firms gained the capacity for independent technological development. This was spurred by the expansion of domestic demand and other needs, but the government's strong policy of encouraging domestic production—as in its preferential purchasing of domestically produced goods—also played an important role. Moreover, incentives in the form of tariff exemptions and subsidies only applied to firms in which foreign stock ownership was below a certain percentage. And, even more directly, a number of control policies were adopted to lower foreign capital participation in domestic firms. Thus, by the end of the 1930s, capital, management, and production in most venture firms had been transferred to Japanese nationals.

Localization Policy

The heavy electrical machinery industry exemplifies industrial development via joint-venture companies. The rapid electrification that took place in Japan in the 1900s lured foreign portfolio investment and at the same time raised the domestic demand for heavy electrical equipment such as motors and dynamos. To meet this demand, major electrical machinery firms were set up as joint ventures.

Once this happened, import substitution rapidly occurred in the industry. From the 1920s to the first half of the 1930s, import dependence on various kinds of heavy electrical equipment rapidly declined (Table 7.5). Even during the rush to build the large-scale thermal- and hydraulic-power dynamos after 1933, large-sized dynamos could be entirely supplied by domestic production. This was the result of the rationalization and cost-reducing programs initiated during the recession in the latter half of the 1920s. Moreover, in 1930, under a Ministry of Communications ordinance, the use of domestically produced equipment was subsidized. The ordinance specified, however, that only firms that had less than 50 percent of their stock owned by foreign interests were to be considered domestic firms and were thus eligible for product subsidies. As a result, each joint-venture firm tried to develop technology on its own to reduce its foreign-equity participation.

The automobile industry exemplifies another industry established by Japan's powerful localization policy. In 1929, domestic demand for automobiles was 35,000 units, of which 84 percent was imported as disassembled parts and components to be re-assembled in Japan and 14 percent was imported as finished automobiles. Domestic production could meet a mere 2 percent of total demand. Consequently, the Japanese government adopted a policy of subsidization to nurture domestic firms and through diverse measures was able to control the activity of foreign firms. In 1932, for example, the yen was depreciated by 43 percent, tariffs on automobile components and parts were raised, and increases in the number of units assembled in Japan were controlled. As a result, with the enactment of the Remittance Control Law

Table 7.4
DFI in Japanese Manufacturing Industries: 1899–1940

Industry	Name of firm	Year established	Foreign parent firm	Foreign equity participation
Electrical machinery	Nihon Denki	1899	Western Electric	54; 32[a]
	Tokyo Denki	1905	General Electric	55[b]
	Shibaura-seisakujo	1908	General Electric	24[b]
	Fuji Denki	1923	Siemens	30; 30
	Mitsubishi Denki	1924	Westinghouse	40; 4
	Toyo-Otis Elevator	1932	Otis Elevator	66; 70
	Sumitomo Denki	1932	I.S.E.	13; 7
	Tokyo-Western	1929	ERP	100; 0
Rubber products	Yokohama Gomu	1917	Goodrich	50; 9
	Chuo-gomu	1917	Dunlop	100; 99
Automobiles	Japan Ford	1925	Ford	100[c]
	Japan GM	1927	General Motors	100[c]
Sheet glass	Nihon Itagarasu	1918	Libby Owens	34; 17
Artificial fibers	Asahi Kenshoku	1924	Glanzsoff	25
	Nihon Bemberg	1929	J.P. Bemberg	25; 5

Industry	Name of firm	Year established	Foreign parent firm	Foreign equity participation
Phonograph records	Nihon Chikuonki	1927	Columbia	59; 2
	Nihon Victor	1929	R.C.A.	68; 25
Other machinery	Nihon Seiko	1907	Vickers-Armstrongs	50; 6
	Toyo Kikan	1928	Babcock & Wilcox	66; 66
	Kyozo Seisaku	1928	United Steel and Signal	20; 13
	Toyo Carrier	1930	Carrier Corporation	50; 46
	National Kinsen-Torokuki	1935	National Cash Register	70; 70

Notes:

a. First item is the percentage share at the time of establishment; the second is the percentage share in 1941.

b. Merged to become Tokyo Shibaura Denki in 1939. International Electric (33%; 16%).

c. Stopped production in 1939.

Source: Kogyo Ginko (Industrial Bank of Japan) (1950), "Gaikoku Gaisha no Honpo Toshi (Japanese Investment in Foreign Companies)," in Ministry of Finance (1950(5):64–67).

Table 7.5
Decreased Import Dependence on Heavy Electrical Machinery (%)

	1922–27	1928–32	1933–37
Water turbines and wheels	66.0	48.0	21.0
Hydraulic power dynamos	59.0	42.0	14.0
Steam turbines	97.0	82.0	23.0
Thermal-power dynamos	88.0	80.0	21.0
Transformers	46.0	25.0	0.5

Note: Import dependence is determined by the ratio of the number of units of newly built domestic equipment to the number of units of imported equipment.
Source: Takeuchi (1972).

of 1939, General Motors and Ford ceased re-assembly of automobiles in Japan. In 1939, 165,000 automobiles were produced domestically, representing 65 percent of total domestic demand. Then, in 1941, because of the war between the United States and Japan, all imports were halted.

The localization policy was implemented so that Japan could take the best advantage of DFI, that is, the transfer of new technology to this newly industrializing country.

Eight

Trade and Industrial Policies
During the High-Growth Period

This chapter analyzes Japan's trade policy during the so-called high-growth period of the Japanese economy from the end of postwar reconstruction to the first oil crisis (1955–73). The objective is to identify the characteristics that distinguish Japan's trade policy during the high-growth period from previous periods. The high growth that characterized the period 1955–73 is attributed to the successful policy of nurturing growth industries. There is a vital connection between this policy and the growth of trade. However, Japan's trade policy should not be viewed as a consistent policy that was adopted methodically over the high-growth years, but rather as one that gradually evolved from an initially protective policy to one of trade and capital liberalization.

Japan was able to reap benefits from the postwar liberalization and the gradual economic integration of the Western developed nations. As a late entrant into an international system characterized by division of labor, Japan had to agree to work toward liberalization as a precondition for entry into the system. After the high-growth period, Japan's continuing development and export expansion led to trade friction with Japan's developed trade partners, which provided further incentive to hasten the adoption of liberalization measures.

Japanese government policy characteristically allowed industries a period of adjustment before exposing them to international competition, thus delaying the advent of liberalization. Once trade and capital liberalization began, the government's ability to regulate the activity of private firms weakened. Ultimately, this led to a transformation of Japan's industrial and trade policies during this period. As a result of trade friction, even the export policy in the high-growth period gradually weakened.

PARTICIPATION IN
WORLDWIDE ECONOMIC INTEGRATION

For Japan, the recovery of the international trade system in the post–Second World War period meant a second opening. As was the case a century before, worldwide economic integration was in progress. According to Haberler (1964), it was, broadly speaking, a period of economic integration involving phased trade liberalization, as well as the easing of controls on international investment. Table 8.1 summarizes Japan's participation in international trade relative to the progress of worldwide economic integration.

Although the Havana Convention did not achieve its objective of establishing the International Trade Organization (ITO), the 1947 negotiations in Geneva opened the doors for the establishment of the General Agreement on Tariffs and Trade (GATT) Secretariat, which performed the functions of the proposed ITO Secretariat. The beginning of the postwar period was characterized by continuous negotiations on tariff reductions for specific commodities and by the easing of trade and foreign-exchange control measures that had been adopted in the 1930s.

At the same time, in Europe the European Atomic Energy Community (EURATOM) and the European Coal and Steel Community (ECSC), the predecessors of the European Economic Community (EEC) of the same six member countries, began their activities; the remaining seven countries, encouraged by the EEC, banded together to form the European Free Trade Association (EFTA). In 1961, for the first time, the major Western European nations adopted the position of the IMF's Article 8 countries, so that foreign exchange controls could no longer be used for balance-of-payments reasons, and convertibility of the major currencies was revived. The EEC countries dismantled their tariff barriers against member countries during the 1960s, thus promoting the economic integration of Western Europe. At the same time, they established common tariff barriers vis-à-vis nonmember countries and also adopted a common agricultural policy. In 1973, the United Kingdom joined the EEC, furthering the trend toward European economic integration.

In response to the trend toward economic integration in Western Europe, U.S. President Kennedy, desiring to promote the economic integration of the free world's economies, initiated the package of tariff-slashing negotiations known as the Kennedy Round. Moreover, the Organisation of European Economic Co-operation (OEEC), which had been established to funnel U.S. aid to Western Europe, was reorganized into the present-day Organisation for Economic Co-operation and Development (OECD) to coordinate economic policy among developed countries.

As a result of a number of negotiations, Japan was allowed to join GATT in 1955 and was able to share equally the existing GATT concessions, including the tariff concessions, of other member countries under the most favored nation (MFN) clause, particularly of the United States, that had been agreed to in previous negotiations. However, Japan was initially allowed to temporarily postpone trade and foreign exchange liberalization.[1] The two GATT principles regarding tariffs are (1) reciprocal reduction of tariffs among member countries, and (2) nondiscriminatory treatment of member-country tariff reductions (MFN clause). That is, in the case of general tariff negotiations, bilateral negotiations on a number of commodities must occur simultaneously among the member countries, and each country's tariffs that were agreed upon during such negotiations must be applicable to all member countries, including its new member Japan. The MFN clause allowed Japan to take advantage of three general negotiations prior to its entry into the GATT (1947, 1949, and 1950–51) as well as of the fourth and fifth general negotiations of 1956 and 1960–61 in which it did not actively participate. Although discriminatory treatment of Japan by a number of European countries, such as France and Belgium, continued with the suspension of MFN treatment under GATT's Article 24, it cannot be denied that Japan's trade expansion resulted partly from a "free ride" in progressive tariff reductions, especially those undertaken by the United States. Japan finally joined the OECD in 1964 but was able to completely postpone capital liberalization until 1967.

Table 8.2 shows the growth of industrial production and trade for developed and developing countries during the high-growth period. The data, which includes part of the postwar recovery growth period, shows that growth of industrial production for developed countries averaged between 4 and 7 percent due to the high growth of the major developed countries, the United States and the countries in Western Europe. Moreover, growth of the EEC member countries—the core of Western Europe—during the first two periods was also high (7.6 and 6.7%, respectively). A comparison of the growth performance of the two periods 1953–60 and 1960–70 with that of the 1970s in Table 8.2 shows a drastic change in the international economic environment. Growth of trade in industrial goods largely exceeded that of industrial production in the 1960s, reflecting a steady trend of international trade liberalization in industrial goods trade. Thus when Japan's industrial production rose annually by 14.5 percent in the 1950s and by 13.1 percent in the 1960s, growth in industrial exports was even higher, at 15.9 percent and 15.8 percent for the 1950s and 1960s, respectively.

FOREIGN EXCHANGE MANAGEMENT AND INDUSTRIAL POLICY

What was the role of government in the Japanese economy during the high-growth period? Scholars are divided in their opinions (see Patrick and

Table 8.1
Japan's Participation in Worldwide Economic Integration after the Second World War

Month/year	World	Month/year	Japan
Oct. 1947	IMF and GATT established		
July 1948	OEEC established		
		Dec. 1949	Basic exchange rate set (360 yen to the U.S. dollar)
July 1952	ECSC established	Apr. 1952	Peace treaty effected
		Apr. 1954	General revision of tariffs
		Sept. 1955	Joined GATT
Mar. 1957	Rome treaty concluded		
Jan. 1958	EEC and EURATOM established		
Mar. 1960	EFTA established	June 1960	Master Plan for trade and foreign exchange liberalization announced
Jan. 1961	Intra-EEC tariffs on industrial goods reduced by 10 percent	Feb. 1961	Convertibility of major European currencies revived
Sept. 1961	OEEC reorganized as OECD	Apr. 1962	"Negative list" formula for import control implemented
July 1962	Common agricultrual policy begun for EEC		

Month/year	World	Month/year	Japan
Oct. 1962	U.S. Trade Expansion Act effected	Feb. 1963	Reclassified under GATT Article 11
		Apr. 1964	Joined OECD; reclassified under IMF Article 8
May 1967	Kennedy Round tariff negotiations concluded	July 1967	First liberalization of DFI in Japan
		Apr. 1968–Apr. 1973	Kennedy Round tariff reduction implemented
July 1968	Intra-EC tariffs abolished and common extra-EC tariffs effected	Aug. 1971	Generalized Scheme of Preferences (GSP) implemented
		Nov. 1972	Unilateral tariff reduction of 20 percent
Jan. 1973	EC enlarged (U.K. and three other countries join)		

Source: MITI (1982).

Rosovsky 1976; Shinohara 1982; Komiya et al., eds. 1988). Few in Japan claim that the government played the role of prime mover, with private firms merely following orders in a "Japan, Inc." type of relationship (Patrick and Rosovsky 1976: chap. 1). In Japan, governmental guidance did not resemble that in some developing or socialist countries. Rather, the government–business relationship found in Japan has been unique—one that is unknown in the United

Table 8.2
World Industrial Production and Trade in Industrial Products:
Market Economy Countries

Year	Industrial production (growth rate, %)		Industrial product exports[a] (growth rate, %)	
	Developed countries	Developing countries	Developed countries	Developing countries
1948–53	6.6	4.0	—	—
1953–60	4.2	7.2	6.8[b]	3.5[b]
1960–70	5.8	6.2	9.3	9.8
1970–79			6.0[c]	11.3[c]
1970–80	3.0[c]	5.9[c]		

Year	Industrial product exports[a] (US$ billions)		Industrial product exports[a] (growth rate, %)	
	To developed countries	To developing countries	To developed countries	To developing countries
From developed countries				
1960	37.7	16.4	} 11.5	5.8
1970	128.0	33.5	} 5.6	7.4
1979	572.3	191.8		
From developing countries				
1960	2.5	1.2	} 9.1	11.0
1970	8.9	3.6	} 10.0	13.5
1979	57.5	31.6		

Notes:
a. Industrial products include Standard International Trade Classification (SITC) 5–8.

b. Includes growth rate of all commodity exports. The growth rate of industrial products from developed and developing countries combined was 7.3 percent.

c. The growth rates for the columns under Industrial Production were available for the period 1970–1980, while those for Industrial Product Exports were available only for the period 1970–1979.

Sources: United Nations, *Monthly Bulletin of Statistics,* various issues.

States or Europe. The government has had a protective attitude toward private firms, which have basically cooperated with the government. Furthermore, there have been many opportunities for communication and information exchange between them, and many scholars agree that industrial policy has been adopted on the basis of consensus. Opinions diverge, however, as to the degree of government leadership and its effectiveness. Even during the high-growth period, there was no single industrial policy. The changes that took place at that time must therefore be examined carefully.

Governmental guidance was relatively strong during the postwar reconstruction period under the priority production policy (1947-50). In order to revive the coal, iron and steel, and electric power industries, the government assumed authority and heavily subsidized these industries. But the policy generated huge fiscal burdens and inefficiency in assuring the supply of goods (see the discussion on steel in Chapter 5). During the industrial rationalization period (1950-61), greater stress was placed on achieving industrial efficiency and strengthening international competitiveness. The government adopted a promotion policy for growth industries such as iron and steel, machinery (machine tools and other types of machinery), electronics, and petrochemicals. This approach was a model for the one adopted by the Industrial Structure Council (1961-) in the 1960s. These industries pulled the economy onto the path of high growth, and the success of this industrial policy, which the OECD labeled a "picking-the-winners" policy, has attracted attention both in Japan and abroad (see Chapter 9).

In selecting industries to promote, two criteria were employed: the industries had to have high income elasticity and show high productivity increases. These industries included the priority growth sectors, which were promoted by a concentration of public and private resources that induced investment by private firms expecting high growth under the Income Doubling Plan of 1961-70. However, the policy was broadened into a promotion policy for industry in general and included industries such as nonferrous metals and petrochemicals in which comparative advantage was difficult to achieve because of Japan's lack of resources.

The government's intervention in the market can be broadly categorized by the priority policies adopted for specific industries and the enactment of various types of regulatory measures. Priority policies include the many incentives granted to industries, such as direct lending by government financial institutions (including the Bank of Japan's low-interest financing of equipment investment and working capital through private banks), special tax measures such as tax deductions and grace periods for repayment of loans, and direct subsidies.[2] But the peculiarity of Japanese industrial policy was that, despite the abundance of incentives, many of these measures had little quantitative importance. Although the incentives were initially attractive, they lost much of their appeal as firms began to improve their capital financing ability.

Some of the government's regulatory measures had no direct legal basis, as in the case of administrative guidance measures. These measures tried to limit competition from outside an established industry by regulating the entry of firms into specific industries. They were intended to end "excessive competition" in industries as well as to maintain a stable market and promote structural reorganization.[3] But administrative guidance, which relies largely on persuasion, has its limitations and entails costs. Altering market behavior through administrative guidance was not very effective. Regulations having a direct legal basis proved more effective, particularly the foreign exchange and trade controls. These controls were adopted at the beginning of the 1950s to maintain balance-of-payments equilibrium. However, because the IMF allowed these controls to continue throughout the 1950s, they also served as an instrument of industrial protection (that is, infant industry protection during the period of industry rationalization) and gave the government leverage to control private firms. Thus foreign exchange management became an important foundation of industrial policy in Japan.

Foreign exchange was managed in the following manner. First, under the Foreign Trade and Foreign Exchange Control Law,[4] foreign exchange owned by the private sector was held at foreign exchange banks under the control of the Ministry of Finance.[5] Licenses were needed to buy the foreign currency that was used to pay for commodity imports. These licenses were classified into three categories, depending on the type of imports involved. The first was the Import Quota category (IQ), in which the value of the import quota was predetermined according to the type of goods. Under this category, foreign exchange quotas were allocated among users. The second category was the Automatic Import Quota (AIQ), in which the import quota was variable and the foreign exchange allocation was approved so long as there was no interference with foreign trade and domestic economic development. The third category was the Automatic Approval (AA), in which requested values of foreign exchange were approved automatically and on a nondiscriminatory basis.[6]

In the 1950s, many commodities fell under the IQ classification. Imports of coal, scrap iron, raw cotton, and other raw materials that were indispensable to the operation of the iron and steel industry, the cotton-spinning industry, and other industries were put on the IQ list. The limited amount of imported raw materials were then rationed among firms according to such criteria as equipment capacity or operation levels. For instance, during the recessionary period of 1957 when there was a glut in the steel market, the Iron and Steel Bureau of MITI set up a rationing cartel for imported scrap iron. The cartel designated the production volume for specific commodities, and each firm had to reduce production by between 10 and 40 percent in order to prevent further price drops. Similarly, in 1957 MITI's textile bureau controlled the volume of cotton-spinning production by rationing raw cotton to only 8.38 million of the 92 million spindles registered. Although rationing of raw material imports was the strongest and most effective regulatory measure used to back administrative guidance under MITI's industrial policy, import allocations on raw materials were discontinued in 1961, and the manner of enforcing industrial policy changed.[7]

PHASED IMPLEMENTATION OF LIBERALIZATION

By 1960, Japan was ready for trade and foreign exchange liberalization. In June, the government, through its Economic Planning Agency, announced its "Master Plan for Trade and Foreign Exchange Liberalization (*Boeki Kawase Jiyuka Keikaku Taiko*)."[8] The motives behind this liberalization movement included international pressure stemming from the strong trend in international economic liberalization, the improvement in Japan's balance-of-payments position in the previous few years, and increases in foreign exchange reserves—as well as the expectations of higher productivity resulting from the rationalization efforts of firms. However, out of prudent concern for industry protection, liberalization was implemented in stages.

According to the Master Plan, traded goods were divided into four categories:

(A) Goods to be liberalized at an early date;

(B) Goods to be liberalized in the near future (that is, within three years);

(C) Goods requiring a longer period of time before liberalization; and

(D) Goods for which a suitable time period for liberalization was difficult to determine.

The liberalization of imports such as raw cotton and wool (category A goods) was expected to contribute to cost reduction in industries utilizing them as inputs. Thus, goods such as textiles and iron and steel, whose domestic industries were already internationally competitive, and those goods not directly competing with domestically produced goods were put under category A or B. Toward the end of the 1950s, because of the strides made in domestic production, synthetic textiles were also put under category B. Included under category C were those goods for which technology development was under way or those goods belonging to the core sectors of the machinery industry where nurturing was necessary. These commodities included machine tool equipment or implements, automobiles, heavy electrical equipment, and chemical machinery parts. Category D included such agricultural commodities as wheat, rice and other starches, and dairy and edible meat products.

Table 8.3 shows the products whose trade was liberalized after 1960. The progress of liberalization under the Economic Planning Agency's Master Plan can be clearly seen in the trends revealed in the table. It is also important to note how the stages of development in domestic production are reflected in the timing of the liberalization of various commodities such as automo-

Table 8.3
Phased Implementation of Trade Liberalization

Year	Rate of trade liberal- ization[a] (%)	Number of restricted products[b,c]		Major products liberalized
		AIQ	IQ	
1960	44			Coffee beans, movie film
1961	70			Raw cotton, radio receivers, instant coffee, and watches
1962	88	254		Socks, sheet glass, fountain pens, crude petroleum
1963	92	192	155	Bananas, crude sugar
1964	93	162	123	Lead, zinc, electric generators
1965	93	161	122	Automobiles
1966	93	167	124	Cocoa powder, streptomycin
1968	93	164	121	Perfume, cream
1969	93	161	118	Brandy
1970	94	133	90	Wine, margalin working machinery, electric generators (more than 400 kWh), chassis fitted with engine, woolen fabrics
1971	95	87	40	Pork, candy, black tea
1972	95	86	33	Ham and bacon, refined sugar, heavy and light petroleum
1973			31	Electrical calculators, some marine products
1974			29	Malt, integrated circuits
1975			27	Electronic computers and parts
1977			27	Tobacco

Notes:
a. Percent share of AA category using 1959 import composition.

b. Numbers in terms of the four-digit Brussels Tariff Nomenclature (BTN).

c. By August 1988, the number of restricted products (both AIQ and IQ) was reduced to 22, which included 21 agricultural products and coal.

Source: Ministry of Finance, *Nihon Gaikoku Boeki Nempyo* (Foreign Trade Annual) (1978).

biles, integrated circuits, and electronic computers. For instance, the liberalization of automobiles took place in 1965 when the import/demand ratio was 2 percent and the export/production ratio was 16.8 percent. In 1971, when half of the intended capital liberalization measures had been achieved, these ratios were 0.8 percent and 38.4 percent, respectively, clearly demonstrating a carefully designed liberalization plan. The exception was the liberalization of the computer industry, which was achieved hastily and put into effect in 1975 when the import/demand ratio stood at 20 percent and the export/production ratio was still 4.5 percent.

The extent of liberalization can be measured by estimating the proportion of goods in the AA and AIQ categories to all goods, using the 1959 import value composition. In 1963 liberalization was about 92 percent complete. However, this estimate should be viewed with reservation because of a large change in import composition that occurred after 1959. In particular, the IQ category includes commodities under import control, although these were mostly agricultural and included only 27 products in 1983, that in fact belong in category D.[9]

Tariff Policy Reform

Tariff policy reform went hand in hand with trade liberalization (see the discussion on tariff and nontariff restrictions in Chapter 7). In place of the direct controls mandated by the discontinued quota system, the use of tariffs as a tool of industrial policy increased. Because existing tariffs were unsuitable for the level of development of the country's industries in 1961, tariff law reform was undertaken in June of that year (Ministry of Finance 1963). Tariff rates were thus altered to account for the competitiveness of specific industries, and the Brussels Tariff Nomenclature (BTN) classification used in the United States and Europe was adopted. As a result, tariff rates on agricultural commodities, petrochemicals, and some types of machinery were raised.[10] The tariff rates on both total imports and dutiable imports rose in 1965–67 (see Figure 7.1).

What type of tariff structure emerged as a result of the reform? Table 8.4 shows estimates of the nominal as well as effective protective rates on selected commodities in major industries based on the tariff rates prevailing on April 1, 1962 (Japan Tariff Association 1962). The nominal tariff rates are expressed as a percentage of the commodity unit price, whereas the effective protective rate is calculated in terms of the percentage of value added of labor and capital inputs in the production of the given commodity. This estimation proce-

Table 8.4
Tariff Structure at the Start of Trade Liberalization: April 1962

Sector[a]	Nominal Rate (%)	Effective Protective Rate (%)
Metals and products		
Iron ore, scrap iron[b]	0	—
Coal products	5.0	—
Crude petroleum	10.0	—
Pig iron	10.0	24.4
Steel ingots	12.5	47.0
Hot-rolled steel	15.0	35.1
Steel pipe	15.0	18.9
Nonferrous metal ore	0	
Nonferrous metal	10.0	25.2
Copper products	22.2	63.7
Aluminum	19.3	40.7
Machinery		
Metal-working	19.7	20.9
General parts	20.0	22.9
Optical	24.1	28.7
Watches and clocks	30.5	43.2
Heavy electrical	17.5	17.5
Automobiles	36.0	66.5
Textile products of natural fiber		
Wool, raw cotton	0	
Cotton yarn	5.0	9.9
Wool yarn	10.0	41.0
Cotton fabric	16.0	36.2
Woolen fabric	20.0	40.0
Knitwear	23.0	49.2
Apparel and accessories	27.8	48.8
Textile products of synthetic fiber		
Synthetic textile material	25.0	31.0
Synthetic fiber	25.0	33.8
Synthetic fabric	25.0	26.3
Knitwear	23.2	24.7
Apparel and accessories	27.8	51.5

Notes: Nominal rates as of 1 April 1962. Effective protective rates are calculated by the following formula using input-output coefficients of 1961:

$$T_j = (t_j - \sum_{i=1}^{m} a_{ij}t_j)/(1 - \sum_{i=1}^{n} a_{ij})$$

where T_j and t_j denote effective and nominal rates, respectively.

a. Commodities in each sector are ranked by amount of processing required.

b. Effective protective rates for raw materials were not estimated and are indicated by dashes.

Source: Calculated by author.

dure is used because it is more accurate in estimating the extent to which tariff protection raises the value added of inputs to production (Yamazawa 1969). The following findings can be ascertained from Table 8.4:

- The escalating structure of the nominal tariff rates (that is, rates are lowest at the raw material stage and rise with further processing) is clearly evident for the sectors directly related to raw materials, such as metals and natural fibers;

- The structure of effective rates is obscure. For instance, even if the nominal tariff rates are high, the effective protective rates decline when nominal tariffs on inputs are also high, thus raising the value added (compare, for example, cotton and synthetic fabrics). In commodity groups such as metals and natural fabrics, there is no significant rank correlation between nominal tariff rates and effective protective rates. This is also seen in Balassa's (1965) international comparison of developed countries' tariff structures.

- High effective protective rates are observed in the primary processing stages close to the raw material stage. For crude steel and cotton fabrics, for example, nominal tariff rates are not high but effective protective rates are. Because of the zero tariff or low tariff rates on imported industrial raw materials by developed industrialized countries, even low nominal tariff rates on processed primary goods yield high real protective rates.

- In the machinery and textile groups, luxury consumer goods carry high nominal tariff rates and thus high effective protective rates as well.

- For goods such as machine tools and heavy electrical equipment, synthetic fiber materials, and filaments, for which the liberalization Master Plan intended rates to be low for both nominal and effective protection, tariffs did not replace the quota system.

Figure 7.1 clearly shows that tariff rates were highest during the period 1960–65. Tariffs were later reduced during the Kennedy Round negotiations (1967–71), the implementation of the Generalized Scheme of Preferences (GSP) for developing countries (1971–), the two unilateral tariff reductions that were undertaken primarily to prevent further yen appreciation (1972–, 1976), and the implementation of the Tokyo Round agreements on tariff reductions (1980–87), under which Japan's tariffs on mining and industrial products declined to a level comparable to that of the European Community (EC).

Figure 8.1 compares the distribution of tariffs on mining and manufacturing products of Japan, the United States, and the EC. Of particular interest is the downward shift in the distribution after the Tokyo Round. The distribution of tariffs for Japan, the EC, and the United States is concentrated in the 5 to 10 percent range. However, changes in the distribution for the United

Figure 8.1
Changes in the Frequency of Tariffs on Mining and Manufacturing Products:
Comparison of Japan, the EC, and the United States

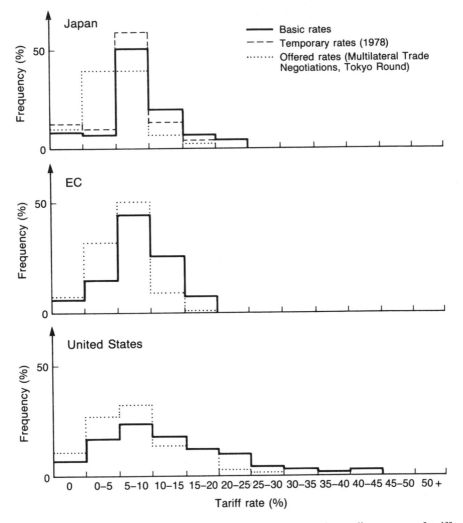

Note: Individual commodities with different tariff rates are grouped according to range of tariff rate within which it falls.

States contrasts with that for the EC. Prior to the Tokyo Round, the distribution of tariffs on mining and manufacturing products for the EC ranges between 0 and 20 percent and is particularly concentrated in the ranges between 5 and 15 percent. However, with the tariff reductions under the Tokyo Round, the distribution shifts downward to between 0 and 15 percent, concentrating especially in the ranges between 0 and 15 percent and between 0 and 10 percent. On the other hand, the distribution for the United States ranges between 0 and 45 percent; with the tariff reductions, the distribution shifts downward, spreading over the ranges between 0 and 30 percent. Japan's distribution is between those of the EC and the United States. Japan had two rates before the Tokyo Round: basic rates that appeared in the official tariff table, which were binding by GATT rules and could not be raised without negotiation, and temporary rates, which were rates that were lowered temporarily on many imported industrial products (the two unilateral tariff reductions). Although the Tokyo Round negotiations to reduce the basic tariff rates were completed, the tariff distribution actually imposed in 1978 was that of the temporary rates. Before the Tokyo Round, Japan's unilateral tariff reductions had caused a shift toward the EC type of distribution. After the Tokyo Round, distribution of tariffs for the EC and Japan became even more similar.

Liberalization of Direct Foreign Investment in Japan

Even after becoming a member of the OECD, Japan was allowed to postpone the date of complete capital liberalization. In July 1967, the first liberalization measure was adopted, and liberalization gradually proceeded until the fifth liberalization measure of May 1973. Liberalization was accomplished by shifting from the individual (case-by-case) investigation system that was set up under the foreign exchange laws to the automatic approval system. Thus, foreign capitalization of a new firm's equity acquisition could be approved up to 50 percent for category 1 industries or up to 100 percent for category 2 industries.[11] Just as liberalization gradually moved industry categories from the individual investigation to the liberalized system, they were also moved from category 1 to category 2 of liberalized industries.

The government was extremely careful in choosing the industries to be liberalized. During the first stage of liberalization, category 1 listed 33 industries, whereas category 2 included industries such as iron and steel, cement, weaving, and shipbuilding, in which domestic firms were competitive internationally. Thus there was hardly any possibility of foreign capital flows into the 17 industries included on the category 2 list. During the second liberalization stage that began in March 1969, 160 industries were included under category 1 and 44 industries under category 2. This increase in the second stage represented a fourfold increase in the total number of liberalized industries as compared to the number of liberalized industries in the first stage. During the third stage of liberalization in September 1970, there was another large increase in the number of liberalized industries, with 447 industries included under category 1 and 77 industries under category 2. The total value of shipments from the industries in both categories made up 75 percent of the manufacturing sector's total shipments.

By April 1971, the automobile industry was fully liberalized. In August 1971, under the fourth stage of liberalization, a shift to the "negative list system," in which only nonliberalized industries were announced, was undertaken. Under the fifth stage of liberalization of May 1973, with the exception of 22 industries (7 industries required individual investigation and 15 industries were from category 1), all industries were liberalized. However, foreign stock ownership in existing firms continues to be closely monitored, and regulations are stricter on takeover bids and stock held by foreigners.

The remaining regulations and the cautious liberalization process described above show the exclusive nature of Japan's domestic investment policy and its protection of domestic firms. Indeed, the cautiously planned postponement of trade and capital liberalization gave private firms the time needed to strengthen their international competitiveness and technological development. The success of this strategy is evident, because upon liberalization, Japanese firms were already competitive (Shinohara 1982, Pt. 1). However, it is partly a result of this success that Japan and its trading partners are now experiencing trade friction. For instance, if American and European firms had been able to enter Japan's domestic automobile and electrical machinery industries and had taken part in the export expansion to the United States and Europe along with Japanese firms, the trade problems of today might have taken a different course, and international industrial cooperation would probably have proceeded more smoothly.

EXPORT-PROMOTION POLICIES

In the 1950s, with the reopening of private firms to normal export trade, Japan was plagued by a scarcity of foreign exchange and its related problems. In particular, after the end of the export boom during the Korean War (1950–53) the number of exportable goods was limited. Only light industrial goods such as silk cloth and cotton fabrics were highly competitive internationally, whereas pre–Second World War exports such as iron and steel, textile machinery, and chemical fertilizers, which had been destined only for the East Asian markets such as Manchuria, Korea, and China, were no longer competitive. The dim prospects of the postwar export markets were worrisome. Given this background, policymakers became conscious of the need to nurture export industries and adopted a number of measures to promote exports (Table 8.5). These took the form of preferential export financing, export-promoting fiscal policy, and the creation of export-promoting institutions, each of which is discussed in the following sections.

Preferential Export Financing

The procedure for export financing is as follows: When exporters ship their merchandise, it is accompanied by a bill of lading against which a usance export bill can be issued, allowing the exporter to recover export funds. Even before lading, advance export financing can be obtained on the basis of the export contract; thus, the needed cash is available for output processing and

Table 8.5
Export-Promotion Policy

Preferential Export Financing		
A	Export advance-bill system	11/1949–6/1960
A'	Export trade-bill system	7/1960–6/1972
B	Foreign currency-secured loan system	2/1953–8/1961
B'	Foreign exchange loan system	9/1961–3/1972
C	Foreign exchange bill rediscounting system	12/1965–6/1972
D	Yen usance bill rediscounting system	5/1970–6/1972
E	Japan Export–Import Bank's long-term trade credit	1954–1968
Special Tax Measures		
F	Export-income exemption	1953–63
F'	Tax exemption on export-income increase	1957–61
G	Export-increase depreciation system	1964–71
H	Tax exemption on technology export income	1959–
I	Depreciation allowance on opening of overseas branches	1958–63
J	Overseas market development reserve fund	1964–72
K	Overseas investment loss reserve fund	1964–74
L	Special depreciation allowance for export-contributing firm	1968–70
Export-Promoting Institution		
M	Export insurance system	1950–
N	Japan Export Bank (Japan Export–Import Bank)	1951–
O	Japan Export Trade Organization (Japan External Trade Organization)	1954–
P	Supreme Export Council	1954–
Q	Acknowledgment of export contribution	1963–72

Source: MITI (1982).

freight charges. Although the major portion of the export financing is denominated in foreign currency, it could be converted into yen by having the promissory note discounted at foreign exchange banks.

Preferential export financing consisted of the Bank of Japan charging an official rediscount rate on export bills or collateral loans from foreign exchange banks that was lower than the official discount rate for other commercial bills. Foreign exchange banks then set their own rate on export bills at the official rediscount rate plus a commission fee. Thus, export bills enjoyed lower rates than other commerical bills.

The export advance-bill system was adopted in 1949 but was changed to the export trade-bill system in 1960 (see A and A', Table 8.5). However, in the case of undelivered letters of credit, the Bank of Japan used the discounted bills of the foreign exchange banks as guarantees and lent yen funds at a higher rate than the rediscounting rate. In the case of usance export bills after lading, short-term loans could be obtained from the foreign exchange banks under the acceptance system. The system of foreign currency-secured loans and funds (see B and B', Table 8.5) provided more profitable financing for exporters. The usance export bills purchased by foreign exchange banks from exporters were exchanged for yen-denominated promissory notes, which were then used as collateral to draw the appropriate value of yen loans from the Bank of Japan at low international rates of interest. Under this setup, foreign exchange banks became buyers of foreign currency-denominated bills and sellers in the forward exchange market, causing a trend toward lower quotations. To control this trend, the foreign exchange-bill transaction system (see C, Table 8.5) was adopted in the second half of the 1960s so that foreign currency-denominated bills could be bought.[12]

Column 2 in Table 8.6 shows the Bank of Japan's preferential rates. The rate for export advance-bills of the foreign exchange banks (that is, eligible for the Bank of Japan's rediscounting [column 5, Table 8.6]) changed in response to changes in the Bank of Japan rate and was kept higher than that for ordinary commercial bills (column 4, Table 8.6). The Bank of Japan's preferential export margin (column 1 minus column 2, Table 8.6) ranged from 1.4 percent to 2.1 percent. Characteristically, during periods of financial restraint (such as June 1957 and September 1961), export loan rates, in contrast with the increase in official lending rates, were either not changed or were actually lowered, so that the preferential margin increased. Thus with the overheating of the economy during the high-growth period and the balance-of-payments deficits, financial restraints were applied simultaneously with export promotion.

Although the lending rate for foreign exchange loans for postlading finance (column 3, Table 8.6) was low (2.56%) when the system first began, the lending rate rose in the second half of the 1960s in response to the rise in U.S.

interest rates. Nevertheless, preferential export financing was generally strengthened in the 1960s. The facilities for the foreign exchange funding system discussed previously were enlarged and export bill preferential margins were widened. The utilization of preferential export financing, denoted by the ratio of Bank of Japan export-related loans to the export-related loans of all banks, rose from about 30 percent in the early 1960s to about 50 percent in the period 1967–71.[13]

In the 1970s, however, the ballooning of current account surpluses, together with the policy adopted to prevent yen appreciation, forced a drastic reduction of the preferential export margins, and in August 1971, the margins were

Table 8.6
Preferential Export Financing: 1955–72

Month/year	Bank of Japan			Foreign Exchange Banks	
	Discount rate of commercial bills (1)	Discount rate of export advance bills (2)	Loans against foreign exchange assets[b] (3)	Discount rate of commercial bills (4)	Discount rate of export trade bills (5)
Aug. 1955	7.30	5.84	—	7.67	6.94
June 1957	8.40	5.84	—	8.40	6.57
Sept. 1958	7.30	5.48	—	7.30	6.21
Feb. (Mar.)[a] 1959	6.94	5.11	—	6.94	5.84
Dec. 1959	7.30	5.48	—	7.30	6.21
Aug. 1960	6.94	5.22	—	6.94	5.84
Jan. 1961	6.57	4.75	—	6.57	5.48
Sept. (Oct.)[a] 1961	7.30	4.38	2.56	7.30	5.11
Mar. 1963	6.21	4.02	2.56	6.21	4.75
Mar. 1964	6.57	4.02	3.29	6.57	4.75
June 1965	5.48	4.02	3.65	5.48	4.75
Sept. 1969	6.25	4.25	4.00	6.25	5.00
May 1970	6.25	5.25	5.00	6.25	6.00
Aug. 1971	5.25	5.25	5.25	5.50	6.00
Dec. 1971 (Jan. 1972)[a]	4.75	4.75	4.75	5.00	5.50
June 1972	4.25	4.25	—	4.50	5.00

Notes:
a. The change in the Bank of Japan's rate was followed by rate changes at foreign exchange banks in the month shown in parentheses.
b. This measure started in 1961 and ended in 1971.
Source: Bank of Japan, *Keizai Tokei Nempo* (Economic Statistics Annual), various issues.

cancelled altogether (see Table 8.6). The preferential export financing system was finally discontinued in June 1972.[14]

Whereas export financing of small and medium-sized firms came from small and medium-sized finance corporations, long-term loans for shipping and plant exports were extended by the Japan Export–Import Bank (Ex–Im Bank). The latter provided cooperative financing together with commercial banks, in which the Ex–Im Bank usually financed 70 percent of the loan and extended loans at a lower rate (4%) than the rate charged by commercial banks (8%).

Fiscal Policy for Export Promotion

In order to promote exports in the 1950s, a special tax measure, the export-income exemption (see F, Table 8.5), was adopted. The exemption allowed exporting firms to claim income tax exemptions equal to a fixed percentage of their export values (1–5%). It was strengthened in the late 1950s into the system of accelerated tax exemptions on export income (F', Table 8.5) and income for technology exports (H, Table 8.5) and subsidies for the opening of overseas branches (I, Table 8.5).

Due to the prohibition on export subsidies under GATT Article 16, this straightforward export subsidization system was discontinued in 1963. Indirect tax-exemption measures were, however, adopted to take its place. For example, the accelerated depreciation allowance for export income (G, Table 8.5) increased the accelerated depreciation rate of exporting firms, and the overseas market development reserve fund (J, Table 8.5) allowed a fixed proportion of sales to be set aside for losses. As a proportion of actual exports, the indirect export subsidies did not differ much from those of the tax deductions. However, existing measures were strengthened and new measures were adopted, such as the promotional measures for technology exports (for proprietary rights, copyright, consulting roles) and overseas investment (H and K, Table 8.5).

In 1966, premium rates under the accelerated depreciation allowance system were reduced and the reserve fund for overseas market development was increased. In 1968, the premium accelerated depreciation for firms contributing to the country's export growth was strengthened. However, as a result of the accelerating trend in exports, between 1970 and 1972 certain measures (G, J, and L, Table 8.5) were discontinued, although technology export and overseas investment-related measures were retained.

Table 8.7 presents the values of subsidies under the major fiscal policies for export promotion (value of presumed deductions). Since these incentives apply to all export commodities, the ratio of the total value of subsidies (line 5) to the value of total exports (line 6) can be calculated (line 7). For the period 1956–70, the ratio is about 1 percent for all industries. Since both lines 5 and 6 are for a five-year period, the ratio is the yearly average over the period. Similar estimates are given for the iron and steel industry, including the ratio of total subsidies to iron and steel exports. From 1950 to 1960, the ratios are similar to those of all industries but increase during the period 1966–70 for iron and steel. Since iron and steel were growth export commodities dur-

Table 8.7
Reduction of Tax Revenues under Export-Promotion Measures
(¥100 millions, %)

	1950–55	1956–60	1961–65	1966–70	1971–75
A. All Industries					
1. Export-income exemption, tax exemption on export-income increase	122	582	792	1,483	515
2. Overseas market development reserve fund	—	—	234	475	439
3. Technology export-income depreciation	—	—	18	198	362
4. Overseas investment loss reserve fund	—	—	63	60	889
5. Total (1–4)	122	582	1,107	2,216	2,205
6. Total exports	30,143	56,686	106,823	246,570	590,81
7. Implicit subsidy rate (%) (5 ÷ 6)	0.40	1.03	1.04	0.90	0.37

	1953–55	1956–60	1961–65	1966–70
B. Iron and Steel Industry				
8. Export-income exemption	804	4,567	4,882	—
9. Tax exemption on export-income increase	—	—	—	58,025
10. Overseas market development reserve fund	—	—	—	11,329
11. Technology export-income depreciation	—	—	—	2,303
12. Total (8–11)	804	4,567	4,882	71,656
13. Steel exports	203,858	476,537	580,739	3,343,164
14. Implicit subsidy rate (%) (12 ÷ 13)	0.39	0.96	0.84	2.14

Sources:
A. Tsuruta (1982:60).
B. Tecson (1985).

ing this period, the strengthening of fiscal policy to promote exports was strongly reflected in the exports of these goods.

The tariff rebate system for export goods was a system of rebates on tariffs paid on imported materials used in export production. Adopted first in 1966, this new export tariff rebate system employed a fixed rate of tax rebates for 61 commodities in order to avoid the complexities of separate computations. Essentially, if the rebate was within the limits of the value of the tariff rate, it was neutral with respect to resource allocation so that even GATT allowed it. In the case of fixed average rates, however, the portion that exceeded the tariff rate was considered an export subsidy. Under the new system, the value of such tariff rebates was 16.6 million yen as opposed to the 1.56 billion yen for total commodity exports (or about 60% of total exports), so that the tariff rebate rate was 0.11 percent. The tariff rebate rates for specific commodity groups were 0.13 percent for textile goods (average of 12 commodities) and 0.09 percent for metals (average of 14 commodities). This is because value-added rates were higher in Japan and there were many imported raw materials with few or no tariffs. In consideration of GATT criticism, the average tariff rebate was reduced, leading to the low average rates (Nihon Kanzei Kyokai 1965).

Export-promoting Institutions

In the early 1950s, with the reopening of direct private export trade, a number of export-promoting institutions were established by the government. These institutions provided a useful infrastructure for the export growth of the late 1950s, although it is difficult to quantify their promotional effects. Many of them continue to function, although in the 1970s their objective shifted from simple export promotion to other important areas of overseas investment, resource development, and import promotion.

One such institution is the export insurance system, which was set up in 1950. Under the export insurance system (M, Table 8.5), the government made up part of the losses incurred by exporters resulting from unforeseen events overseas. The system's scope of responsibility was widened in 1956 to include foreign investment. Another institution, the Japan Export–Import Bank (N, Table 8.5) (originally the Japan Export Bank), was established to extend long-term financing to ship and plant exports. Gradually, resource development imports and the financing of foreign investments increased. A third institution, the Japan External Trade Organization (O, Table 8.5) (originally the Japan Export Trade Organization), concentrated its efforts on surveying overseas markets to promote exports. Today its activities include resource development, economic cooperation, import promotion, and the promotion of the internationalization of domestic firms.

The Supreme Export Council (P, Table 8.5), a semiprivate agency, was originally set up in the mid-1950s to set annual targets for exports and to discuss export-promotion policy. The export contribution of various firms was evaluated using a point system that estimated the level of the firms' export performance (Q, Table 8.5). Beginning in 1968, firms contributing to exports were allowed premium accelerated depreciation allowances and increases in foreign currency reserve funds, which were, in effect, export subsidies. In 1969, however, the Supreme Export Council was reformed into a trade council; the Council's activities were discontinued, and by 1972, all of the measures that had been in effect were eliminated. In 1982, the Supreme Export Council was revived but this time its goal was to concentrate on generating policies for import expansion.

A number of scholars have stressed the resource misallocation effects of the government's export-promotion measures. Indeed, the menu of incentives was abundant and was retained until the early 1970s, despite changes in form, because of pressure from special interest groups. However, to what extent these promotion measures affected Japan's export expansion is another question. Estimates of the impacts of the subsidies involved in the preferential export financing and fiscal measures per unit value of exports need to be analyzed.

In the case of preferential export financing, the rate of reduction in interest payments per unit value of exports can be estimated. Assuming that export bills are normally three-month bills, the interest rate paid is one-fourth of the annual rate, and the rate of reduction in interest payments is one-fourth of the preferential margin. In the case of advance export financing, it is at most 0.5 percent; for postlading financing, 1.2 percent, or a total of less than 2.0 percent. Although the Japan Export–Import Bank's financing was long term, with a large preferential margin, it is disregarded here because this type of financing was limited to shipping and plant exports. Moreover, as shown earlier, the rate from special fiscal measures was at most 2 percent so that the combined financial and fiscal rate was about 4 percent. It is difficult, however, to measure the degree of the export-promotion effect of a subsidy rate of this magnitude.

One approach to measuring the export-promotion effect of a subsidy is to compare it with the export-promotion effect of other variable changes such as yen depreciation. In the second half of the 1960s, the exchange rate was 360 yen to the dollar (the yen was considered undervalued in many respects). Due to the yen's appreciation under the Smithsonian Agreement of December 1971, the value of the yen rose by 14.4 percent (that is, to 308 yen to the dollar), and, between March and October 1973 (before the first oil crisis), under the fluctuating exchange-rate system, its value increased by 26.4 percent (to 265 yen to the dollar). In any case, the rates of appreciation greatly exceeded the export subsidy rate estimate.

Another approach is to compare the export-promotion policy with those of contemporary developing countries. Many of today's developing countries are already employing preferential export financing, export-promoting fiscal measures, and a system of tariff rebates for export production. In South Korea, at the commercial bank level, the export bill preferential margin averaged 18.4 percent during the period 1966–70 and 8.5 percent during the period 1975–78. Assuming that these were three-month export bills as in Japan, the interest rate reduction in preferential financing was one-fourth of the preferential margin, or 4.6 percent for the period 1966–70 and 2.1 percent for the period 1975–78. Moreover, the value of domestic tax exemptions related to exports was on average 9.8 percent during the period 1966–70 and 9.2 percent during the period 1975–78.[15] The ratios of tariff rebates on exports to the value of exports were 12.6 percent and 8.8 percent for the respective time periods in South Korea. This is because value added was low and import tariff rates were high.

Compared with the policies adopted by South Korea, Japan's export-promotion measures were modest. The promotion effects were probably greater than is implied by actual export figures in the 1950s, when quantitative controls on financing were severe. However, after the 1960s the effect might not have been that great.

In the 1960s, when such export measures were being adopted, voluntary export restraint measures were applied on export commodities that encountered import restrictions and demands for export control in U.S. and Western European markets. This is discussed in detail in Chapter 9.

Nine

Trade Conflicts
and Structural Adjustment

This chapter analyzes the dramatic changes in the Japanese economy in the 1970s and 1980s. In these two decades, the world experienced serious fluctuations in prices and supplies of petroleum and other primary commodities. The major industrial countries have been affected by sudden constraints in raw materials and energy inputs, which they have tried to overcome by implementing new policies and adjusting their industrial structures. Some countries have fared better than others, but huge trade imbalances have occurred. Japan, with its high import dependence, was seriously affected by the fluctuations in commodity prices, but it made appropriate adjustments and recovered quickly from the setback in growth.

Along with the improvement in Japan's economic growth performance, the country also did well in export growth. Japan's share of world exports increased from 6.6 percent in 1970 to 9.8 percent in 1987, while that of the United States decreased from 14.9 percent to 10.6 percent.

Japan's persistent trade surplus has been the source of several conflicts with its major trading partners. Although Japan has been investing its current account surplus abroad, it needs to restructure its economy so that its external balance is not significantly out of line with its partners. The convention of adjusting policies at the border alone is not enough. Because Japan is now well recognized as a major economic power, Japan's strategy and approach to its domestic and external activities should be completely reoriented. The country has now entered the stage where it shares a leading role with the United States and Western Europe in research and development (R&D). Japanese firms are moving from the traditional goal of expanding shares in existing markets to exploring new markets.

Japan has begun to make adjustments and restructure its economy, and this trend will continue in the 1990s. The restructuring and adjustments of the Japanese economy in the next decade may be undertaken in the multilateral context of the Uruguay Round and Pacific cooperation.

GLOBAL ADJUSTMENT
AND DIVERGENT PERFORMANCE

In the 1970s and 1980s, there were large fluctuations in global supply and demand conditions for major inputs. In the late 1960s and early 1970s, prices of petroleum and other primary products increased dramatically. The sudden rise in commodity prices contributed to upward pressures on the price levels of many countries, and runaway inflation and the threat of unemployment were serious concerns in the latter half of the 1970s. In response to these conditions, deflationary policies were instituted by the industrialized countries in the early 1980s. By 1987, commodity prices had declined to pre-1980 levels. Figure 9.1 shows the cyclical changes in commodity prices and the volatile growth performance of the industrialized countries, although their aggregate, annual average figures show a much smoother pattern of change. The patterns of change are described in greater detail below.

Fluctuation and Policy Response

A quadrupling of petroleum prices between October 1973 and early 1974 ended the period of steady and high economic growth and stable prices that had continued in the world economy since the mid-1950s. Even before this, however, other commodity prices had begun to increase in the late 1960s, although less drastically, and wages were rising in most industrial countries throughout the 1960s. The rise in prices of many commodities and labor largely resulted from the excess demand for productive resources toward the end of the rapid-growth period, which led to accelerated inflation. International monetary disturbances in the late 1960s, which in 1971 eventually led President Nixon to suspend the official convertibility of the U.S. dollar, added to excess international liquidity and aggravated the inflationary trend.

The oil shock of 1973 not only caused rapid inflation, but it also contributed to large trade imbalances, heavy deflationary pressures, and negative growth in the major developed countries. To restore the level of output and employment, governments undertook active fiscal expansion. Although medium economic growth was restored by the latter part of the 1970s, inflation continued to be a problem and in fact was further accelerated by the second oil shock of 1979–80.

Governments responded to the second oil shock with deflationary measures. The U.S. Federal Reserve, for example, tightened the U.S. money sup-

Figure 9.1
Fluctuations in the Global Economy

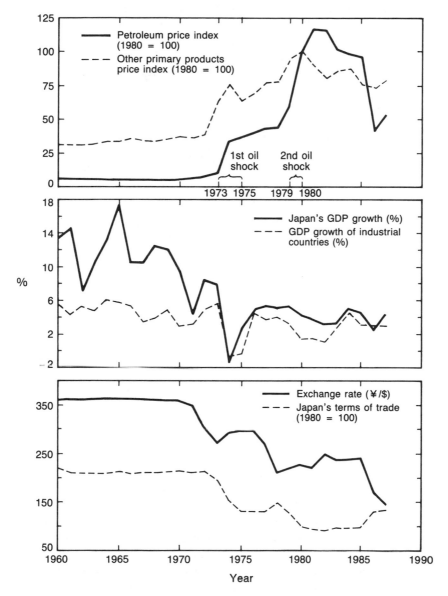

Source: IMF (1988).

ply, but this led to much higher interest rates than had been planned. The higher interest rates attracted substantial inflows of money to the United States, which caused the U.S. dollar to appreciate. Japan and the EC countries followed the United States in tightening their monetary policies, partly to curb their own inflation and partly to discourage the outflow of money and stop the depreciation of their currencies. But the overall tightening of money supply by the United States, Japan, and the EC countries resulted in very high global interest rates and the U.S. dollar remained overvalued.

Although all of the countries responded with deflationary measures, the fiscal responses to these conditions varied among the industrialized countries. Japan adopted an austere fiscal policy and succeeded in reducing its fiscal deficits. Moreover, Japanese production, faced with stagnant domestic demand, became even more oriented toward the export market, which resulted in a huge trade surplus. Despite the trade surplus, the undervaluation of the yen continued because of capital flows to the dollar market.

In contrast, the United States continued with fiscal expansion and accumulated deficits in both its current accounts and fiscal budgets. Among the EC countries, examples of both types of responses were found. West Germany's performance was similar to that of Japan, whereas that of the United Kingdom and France was closer to that of the United States.

The agreement in September 1985 by the Group of Five (Japan, the United States, the United Kingdom, West Germany, and France), however, changed this. High interest rates and the overvalued U.S. dollar were quickly adjusted. The downward adjustment of interest rates occurred first as inflation slowed and tight monetary policies were eased in the major industrialized countries. Although the fluctuations in the world economy have returned to their pre-oil shock levels, the large imbalances between the developed economies remain unresolved.

Disparity in Economic Performance

The economic growth and trade performance of the developed countries prior to 1973 stand in marked contrast to their performance after the first oil crisis. The average GDP growth rate of all developed countries was 4.8 percent in the period 1960–70, but fell to 2.3 percent over the period 1974–83. Similarly, average annual growth of total exports was 8.2 percent in the former period, but dropped to 6.3 percent in the latter period.

Table 9.1 compares the macroeconomic performances of five developed (Japan, the United States, the United Kingdom, West Germany, and France) and two Asian developing (South Korea and Thailand) countries over four five-year periods. The four five-year periods are the high-growth period (1966–70), the recovery from the first oil shock (1975–79), the period of dis-

Table 9.1
Growth and Trade Performance Variation During Global Adjustment

	Japan	United States	United Kingdom	West Germany	France	South Korea	Thailand
Growth rates of real GDP (period average, %)							
1966–70	11.0	3.0	2.5	1.7	6.4	12.7	8.6
1976–79	5.2	4.2	2.7	3.9	3.5	10.6	8.0
1980–84	3.9	1.9	0.7	3.6	1.5	5.9	5.5
1985–87	3.9	3.3	3.5	2.2	2.0	9.4	4.3
Balance of trade (annual, period average, US$ billions)							
1966–70	84	955	−2,692	3,811	−1,185	−901	−446
1976–79	4,160	−27,302	−9,753	14,792	−4,517	−2,312	−1,190
1980–84	11,742	−62,209	−5,558	14,664	−14,029	−3,039	−2,829
1985–87	70,044	−163,978	−16,657	47,829	−7,042	2,846	−1,247

Source: IMF (1988).

inflationary policies (1980–84), and the period of readjustment (1985–87). The last period is cut short because data are unavailable for later years. During the global adjustment following the first oil shock, economic growth of the five industrialized countries did not differ greatly, reflecting the stagnant economies of Japan and West Germany and the more dynamic economies of the others. But a significant difference can be found in the trade balances between the two groups.

South Korea and Thailand, which experienced high growth beginning in the 1960s, continued to experience rapid growth throughout this period (see Table 9.1). In general, the Asian NIEs experienced a growth rate of 8–10 percent, and the ASEAN countries 6–8 percent on average. In the early 1980s, however, the slowdown in the world economy seriously affected the Asian developing countries. While their exports to the developed countries' markets stagnated and their export earnings decreased drastically, their demand for imports grew as their development needs expanded. As a result, many of the Asian developing countries incurred large trade deficits. To avoid further accumulation of foreign debt, many countries were forced to cut back on their development programs. Both the Asian NIEs and ASEAN countries experienced setbacks in their growth between 1982 and 1985. However, since the end of 1986, these economies have been recovering and their trade balances have improved steadily.[1] South Korea's deficit turned to a surplus in 1986, and Thailand's deficit improved in 1987–88. Japan's recovery has also benefited from the continued rapid growth of its neighbors.

TRADE CONFLICTS AND COUNTERMEASURES

Sectoral and Overall Conflicts

In recent years Japan's better trade performance has caused conflicts with its trading partners, but trade conflict is not a new phenomenon. In the 1920s and 1930s, Japanese cotton and silk fabric exporters encountered prohibitive restrictions in India, Canada, and Australia. In the early 1950s, restrictions were imposed on selected goods, including canned tuna, sewing machines, pottery and cotton fabrics, by the United States and unbleached cotton fabrics by the United Kingdom. Trade conflicts spread to iron and steel in 1966, to televisions in 1968, and to synthetic fabrics in 1969. Complaints were made about Japan's cheap export prices and the rapid increases in their exports, and antidumping suits were filed. In the 1970s and early 1980s, complaints were also heard with regard to industrial machinery (1978), automobiles (1981), and VCRs (1981).

As Japan caught up with the industrialized countries in terms of industrialization and development, trade conflicts increased, especially as new exports were developed. Every export was shipped to the industrialized countries' markets to compete with domestic products. American and European producers demanded protection, and the conflict was often settled with voluntary restrictions placed on Japanese exports, monitoring of export prices, and more tightly controlled trade arrangements. Textiles are a prime example. From 1969 to 1971, the United States was in serious conflict with its trading partners over the unrestricted import of textiles into the United States. The conflict culminated in a voluntary export restraint (VER) arrangement and later became a focal point of negotiations between the United States and the Asian NIEs. These negotiations eventually resulted in a managed trade network under the 1974 Multi-Fibre Arrangement (Destler et al. 1979; Yamazawa 1988a). Many export commodities destined for the United States or Europe are still governed by VERs, which indicates continuation of the conflicts between Japanese exporters and American or European producers in particular sectors.

In the 1980s, however, a conflict emerged in the overall trade relationship between Japan and its major trading partners. The export strategy of Japanese firms, as well as the trade and industrial policy of the Japanese government, became targets of criticism at summit and OECD ministerial meetings. The Japanese government received complaints from the EC (in September 1981), the United Kingdom (in October 1981), and the United States (in December 1981) about their persistent trade deficits with Japan. Complaints were also heard about the complicated distribution system of the Japanese market and the commercial practices that prevent foreign access. The trading partners demanded market liberalization and import expansion.

Japan responded with a series of trade liberalization programs including unilateral tariff reductions, expansion of import quotas, improved import financing, and the dispatch of import missions. In July 1985, the Japanese government announced an Action Program—the seventh in a series of trade liberalization programs since 1972—to further reduce barriers and promote imports. The Action Program included the reduction or elimination of tariffs on over 1,800 items as of January 1986, and a package of liberalization and simplification measures in standards, certification, and government procurement procedures. This program goes beyond previous trade liberalization programs in its principles and scale and is expected to increase imports and reduce surpluses in the long run.

Factors Causing Trade Conflicts

The factors causing trade conflicts are complicated and interrelated. First, individual sectoral conflicts result mainly from the catching-up industrialization process of developing countries and the resulting adjustment difficulties faced by the importing industrialized countries. International competitiveness comes not only from cheap labor costs, but also from dynamic gains such as the new technology and economies of scale acquired in the catching-up process. The prolonged process involved in reallocating employment between sectors in mature economies adds to the difficulty of adjusting to changing comparative advantage. Trade conflicts have now spread to some high-tech industries where the importing countries wish to protect domestic production for security or other strategic reasons.

Second, large trade imbalances have been generated in the process of adjustment to the changing conditions and comparative advantage positions. This is most evident in the conflicts between Japan and the United States. Japan's trade surplus with the United States was around US$12–$13 billion in 1981–82, but increased rapidly to reach US$51.4 billion in 1986. The United States made stronger demands for further liberalization of the Japanese market and a reduction of the bilateral imbalance to a tolerable level. The increasing bilateral trade imbalance between Japan and the United States simply reflects the increasing imbalances of these two countries with the world, which, as Bergsten and Cline (1987) correctly analyzed, can be attributed to the macroeconomic policies of the two countries. Japan's trade surplus with the world expanded from around US$20 billion in 1981–82 to US$93 billion in 1986, whereas the U.S. trade deficit with the world expanded from US$28 billion in 1981 to US$148 billion in 1986.

The prolonged trade imbalances between the United States and Japan have, however, aggravated the sectoral conflicts between the two countries, and trade negotiations and VER agreements have continued to proliferate. The conflict over semiconductors was concluded in August 1986 with a new compromise agreement on American price surveillance of Japanese manufacturers. But, in March 1987, the U.S. government invoked Article 301 of the U.S. Trade Act because of an alleged violation of the antidumping provision by a Japanese producer, and prohibitive tariffs were imposed on the imports of related Japanese products.

Market-Oriented Sector-Specific (MOSS) talks were also held to discuss the liberalization of the Japanese market. At first, the talks dealt with four sectors—namely telecommunications, medicine and medical equipment, electronics, and forestry products. In subsequent discussions, the talks have been expanded to include principles such as equal access in the bidding process for construction projects, which American construction companies have sought in their efforts to bid on construction projects such as the Kansai International Airport project. The American demand for Japanese market liberalization has been most forthright with respect to agricultural products. The United States submitted Japan's residual import restrictions on 12 agricultural products to the GATT panel, which decided that in 10 of the 12 cases Japan had violated GATT rules. The U.S. Rice Millers Association also denounced Japan's policy of rice self-sufficiency.

These demands for Japan to liberalize its markets are well founded, and the Japanese government has begun to accommodate them as announced in the Action Program and the Maekawa Report. These changes are beneficial to the Japanese economy. Trade conflicts with the United States, together with the rapid appreciation of the yen, have directly prompted the restructuring of the Japanese economy.

Trade Conflicts with Asian Countries

Japan's trade conflicts are not confined to the United States and Western Europe. Consistent trade surpluses with the Asian NIEs and some ASEAN countries have raised major issues at bilateral governmental talks and the Japan-ASEAN Forum. Japan's trade surplus basically reflects the strong import demand for machinery, parts, and industrial materials needed by these countries in their development. It also reflects the different stages of development of Japan and these Asian countries. Thus the demands made of Japan focus on the expansion of imports to Japan, improved market access for major ASEAN exports such as boneless chicken, bananas, and plywood, and an improved Generalized Scheme of Preference (GSP). Since these Asian countries are aiming to catch up in their industrialization, Japan was also asked by the NIEs and ASEAN countries to increase imports of new manufactured products (Indonesia), invest in new industries (Thailand), and provide better access to high technology (South Korea and Taiwan).

The Action Program included some official measures to respond to these demands and requests. But like producers in the United States and Western Europe, Japan's domestic producers complain about increasing imports, especially as the exports of the Asian countries become more competitive in world markets. The increased competition between Japan and its Asian neighbors has been accelerated by the rapid appreciation of the yen, but this competition has also tended to promote Japan's economic restructuring.

JAPAN'S MACROECONOMIC POLICIES
AND PERFORMANCE

In the 1970s and early 1980s, macroeconomic policies focused on overcoming the two oil shocks, but lately they have been increasingly geared toward correcting external imbalances and mitigating trade conflicts. The macroeconomic policies in both periods have helped to provide a framework for the restructuring of the Japanese economy, with individual firms changing their strategies and behavior accordingly.

Table 9.2 displays the basic characteristics of Japan's macroeconomic performance during the 1970s and 1980s. The effects of the first and second oil shocks are distinctly revealed by the fluctuations in the growth rate of real GDP and in the current account balance. Negative growth was recorded in 1974, and positive growth, though very low by Japanese standards, was recorded in 1975, with current account deficits in both years. Between the two oil shocks, during 1976–78, the economy recovered. Medium growth was maintained and a current account surplus was accumulated. Growth rates declined again in 1979–80 (though not as much as in 1974–75), and the current account deficit was US$10 billion for both years. After 1981, growth reached a low of 3 percent, but the current account surplus attained in 1981 continued to expand. In 1984 and 1985, the economic growth rate increased with further increases in the current account. In 1986, although the growth rate dropped to 2.6 percent, the current account surplus ballooned to US$86 billion, which in 1986–87 led to a drastic change in macroeconomic policies.

The relationship between two growth rates in Table 9.2—the growth rate of national expenditure and the growth rate of GDP—invites further investigation. National expenditure is the sum of consumption, investment, and government expenditure. If the growth rate of national expenditure is multiplied by the ratio of national expenditure to GDP, it will give the contribu-

Table 9.2
Pattern of Japan's Economic Growth: 1974–87

	Growth rate of real GDP (%)	Growth rate of national expenditure (%)	Current account (US$ billions)
1974	− 1.4	− 0.5	− 4.7
1975	2.7	1.8	− 0.7
1976	4.8	4.0	3.7
1977	5.3	4.4	10.9
1978	5.2	6.0	16.5
1979	5.3	6.5	− 8.7
1980	4.3	0.8	− 10.8
1981	3.7	2.1	4.8
1982	3.1	2.8	6.9
1983	3.2	1.8	20.8
1984	5.1	3.7	35.0
1985	4.9	3.8	49.2
1986	2.4	3.8	85.8
1987	4.2	5.0	87.0

Source: Calculated from national account and balance-of-payments statistics in the 1980 constant price series (Bank of Japan, *Keizai Tokei Nempo* [Economics Statistics Annual], 1988).

tion of domestic demand to overall growth of real GDP.[2] For the period under study, this ratio is 0.98-1.01, which indicates that the growth of national expenditure closely approximates the entire contribution of domestic demand to overall growth. The difference between the two growth rates gives the contribution of external demand (exports minus imports of goods and services), which is associated with the change in the current account balance. If the current account increases, then the contribution of external demand is positive, and if it decreases, then the contribution of external demand is negative. Table 9.2 shows that the current account position improved and that its contribution to overall growth was positive from 1975 to 1978 and from 1980 to 1985, but negative for 1979 and 1986-87.[3] This macroeconomic performance directly resulted from changes in the macroeconomic policy mix, which is reviewed below.[4]

High-Growth Period

The period 1955-70 was characterized by a clear policy mix. The exchange rate was pegged at 360 yen to the U.S. dollar and was allowed to fluctuate within a 1.5 percent band. Capital did not move freely across the border. Fiscal policy had almost a neutral effect on the business cycle under the balanced budget principle. Monetary policy was therefore used to deal with both the balance of payments and the business cycle. Fortunately, the policy goals often synchronized with each other. Economic booms coincided with balance-of-payments deficits because of the increasing imports of raw materials for industrial production. The Bank of Japan tightened its money supply by mainly raising official rediscount rates combined with a tighter discount window for lending to firms. During the recession, export sales rose and an external payment surplus resulted, which led to the easing of the money supply. The balance of payments tended to constrain continued excessive growth, and under the IMF regime the Japanese government was only concerned with its own external and internal balances. Since the early 1970s, however, the macroeconomic policy mix has been quite different.

Smithsonian Agreement

In December 1971 the Smithsonian Agreement set the yen-dollar exchange rate at 308 to 1, and in March 1973 the yen was floated with other major currencies. Since then, changes in the value of the yen vis-à-vis other major currencies have played a major role in adjusting external imbalances, but the time lag in adjustment (the J-curve effect) has often been much longer than expected. Capital movement has become more sensitive to international differences in interest rates and has often caused erratic movements in exchange rates. This, in turn, has led central banks to maneuver their monetary policy to achieve internal balance.

A balanced budget could no longer be maintained in Japan because expenditures tended to increase as inflation increased and revenues decreased due to the depressed economy. The financing of the accumulating budget deficits required an increasing share of revenues, which, in turn, reduced available revenue for other expenditures. All macroeconomic policy measures became severely constrained.

First Oil Shock and Recovery

The effect of the first oil shock on Japan was more severe than on any other industrialized country. Following the quadrupling of petroleum prices in 1973-74, wholesale and consumer prices rose by 28 and 23 percent, respectively. To cool the inflationary pressure, the Bank of Japan tightened the money supply by raising its rediscount rate to 9 percent. Government expenditures became inflated and, combined with decreased tax revenues, resulted in huge fiscal deficits. Business activities were curtailed both by limited oil supplies and a tightened money supply. This slowed Japan's industrial activity by as much as 17 percent, and GDP growth became negative.

In the period 1973-75, Japan had a huge current account deficit, which together with the oil price hike, lowered Japan's terms of trade by 42 percent (see Figure 9.1). Stagnant domestic demand led to the promotion of exports to achieve a positive growth rate. The Bank of Japan managed to keep the exchange rate at between 284.90 and 307.00 yen to the dollar during 1975-76 as compared to about 253.00 yen to the dollar in 1973-74. In 1976, growth recovered to around 5 percent and the current account showed a surplus; thus, monetary policy was gradually relaxed. Japan was criticized, however, for undervaluing the yen. From early 1977, the Bank of Japan allowed the yen to continue to float on the market, and by November 1978 the yen was trading at 175.50 to the dollar. Japan was also requested at the London Economic Summit in May 1977 to adopt an expansionary policy to stimulate domestic demand and increase imports, so as to play a "locomotive" role, together with the United States and West Germany, in leading the world's recovery from the oil shock. The Bank of Japan's rediscount rate was lowered to 3.5 percent, and the fiscal deficit was continued.

Second Oil Shock and Disinflationary Response

The macroeconomic policy mix that was geared to international harmony was terminated by the second oil shock, which occurred as incremental price increases in 1979-80. All countries became concerned about the state of their own economies. The United States led the disinflationary response to the second oil shock with high interest rates. This invited capital inflows, which resulted in an overvalued dollar. The yen-dollar exchange rate rose to as high as 263.65 to 1 in February 1985. The Bank of Japan's rediscount rate was raised to 9 percent in March 1980, and an austere fiscal policy ("zero ceiling" on all government expenditures) was introduced in Japan to reduce the public debt from 4.5 percent of GNP in 1982 to 2.1 percent in 1985.

Although Japan was able to adjust more readily to the second oil shock and the setback in economic growth in Japan was much less than in other industrialized countries, growth slowed to around 3 percent. The disinflationary policy mix was continued and production was increasingly oriented toward exports. This was helped by the fiscal expansion and increase in imports of the United States, although the trade conflict between the United States and Japan widened.

Redirection of the Macroeconomic Policy Mix

The agreement of the Group of Five in September 1985 was aimed at correcting the overvalued dollar and resolving trade imbalances. Japan was unhappy with the undervalued yen and welcomed its appreciation to 190–200 yen to the dollar, although no target rate was agreed upon at the summit. The yen's appreciation was initiated by the joint intervention of the Bank of Japan and the U.S. Federal Reserve but its value increased beyond expectations in market trading. In March 1986, when the yen fell below 180 yen to the dollar, the Bank of Japan intervened to halt further appreciation of the yen by buying dollars and selling yen. However, this effort failed to stop the yen's further appreciation.

After 1986, the yen-dollar rate fell repeatedly and rapidly, with short periods of limited stability, until the middle of 1988 when it reached the 120-yen level. Throughout this period, monetary policy remained relaxed. The Bank of Japan's rediscount rate was reduced from 4.5 percent in January 1986 to a historical low of 2.5 percent in February 1987. The rediscount rate was maintained at this low level in case the narrowing interest rate difference between the United States and Japan should invite Japanese capital back from the United States.

The switch to an expansionary fiscal policy was delayed by concerns over fiscal deficits. In September 1986, the Japanese government implemented a public investment program of 3 trillion yen in order to boost domestic demand and achieve a 4 percent growth rate. The growth rate of real GDP, however, turned out to be only 2.6 percent in 1986 and as low as zero in April-June 1987, although it increased after that. In May 1987, before the Venice Economic Summit, the Japanese government pumped an additional 6 trillion yen (about US$40 billion) into the economy in order to boost domestic demand. Private housing investment, private consumption, and company capacity investment were stimulated, and as a result GDP grew at 4.2 percent in 1987 despite the negative contribution of net exports.

The correction of Japan's current account imbalance was delayed because of the J-curve effect. Although the volume of Japanese exports decreased after the middle of 1986, the trade surplus did not decrease in dollar terms until April 1987. The value of imports did not increase because of the decline in oil prices. As a result, the Japanese current account declined continuously after May 1987, and only a small increase was recorded for the current account surplus for 1987 in comparison with the previous year.

Although a huge trade imbalance still remained, the restructuring of the Japanese economy proceeded in the context of the following macro policy mix changes. First, slower growth itself forced firms and industries to undergo structural adjustments. Second, the rapid appreciation of the yen and the improved terms of trade in 1973 before the first oil shock, in 1978, and after 1985 severely affected export-oriented and import-competing industries and drastically altered their comparative advantage. Third, the trade imbalances, trade conflicts, and resulting series of market liberalization measures have encouraged imports and increased domestic competition. Fourth, lively domestic demand encouraged more firms to produce for the domestic market. Fifth, the government's policies were increasingly geared toward international harmony and promotion of the restructuring of the economy.

THE RESTRUCTURING OF INDUSTRIES AND FIRMS

Table 9.3 summarizes the MITI report on structural changes (MITI 1988a). Figures for the period 1975–84 are based on past performance, while those for the period 1990–95 are based on an analysis of current trends. Although the industry classification does not reveal the current trends precisely, Table 9.3 provides a general picture of the changes taking place.

From "Heavy and Big" to "Light and Small"

Table 9.3 shows that the shares of primary, consumer, and basic materials industries declined steadily from 1975 to 1984, and the decline is expected to continue until 1995. Construction and other services sectors, which also declined until 1984, are expected to either remain steady or increase their shares. Machinery production increased rapidly during the period 1975–84 and will continue to increase at a decelerated rate. The increase in services will continue at a faster rate.

MITI's industrial production index presents a more detailed picture of trends by individual sectors (MITI 1988b). Within the basic materials sector, metals and chemical fertilizers recorded severe declines. Aluminum production declined from 1,091 tonnes in 1980 to 41 tonnes in 1987. Crude steel production decreased by 12 percent, urea production by 59 percent, and ammonia production by 29 percent during the same period. Ethylene, representing petrochemicals, decreased by 14 percent from 1980 to 1982, but recovered and surpassed its 1980 level by more than 10 percent. Color film increased by 154 percent.

Within the machinery sector there have also been mixed performances. Shipbuilding declined by 71 percent and steel structures by 16 percent during the

Table 9.3

Changes in the Industrial Structure

(% composition of output at current prices)

	1975	1980	1984	1990	1995
Primary (agriculture, forestry, and fishery)	3.9	3.0	2.7	2.1	1.7
Consumer (food processing, textiles and clothing, paper, and miscellaneous)	14.9	13.7	13.0	10.9	10.0
Basic materials (metals, metal products, chemicals, coal and petroleum products, and ceramics)	16.0	16.7	14.3	11.6	10.6
Machinery (industrial, electrical, transportation, and precision)	12.3	13.7	16.6	16.6	17.0
Construction (construction and mining)	10.7	10.6	8.6	9.6	9.4
Services households and firms (advertising, information, and leasing) and public services (education, medical, and governmental)	14.1	15.1	16.9	21.3	23.7
Other services (utilities, transportation, commerce, and finance)	28.1	27.2	27.9	27.9	27.6

Note: Figures for 1990 and 1995 are forecasts based on an analysis of the trend of changes described in the text.

Source: MITI (1988a).

period between 1980 and 1987, whereas automobile production expanded by 46 percent. Staggering increases have occurred from 1980 to 1987 for such items as watches (133%), computers for general use (153%), industrial circuitry (267%), VCRs (525%), and industrial robots (681%). Within the consumer industries, foodstuff and textile production decreased, while new products increased as much as in other sectors.

The increasing share of services reflects the move toward "a services economy," but changes in its content should be examined carefully. The share of household expenditures as a percentage of total expenditures on services such as restaurants, barbers, education, and medical care increased from 28.3 percent in 1975 to 35.5 percent in 1986, which partly corresponds to the rising expenditures on commodities (consumer industries). It should be noted that the share of intermediary services, which include consulting, leasing, and information services that support business activities, increased rapidly as a percentage of total expenditure. Inputs of these support services tend to increase in all industries as the industries expand, but service input coefficients are twice as high in the machinery industries as compared to the consumer and basic materials industries. The increase in the service input coefficient in the machinery industries is expected to continue and accelerate. The fact that support services formerly provided within individual firms are now procured from outside companies by the firms partly explains the increase in the service input coefficients.

The structural changes mentioned above are often described as changes from "heavy, thick, long, and big" to "light, thin, short, and small." This implies a shift in production from Heavy and Big (H&B) industries such as basic materials to Light and Small (L&S) industries such as household and office equipment and services. It also implies a shift in consumer tastes at the higher income level toward more sophisticated and differentiated goods and shorter cycles of fashion changes.

Table 9.4 shows changes in the export and import structure. Although it only covers commodities, the classification corresponds to that of Table 9.3. The rapid decline of metals exports and the equally rapid increase of machinery exports during the period 1980–87, and especially 1985–87, should be noted. The four individual machinery items listed together increased from 9.0 to 32.1 percent during the period 1970–87, accounting for four-fifths of the increase of machinery's share.

In imports, raw materials decreased steadily over the whole period, while fuels increased until 1980 and then rapidly declined after 1985. The increase in imports of other manufactured goods, consisting of such standardized products as textiles and steel, was evident after 1980 and has been growing more rapidly since 1985. The combined share of chemicals, machinery, and other manufactured goods as a percentage of total imports—the manufactured imports ratio—increased at an accelerating rate in the 1980s to 44 percent. Both the increase in manufactured imports and the decrease in imports of raw materials and fuels correspond to the decrease in domestic production of the consumer and basic materials industries and are related to the shift from H&B to L&S industries.

Retrenchment of "Heavy and Big" Industries

H&B were the leading industries in the high-growth period during which they achieved economies of scale and cost reductions, thereby acquiring international competitiveness. However, the price increases of oil and raw materials decreased their competitive edge, while slower economic growth after the

Table 9.4
Changes in the Export and Import Structure
(% shares of total exports and imports)

	1970	1975	1980	1985	1987
Export structure					
Textiles	12.5	6.7	4.9	3.6	3.0
Chemicals	6.4	7.0	5.2	4.4	5.1
Metals	19.7	22.4	16.4	10.5	7.9
Machinery	46.3	53.8	62.8	71.8	74.6
Office equipment	1.7	1.4	1.8	4.4	6.3
Semiconductors	0.4	0.8	1.8	2.7	3.6
VCRs	—	—	1.5	3.8	2.6
Automobiles	6.9	11.1	17.9	19.6	19.6
Import structure					
Foodstuffs	13.6	15.2	10.5	12.0	15.0
Raw Materials	35.4	20.1	16.9	13.9	14.7
Fuels	20.7	44.3	49.8	43.1	26.2
Chemicals	5.3	3.6	4.4	6.2	7.9
Machinery	12.2	7.4	7.0	9.6	12.8
Office equipment	1.7	0.9	0.7	1.2	1.5
Manufactured goods	12.8	7.4	11.4	15.2	23.4
Iron and steel	1.5	0.3	0.6	1.1	1.7
Textiles	1.7	2.3	2.3	3.0	5.1
Manufacturing subtotal	30.3	18.4	22.8	31.0	44.1

Note: Manufacturing subtotal is the sum of chemicals, machinery, and manufactured goods.

oil shocks forced a low utilization rate of their existing capacities. Interest payments on the underutilized capacities added financial burdens to the H&B firms, so that many opted to reduce existing capacities.

Table 9.5 shows the reduction of iron- and steel-making capacities in the steel industry. Since 1970, five large steel mills have introduced integrated production, utilizing both blast furnaces and converters to produce steel, while smaller mills operate only converters or electric furnaces of a much smaller size. Prior to the first oil shock, Japanese steel mills had planned to increase their capacities, and some furnaces were, in fact, completed after 1973. But the low utilization rate of furnaces led to a reduction in iron and steel production capacities beginning in the late 1970s and intensifying in the 1980s. The reduction was most severe in iron production—the primary processing of ores and scrap iron. Since Japanese iron producers relied entirely on imported materials, their competitive edge was badly affected by the increased price of fuel. Electric steel mills nearly ceased iron production, while integrated steel mills eliminated 19 furnaces and reduced their capacity by 25 percent. On the other hand, in steel production, where Japanese mills have the advantage of producing high-tech finished steel and have a large domestic market, the number of furnaces decreased but the capacity of those remaining fell only slightly, as old, obsolete furnaces were abandoned in favor of new, efficient ones.

Table 9.5
Reduction of Iron and Steel Production Capacity

	1970	1975	1980	1985	1987
Iron making					
Blast furnaces					
No. of furnaces	62	69	65	54	50
Capacity ('000 tonnes/yr.)	76,545	120,308	136,245	123,672	103,064
Electric furnaces					
No. of furnaces	23	20	10	5	2
Capacity ('000 tonnes/yr.)	227	224	94	67	29
Steel making					
Converters					
No. of furnaces	83	98	94	85	85
Capacity ('000 tonnes/yr.)	91,480	125,319	129,967	123,976	124,080
Electric furnaces					
No. of furnaces	739	705	626	555	514
Capacity ('000 tonnes/yr.)	13,599	24,972	28,757	28,389	28,079

Source: MITI in Bank of Japan (1988), *Keizai Tokei Nempo* (Economic Statistics Annual 1988).

From November 1986 to March 1987, the five biggest integrated steel mills announced in succession their plans to further reduce capacity and personnel in order to adjust to the crude steel production target of 90 million tonnes per year. Seven blast furnaces were to be demolished and 52,000 employees out of a total 191,000 were to be laid off or moved elsewhere in 1988–89.

Another cost reduction measure adopted by Japanese steel mills was the more economic use of fuels in the various stages of operation. The energy input per tonne of crude iron ore was reduced steadily from 5,290,000 kcal in 1975 to 4,783,000 kcal in 1980, and to 4,258,000 kcal in 1985. The switch from costly oil to coal was also promoted. In blast furnaces especially, oil was almost totally replaced by blast and coking gases.

A sharp reduction of capacity and personnel was similarly carried out in the aluminum, shipbuilding, chemical fertilizer, and petrochemicals industries. As in iron production, competitiveness in these industries had deteriorated due to the increased costs of raw materials and fuels, and very low operation rates under stagnant demand.[5]

Exploring New Frontiers for L&S

The shift toward L&S is most apparent in the expansion of the machinery industry and in services. Free from the disadvantages of H&B (the large-scale use of energy and resources under increased energy prices and slower growth), L&S has vast technical possibilities in responding to the great variety of demand and changing consumer tastes for more sophisticated equipment. Instead of mass producing a small variety of goods, the L&S approach envisions small-lot production of a large variety of goods. Production must be achieved without increasing costs and with a shorter lead time. Fortunately, the Japanese have a lot of experience and expertise, an established machinery industry, and a large, high-income domestic market in which to test new products.

Not all machinery meets the L&S requirements. Only the electronics, automobile, and some industrial and precision machine industries were able to develop new frontiers and expand production rapidly. Once the technology is standardized for mass production, the Japanese competitive edge is easily eroded and lost to the neighboring NIEs. This has been the case for household electronics and compact automobiles. The domestic market, with its vast spending power and sophisticated tastes, has enabled Japanese manufacturers to explore and test new products. The macroeconomic policy mix shift in 1986 toward boosting domestic demand has accelerated this, with such products as digital audio tape-players (DATs) and furniture components designed for limited room space appearing in stores.

The development toward L&S requires a high precision control system and the effective use of market information. This has, in turn, resulted in an increase in demand for information and lease services, as mentioned above.[6] These services were originally provided by service departments within the pioneering firms. As the demand for the services by other organizations grew, the service departments became independent businesses specializing in these services. In conventional statistics, since these new businesses produce "services to firms," they are classified as such, thereby increasing the output of the services sector.

The restructuring toward L&S is also active in other industries such as textiles and clothing. Clothing production involves the assembly of textiles and accessories and is very sensitive to rapid market changes. In the clothing industry, manufacturers-cum-wholesalers do the planning and marketing. They purchase fabrics, design and cut the fabrics using computers, subcontract the sewing, and ship the finished clothes to markets. They create a basic design and fashion, produce more than a dozen varieties using different colors and sizes, and supply the market with those varieties most in demand. Major clothing producers have at their disposal highly automated sewing factories or subcontracted firms both in Japan and in neighboring countries. Clothing producers try to coordinate production and sales so as to minimize their inventory (the "just-in-time" system). Parent companies and their subsidiaries are linked by a nationwide network of highway and express delivery systems (*taku-kyu-bin*) that provide quick, reliable, and economical transportation of materials and finished goods in small lots. This departs from the old image of labor-intensive clothing production. In a textile industry policy report, the move toward L&S was emphasized as a major factor in the industry's revitalization.

The shift to L&S became evident in the 1980s. Although statistics with conventional classifications do not show this, evidence can be found in the increased use of semiconductor/industrial circuitry, a basic component of microelectronics. The capacity of semiconductors has improved almost a thousandfold. At the same time, prices of semiconductors have been halved over the past decade, enabling their use in industrial and transportation machinery as well as in electronics.

Further evidence can be found in the increased use of point of sales (POS) among the retailers of consumer products. In the POS system, cash registers read the Japanese Article Number (JAN) code attached to each article sold. Sales figures can then be compiled and trends analyzed automatically. The JAN code system was begun in 1978, and by 1982 the number of registered producers and retailers equipped with POS registers was 217 and 78, respectively. However, by 1987, these figures had risen dramatically to 26,438 and 11,711 and include all of the major producers and retailers.

Other areas of exploration (other than microelectronics) are new materials technology (such as fine ceramics and metals with special properties) and biotechnology (such as medicine and agriculture). Their industrial applications have not been readily identified in conventional statistics. The MITI report predicted, however, that by 1995 their potential market size would amount to US$460 and US$53 billion, respectively, compared to US$1.3 trillion for microelectronics (MITI 1988a).

Globalization of Firm Activities

During the macroeconomic changes of the 1980s, Japanese industries and firms had to abandon their conventional strategy of domestic production for export, and turned to exploring new frontiers, such as L&S production, at home. Another response to the macroeconomic changes of the 1980s was the relocation of production abroad, and selling the products in the host market, exporting to a third market, or importing the product back to Japan. As Figure 5.5 shows, many Japanese industries were at the export and mature stages as of 1980, but in the following years some export industries were forced to the mature stage, and some mature industries to the reverse import stage. CPC development was accelerated in these industries so that direct foreign investment (DFI) promoted the restructuring of the Japanese economy. Further analysis is needed to determine the interrelated decisions of both domestic and external redirection in individual industries and their representative firms, but the external redirection of Japanese firms can be classified by means of the aggregate surveys by the Ministry of Finance and MITI.

Japanese DFI, which had earlier been subject to restrictive rules to keep domestic savings in Japan, expanded after the investment rules and regulations were relaxed during the period 1967–70. The first boom in DFI occurred in 1973 (US$240 million), and increased again in the late 1970s after the economy recovered from the first oil shock. DFI exceeded US$10 billion in 1984, and according to Ministry of Finance statistics, it rose again to US$32 billion in 1986–87.

In which industries and to which countries was DFI directed? Throughout the 1960s, Japanese DFI was directed to the development and procurement of such resources as petroleum, lumber, and minerals. During the first investment boom in 1973, Japanese DFI was directed to the relocation of labor-intensive manufacturing to Southeast Asia because of increasing labor costs at home. In that year, the Asian share of total Japanese DFI was 28.6 percent; of total Japanese DFI in manufacturing, 32.5 percent; and of total Japanese DFI in textiles, 58.6 percent.

In the 1980s, however, both the destination and industry composition of Japanese DFI changed. In recent years, the direction of Japanese DFI has shifted toward the developed countries. The shares of Japanese DFI to the United States and Europe made up 40.8 percent and 15.5 percent of total

Japanese DFI, respectively (in terms of values of investment in fiscal year 1986, ending March 1987). For Latin America and Asia, respectively, the shares were 21.2 percent and 10.4 percent. In terms of industry composition, 17.1 percent of Japanese DFI was in manufacturing, of which 25.9 percent was in electric and electronic goods, 21.8 percent in automobiles, and only 1.7 percent in textiles. Greater shares were occupied by the nonmanufacturing sectors, such as finance and insurance (32.4% of total DFI), commerce (8.3%), and other services (7.0%).

The latest official statistics do not, however, cover 1987–88, which is when the second DFI boom occurred. Nevertheless, the shift in the direction of Japanese DFI has been reported in the newspapers. The Nikkei Data Base was employed to provide reports on the overseas projects of Japanese firms from the four newspapers of The Japan Economic Journal Group (including those specializing in reporting on industry and distribution), which were then used to analyze trends. Owing to the use of key words such as *overseas activity, international specialization* and *DFI*, the data include other forms of activities such as OEM (Original Equipment Manufacturing—that is, procuring finished products from other firms and selling them labeled with the brand names of the wholesaler or retailer) and production agreements, technical cooperation, and other business cooperation, which are excluded from official DFI statistics because there is no participating equity ownership.

Table 9.6, which is divided into two parts, summarizes the globalization of Japanese firm activities by the number of projects. Part A describes Japanese DFI by location and industry, and Part B by location and type of business activity as well as periods (three months for the first period and six months for those thereafter). The classification of the data into regions reveals that globalization has proceeded in all Japanese activities.

Part A in Table 9.6 shows that North America and Western Europe were the focal points of Japanese activities, with shares of 42.5 percent and 21.6, respectively. Pacific Asia's (Asian NIEs, ASEAN, and China) share was 33.6 percent. Japan's overseas activities were concentrated in North America, Western Europe, and Pacific Asia. Overseas activities are concentrated in manufacturing, in which electronics, automobiles, and chemicals have the largest shares; textiles has only 5 percent. Nonmanufacturing includes distribution/trading companies, finance, information, and other services. The regional composition of individual industries in manufacturing and nonmanufacturing are similar, implying that Japanese commercial activities are distributed in proportion to the size and prospects of the individual regions. However, the industry composition from one region to the next sometimes differs, reflecting the different emphasis given by Japanese firms to individual regions. In North America, a much greater share of overseas projects is in information and above average shares are in other services and automobile and chemicals production. In contrast, Western Europe has larger shares in textiles, electronics, and distribution. The shares of the Asian NIEs are nearly equal to those of Western Europe. All ASEAN members, China, and Oceania have larger shares in food processing.

In Part B of Table 9.6, Japanese firms are shown to be as active in other types of business as they are in DFI (i.e., local production), and their activities in other areas in later periods have tended to increase (except in technical cooperation). Whereas North America had the largest shares in all types of business, followed by Western Europe in earlier periods, the Asian NIEs and ASEAN have increased their shares significantly. Since 1986, the Asia-Pacific share exceeds North America and Western Europe in production cooperation and DFI. It should be noted that the share of Japanese DFI for the Asian NIEs is now stagnant and has been surpassed by that of ASEAN in early 1988. Both North America and Western Europe have maintained their shares in technical and other business cooperation.

DFI by Japanese firms in North America and Western Europe is directly affected by trade conflicts and restrictions, whereas Japanese DFI in Asia is affected by increasing costs in Japan due to the rapid appreciation of the yen. However, there seems to have emerged a clear change in the global strategies of Japanese firms. They will not limit themselves to operating domestically as they have traditionally, even if the conflicts are resolved and the yen depreciates.

Japanese manufacturers have moved simple, labor-intensive production and production of standardized items to other countries in Asia. The products are then exported directly to other countries or imported back to Japan. This relocation of manufacturing to neighboring Asian countries has been made possible by the specialization of products and production processes in electronics, precision instruments, and automobile parts. The manufacture of sophisticated items in Japan and parts requiring specialized machines and technology-intensive processes is now a priority, and production of such products has been growing. The division in labor between Japan and its developing Asian neighbors has resulted in rapidly increasing trade in parts and intermediate products at various production stages between Japan and the Asian NIEs and ASEAN countries. For example, cheap clothing is now imported from Asia while specialty fabrics manufactured by high-tech production processes are supplied by Japan. While this has contributed to a rapid net increase in manufactured imports to Japan, it also indicates an increasing import dependence of Asia-Pacific countries on Japan. This network of specialization has expanded not only as a result of Japanese firms, but also as a consequence of CPC development and the establishment of an industrial base in the Asia-Pacific region.

Overseas activity of Japanese firms in automobile assembly and electron-

Table 9.6
Globalization of Japanese Firm Activities (by number of projects)

A. INDUSTRY

| Industry | Region | | | | | | World total[a] |
---	North America	Europe	Asian NIEs	ASEAN	China	Oceania	---
Manufacturing							
Foodstuffs	136 (36.3)	62 (16.5)	64 (17.1)	43 (11.4)	45 (12.0)	13 (3.5)	375
Textiles	71 (21.6)	112 (34.0)	70 (21.3)	16 (4.9)	48 (14.6)	4 (1.2)	329
Chemicals	317 (47.5)	144 (21.6)	111 (16.6)	48 (7.2)	33 (4.9)	4 (0.6)	668
Electronics	513 (41.8)	285 (23.2)	260 (21.2)	91 (7.4)	42 (3.4)	2 (0.2)	1,228
Automobiles	337 (48.3)	115 (16.5)	116 (16.6)	45 (6.4)	20 (2.9)	16 (2.2)	698
Subtotal	2,084 (40.3)	1,153 (22.3)	958 (18.5)	371 (7.2)	334 (6.5)	66 (1.3)	5,165

Industry	Region						
	North America	Europe	Asian NIEs	ASEAN	China	Oceania	World total[a]
Nonmanufacturing							
Distribution and trading	105	93	79	20	26	8	348
	(30.2)	(26.7)	(22.7)	(5.7)	(7.5)	(2.3)	
Finance	110	67	57	6	21	8	277
	(39.7)	(24.2)	(20.5)	(2.1)	(7.5)	(2.8)	
Information	175	41	28	2	11	1	259
	(67.6)	(15.8)	(10.8)	(0.8)	(4.2)	(0.3)	
Other services	208	73	45	13	39	12	399
	(52.1)	(18.3)	(11.3)	(3.3)	(9.8)	(3.0)	
Subtotal	846	338	456	65	135	66	1,729
	(48.9)	(19.5)	(26.4)	(3.8)	(7.8)	(3.8)	
Total	2,930	1,491	1,414	436	469	132	6,894

Table 9.6. Continued.

B. TYPE OF ACTIVITY

Activity/period[b]	Region						World total[a]
	North America	Europe	Asian NIEs	ASEAN	China	Oceania	
Local production (DFI)							
9–12/1985	86	28	18	20	23	1	184
1–6/1986	158	64	75	18	23	4	369
7–12/1986	110	52	92	21	19	5	327
1–6/1987	154	68	133	59	18	9	464
7–12/1987	192	83	108	76	18	8	508
1–6/1988	179	63	80	90	20	6	462
Production agreements							
9–12/1985	21	15	4	0	7	0	50
1–6/1986	31	11	13	4	5	1	68
7–12/1986	39	18	36	6	13	1	116
1–6/1987	28	16	46	4	7	0	103
7–12/1987	54	35	38	7	13	2	152
1–6/1988	61	59	38	17	21	6	206

Activity/period[b]	Region						
	North America	Europe	Asian NIEs	ASEAN	China	Oceania	World total[a]
Technical cooperation							
9–12/1985	21	22	16	3	18	6	94
1–6/1986	50	33	26	14	38	3	180
7–12/1986	76	47	32	6	20	0	199
1–6/1987	61	20	50	10	23	5	181
7–12/1987	93	37	32	11	15	6	200
1–6/1988	82	51	25	6	17	11	185
Other business cooperation							
9–12/1985	89	58	19	7	10	5	193
1–6/1986	165	102	22	3	15	6	321
7–12/1986	185	95	34	3	16	10	357
1–6/1987	213	85	41	5	21	8	378
7–12/1987	187	126	53	7	27	10	415
1–6/1988	243	155	52	17	24	10	509

Notes:

a. Columns do not total due to the omission of rest of world.

b. For each activity, the first period covers three months; the remaining periods cover six months.

Source: Overseas Activities of Japanese Firms (OAJF) Project, Hitotsubashi University, Tokyo, compiled from Nikkei Data Base, September 1, 1985–June 30, 1988.

ics production began in the United States and the EEC countries with the rising number of restrictions on Japanese exports of these goods. At present, 60–80 percent of the total value of the output of these Japanese subsidiaries is produced in the host country to satisfy local production content and employment creation requests. Overseas production tends to incur additional production costs, but it also enables Japanese firms to keep up with changing demand and to explore new frontiers in the American and European markets. A MITI survey on the motivations behind overseas operations by Japanese firms endorsed the positive aspects of overseas production.[7] According to the survey, the most important incentives for Japanese firms engaging in DFI in the United States and Europe are:

Motivation Factor	Degree of Importance of Motivation Factor as Measured by the Percentage of all Firms Responding[a]	
	United States	*Europe*
• Fear of trade conflicts	15.3	21.2
• Response to trade restrictions	12.5	18.2
• Sales expansion in local market	86.1	17.2
• Acquisition of technology and market information	12.5	21.2

a. Respondents were asked to give the three most important factors.

Seventy to eighty percent of Japanese firms leave marketing and procurement of parts and materials in local production to their overseas subsidiaries, and a few firms have established R&D facilities overseas. A deluxe television wall set, developed at a Japanese subsidiary operating in the United States for American consumers and now imported to Japan, exemplifies the globalized activities of Japanese firms in recent years. Some major Japanese firms have already divided the world into three regions—North America, Europe, and Asia—and have established headquarters in each area.[8]

The globalization of activities is not confined to Japanese firms. American firms began to globalize in the 1960s, and were followed by the Japanese. Helleiner (1981) described the global operations of American firms as "intrafirm trade." The share of trade between U.S. parent firms and their subsidiaries and between subsidiaries under a common parent firm (including overseas subsidiaries), was 48.8 percent of total U.S. exports to the world in 1983. The share of intrafirm trade for Japan reached 34.0 percent in 1986 (MITI 1988c). The growing significance of intrafirm trade reflects the changing nature of international trade from transactions between independent firms to those within a single firm across borders. Diversified forms of international specialization arise, with firms retaining technology and management know-how within their organizations. The development of telecommunications has enhanced firms' abilities to adopt a global strategy and thereby spread capital and technology worldwide. Whether trade restrictions urged by lobbyists and politicians can continue to work alongside the globalization of business activities is of significant interest.

Foreign Firms Operating in Japan

How has this universal trend of globalization affected the Japanese market? That is, how have foreign firms entering the Japanese market affected the restructuring of Japan's economy and industries?

A MITI survey of foreign firms operating in Japan (that is, firms with more than 50% of its equity shares owned by foreigners) as of the end of March 1985 found that while DFI in Japan has risen much like Japanese DFI abroad, the level of DFI in Japan remains less than Japanese DFI abroad (MITI 1988c). From US$500 million in the 1970s, DFI in Japan has increased to US$1 billion in the 1980s. The main sources of DFI in Japan (in terms of the number of firms as of March 1985) are the United States (48.5%), Europe (35.6%)— which includes West Germany (7.7%), the United Kingdom (7.4%), Switzerland (5.9%), and France (4.7%)—and Asia (11.1%). The breakdown of DFI in Japan by industry is 73.5 percent for manufacturing, with petroleum refining (40.4%), chemicals (12.8%), and electrical machinery (9.8%) accounting for the largest shares. Typically, foreign manufacturing firms import materials and parts and sell their products in the Japanese market. This practice is reflected in the high import/sales ratio of all foreign firms operating in Japan (55.9%) and the low export/production ratio, which was 5.9 percent.

Although the restrictions on DFI in Japan were loosened during the period 1968–73, foreign firms should be encouraged to continue operating in Japan. With DFI, new technology and management are introduced and competition is increased, thereby accelerating Japan's restructuring. In the future, Japan should welcome the Asian NIEs' DFI in manufacturing/marketing and more American and European investment in finance and information services.

AN ASSESSMENT
OF GOVERNMENT INDUSTRIAL POLICIES

The Japanese government's policies have affected the restructuring of Japanese industries and firms by providing the framework in which the restructuring has taken place. This section reviews the industrial and trade policies that directly affect *micro*economic behavior.

Adjustment Assistance to H&B Firms

The core of MITI's assistance after the first oil shock consisted of a series of laws to assist depressed industries in their adjustment. For example, the laws attempted to prevent the basic materials industries, which lagged behind in the recovery after the first oil shock and whose output growth was less than half that of the machinery industry, from impeding those sectors of the economy that were performing well. The laws were enacted to assist depressed industries in reducing their capacities to a manageable size. The 1978 Law of Temporary Measures to Stabilize Specific Depressed Industries provided for the implementation of an adjustment assistance program.[9] The program's plans were as follows:

1. Fourteen industries were designated as qualified for adjustment assistance for five years from 1978 to 1983. They included electric furnace steel making, aluminum smelting, ferrosilicon manufacturing, shipbuilding, the manufacture of four synthetic fibers, three chemical fertilizers, and the manufacture of cotton, wool, and paperboard.

2. For each industry, a Basic Stabilization Program was established jointly by the industry, based on industry-wide consensus, and MITI to identify the extent of excess capacity by forecasting demand and supply.

3. The actual decrease of excess capacity was left to individual firms, with some administrative guidance probably coming from the industry's trade association. Eight industries were instructed by MITI to form a cartel (*fukyo* cartel) with the aim of reducing excess capacity.[10]

4. Financial assistance was given to encourage the adjustment. A special loan to aid the shift to other activities was provided by the Development Bank of Japan. Subsidies were available to pay the cost of retraining surplus workers in H&B production and of reemploying them in other production sectors.

The Smaller Business Switchover Law was enacted to assist the adjustment of industries composed primarily of small and medium-sized firms. Twenty-one industries were designated as depressed and were provided with the financial adjustment assistance indicated in item 4 above for the ten-year period 1976–86.

The impact of these laws on the selected industries was dramatic. For example, excess capacity in aluminum production was reduced by 56.7 percent, in urea production by 44.9 percent, in shipbuilding by 35 percent, and in ammonia production by 26.1 percent. MITI reported that by 1980 most industries had achieved their goals, increased their capacity utilization rates, and improved their management (Peck, Levin, and Goto 1987). However, the improvements were achieved mainly through the recovery of market demand and not by any improvement in management structure as the law intended. As a result, these industries suffered again from structural depression after the second oil shock and appealed for additional help to further decrease excess capacity.

Following the second oil shock, adjustment assistance continued under the 1983 Temporary Measures for the Structural Adjustment of Special Industries Law. Eleven out of the 14 industries that were protected under the 1978 Law of Temporary Measures to Stabilize Specific Depressed Industries and 15 new industries, including ethylene production, qualified for continued adjustment assistance under the 1983 law. Again, most industries achieved the capacity reduction goal and many cartels were cancelled before the target year. The 1978 and 1983 laws were generally successful in their employment adjustments, as few workers were displaced. Despite strong opposition to the continuance of adjustment laws for depressed industries, the Special Measures for Facilitating Adjustment Law, the third in the series, was enacted in 1987 to assist industries such as chemical fertilizers and ferro-alloys.

The adjustment laws for depressed industries have been both a success and a failure. MITI claimed that the laws were consistent with the OECD's criteria of a positive adjustment policy in that the policy measures were well defined, were transparent, and had a time limit for their implementation. In addition, no trade restrictions were imposed. While the policies were consistent with the OECD definition of a positive adjustment policy, their implementation was not in several respects. First, administrative guidance did not clearly encourage individual firms to decrease their capacities, and repeated adjustment assistance contradicted the idea of a time limit. Second, forecasts of supply and demand, the main outcome of the Basic Stabilization Program, often differed from actual figures during worldwide fluctuations. As a result, individual firms modified their capacity decreases according to the actual figures; thus, capacity reduction was inefficient. This argument is supported by Peck, Levin, and Goto (1987) who found that market shares remained unchanged in concentrated industries even after uniform capacity reduction across industries was accomplished. Modifications to the 1987 law allowed decisions on capacity decreases to be left to individual firms without the benefit of a Basic Stabilization Program and cartels.

Nevertheless, the adjustment laws provided the framework for capacity reduction. In fact, ethylene-producing firms continued to suffer from excess capacity until 1983 when the industry was included under the 1983 law and a cartel formed for capacity reduction. Employment adjustment was so successful throughout the economy that only a limited number of surplus workers were displaced in the H&B industries, despite major capacity adjustment.

Industry-Specific Adjustment

Along with the adjustment laws for depressed industries, industry-specific adjustment assistance was provided for declining industries such as agriculture, coal, and textiles. The ministries responsible for each particular industry established advisory councils that included representatives from consumer advocacy groups, the media, and academia, as well as from industry and trade unions. Each of the advisory councils reviewed their industry's supply and demand prospects, studied the adjustment difficulties of the industry, and recommended the adjustment assistance needed for the industry. The assistance was then implemented by the respective ministry in cooperation with prefectural governments. The amount of public funds, the policy recommendations for adjustment assistance, and the role played by government in the adjustment process differed greatly between industries.

Coal and cereals have relied heavily on government assistance in their adjustment. Domestic prices for these commodities were maintained at a level that was much higher than the prices of imports under the strict import quota restriction. Domestic producers were provided with a variety of subsidies to maintain or adjust production levels or cease production. Despite this heavy protection, domestic production and employment have decreased dramatically during the past quarter century, and further adjustments have recently been needed as a result of the rapid appreciation of the yen. For example, coal production and employment declined from 55 million tonnes per year and 260,000 miners in the peak year of 1961 to 17 million tonnes and 26,000 miners in 1987. Another halving of production and employees is planned under the current Eighth Coal Policy (1987–91). For cereals, price supports for rice are being considered and it is widely anticipated that the current ban on rice imports will be modified so that rice can be imported under quota restrictions, with the quotas increasing gradually.

The policy on textiles is a guidepost in the shift to L&S. In the textiles industry, the adjustments have been focused primarily on market mechanisms (Yamazawa 1988a) and on small and medium-sized weaving mills. Since 1953, equipment in these firms had to be registered, and new equipment could only be installed when the old equipment became obsolete. The subsidized scrapping of 10-20 percent of existing capacity was repeated several times. However, complaints about excess capacity, which apparently resulted from the steady increase in productivity per machine and a lack of voluntary (unsubsidized) scrapping, are still being voiced.

Competent medium-sized firms are going ahead with the reorganization of the industry toward L&S, as evidenced by the clothing manufacturers mentioned earlier. This adjustment is necessary because of increasing competition with imports in the domestic market and competition between foreign and Japanese clothing producers in international markets. The increasing competition has been intensified by the rapid appreciation of the yen and the liberal import policy for textiles (without Milti-Fibre Arrangement quota restrictions).

Promotion of L&S

The structural shift to L&S is widely recommended in many of MITI's reports, and competent firms in all industries have begun to respond. However, in the absence of "picking the winner" policies, the shift to L&S at present is not as easy as was the implementation of programs for steel in the 1950s and automobiles in the 1960s.

MITI can play only a guiding role and can provide only moderate financial assistance to small and medium-sized firms. The general promotion of R&D has supported the shift toward L&S. Subsidies to universities and research institutes in Japan are almost identical to those of other industrialized countries. The amount appropriated for R&D has increased steadily despite general budgetary constraints, but R&D still occupies only 3 percent of the central government's budget, which is below that of the United States (5%) and West Germany (5%).

Japan is unique, however, in that the Japanese public and private sectors jointly promote applied research. The National Research and Development Program (often called the Large-Scale R&D Project), which has been in operation since 1966, is run by the Agency of Industrial Science and Technology (AIST) (Tamura and Urata 1988). The program is organized as follows:

- It has accepted only high-risk and lengthy research projects that would not have been undertaken by private firms alone.

- For each project, public-sector research institutes and 10–20 private firms jointly organize an R&D association in which a public-sector institute acts as coordinator.

- A project is usually provided with 10–20 billion yen (approximately US$70–150 million in 1987 dollars) and takes 5–10 years to complete. The results are made public and are available to any interested party on a royalty basis.

- So far, 24 projects undertaken since 1966 show a clear shift from resource development and conservation (such as offshore oil drilling, steel production, manganese nodule mining, and desulfurization) to projects related to electronics (supercomputers, pattern information processing, automated sewing systems, and advanced robotics).

The National Research and Development Program has been successful so far because the research projects have been well defined, and the results of the basic scientific studies have been published. AIST will find it increasingly more difficult, however, to conduct basic studies without the help of other institutes and the private sector. Its noncompetitiveness may be criticized, but this is certainly more than offset by the advantages of avoiding a duplication of R&D efforts when the participants act independently of each other.

Trade Policy

Japan has responded to trade conflicts throughout the 1970s and 1980s by reforming its trade policy. Market liberalization measures and export restraints, which have already been mentioned, are the chief changes. These are examined below in the context of restructuring.

Market liberalization measures include tariff reduction, the abolishment or expansion of import quotas, the improvement of standards and procedures, and the liberalization of services trade (construction, finance, and legal). Tariffs on manufactured goods were reduced substantially through unilateral reductions in the 1970s and previous GATT multilateral trade negotiations (particularly the Tokyo Round). In addition, tariffs on products from developing countries were exempted or halved under the Generalized Scheme of Preferences (Yamazawa 1988b).

Many import quotas on agricultural products have been in effect for a long period of time, and proposals to remove them have met strong resistance from vested interests. Nevertheless, some headway has been made and restrictions on animal skins and leather were removed in 1985. It was also decided at the 1988 Japan-U.S. negotiations that restrictions on beef and oranges would be removed by 1991. The current strict import ban on rice has been criticized both in Japan and abroad, but, as noted earlier, it appears that an import quota system will be in place in the near future.

Standards and procedures governing imports were improved substantially by the Action Program of 1986, and this should help to promote imports significantly. Services fall under domestic regulations, which have been modified to encourage non-Japanese competition. These liberalization measures, which are largely a response to pressures from Japan's trading partners, will contribute to Japan's restructuring, increase competition in the domestic market in the long term, and improve the efficiency of the Japanese economy overall.

Voluntary export restrictions (VERs) have been imposed on many machinery exports, and the manufacturers' efforts to circumvent these barriers have affected the restructuring of L&S industries. At the request of foreign governments the Japanese government coordinates VERs with domestic industries and firms. The total quota is negotiated and distributed among exporting firms. Some VERs were introduced by MITI based on the Trade Administration Law, but many VERs were also introduced through MITI's administrative guidance and coordination of interests among related parties. VERs can settle fierce trade conflicts in the short term but will cause distortions in the long term. Rigid share agreements among rival exporters tend to depress competition and keep prices high, thus injuring consumers and industries using the protected good as an input (for example, steel).

The intended effect of VERs gradually erodes. Firms planning to extend their operations overseas readily relocate their export production either to the export market or to third countries from which they export the products in order to avoid restrictions. In fact, even though restrictions on exports of Japanese cars to the United States began in 1980 and exports from Japan decreased to just short of the export quota of 2.3 million cars, production outside Japan gradually increased to 1.6 million cars for 1988.

A new element complicating Japan's trade policy reform is the increasing demand by Japanese producers to restrict imports from developing countries. Imports of knitwear, steel plating, and cement from the Asian NIEs have increased so rapidly that domestic producers fear that the imports may undermine their efforts to decrease capacity when domestic demand stagnates.

With persistent, huge trade surpluses, however, the Japanese government's attempt to placate these demands is limited. Unlike other developed countries, Japan has not resorted to imposing quota restrictions on textiles and clothing imports, which is allowed under the Multi-Fibre Arrangement, despite repeated requests by the Textile Trade Association. However, when the Knitwear Association initiated an antidumping suit against Korean producers in 1988, MITI negotiated with the Korean producers to adopt VERs. By pursuing these restrictive measures, Japan has, in effect, endorsed similar measures that the United States and EC have sought to invoke against Japan. VERs, however, are short-term solutions, as import competition will eventually resume either through increasing imports of the same product from other Asian countries or increasing imports of more sophisticated products not covered by the VERs.

VERs are trade restriction measures outside the scope of GATT rules, and their abolition is being discussed at the Uruguay Round of multilateral trade negotiations. Instead of relying on VERs, Japan should follow GATT Article 19 and implement temporary safeguard restrictions against excessive import increases. This policy would also be consistent with Japan's restructuring efforts.

Hollowing Out of the Industrial Structure?

The shift fom H&B to L&S is inevitably accompanied by substantial changes in employment. As mentioned above, employment in Japan was reduced considerably in the H&B industries. Are the unemployed being absorbed by the expansion of L&S? If L&S expands less than H&B contracts, then structural unemployment will occur. This argument is used to support the case against "deindustrialization" or "the hollowing out of the industrial structure" and has generated fierce policy debate in Japan and the United States.

Table 9.7 shows the changes in the employment structure by industry from 1975 to 1984 and the projected figures for 1990 and 1995. Both the primary and consumer industries show substantial decreases in employment from 1975 to 1995, but the basic materials industry remains unchanged due to the growth of other sectors. In 1995, the machinery and other services categories will have increased by 1 million from their 1975 levels. Employment in the con-

Table 9.7
Changes in the Employment Structure (millions of persons, %)

	1975	1980	1984	1990	1995
Primary					
(agriculture, forestry, and fishery)	6.63	5.76	5.13	3.87	3.10
	(12.7)	(10.4)	(8.9)	(6.4)	(5.0)
Consumer					
(food processing, textiles and					
clothing, paper, and	6.16	5.65	6.05	5.74	5.34
miscellaneous)	(11.8)	(10.8)	(10.5)	(9.5)	(8.6)
Basic materials					
(metals, metal products,					
chemicals, coal and petroleum	2.92	3.04	2.94	2.96	2.98
products, and ceramics)	(5.6)	(5.5)	(5.1)	(4.9)	(4.8)
Machinery					
(industrial, electrical, transporta-	4.39	4.65	5.36	5.26	5.40
tion, and precision)	(8.4)	(8.4)	(9.3)	(8.7)	(8.7)
Construction					
(construction and mining)	4.91	5.59	5.36	7.13	7.88
	(9.4)	(10.1)	(9.3)	(11.8)	(12.7)
Services					
households and firms (advertis-					
ing, information, and leasing)					
and public services (education,	11.28	14.39	16.03	18.49	20.5
medical, and governmental)	(21.6)	(26.0)	(27.8)	(30.6)	(33.1)
Other services					
(utilities, transportation,	15.93	15.49	16.78	16.98	16.94
commerce, and finance)	(30.5)	(28.8)	(29.1)	(28.1)	(27.3)

Note: Figures for 1990 and 1995 are forecasts based on an analysis of the trend of changes described in the text. Numbers in parentheses are percentages of column total.
Source: MITI (1988a).

struction industry will have increased by almost 3 million (60%), while services employment will have nearly doubled. Although the growth of employment in the expanding sectors will be smaller or even negative under slower growth, the employment increase in the L&S industries will be large enough to absorb employment cuts in the H&B industries.

More important is the problem of matching the skill requirements of one group with another. A survey of positions requiring skilled labor conducted by the Ministry of Labor in November 1987 reported different rates of unfilled employment opportunities in L&S industries due to a shortage of qualified skilled laborers and an excess supply in steel and other basic materials industries (*Nihon Keizai Shinbun* [The Japan Economic Journal], October 1988). The shares of vacant positions by industry were 13.5 percent for construction, 9.1 percent for services, and 5.2 percent for manufacturing as a whole. Skilled labor is industry-specific and thus not easily transferred from one industry to another. To bridge the gap, improvements in retraining and placement are necessary.

Toward Institutional Reform

Because restructuring efforts by individual firms and industries are confined by the institutional framework within which they operate, institutional changes are sometimes required to promote further restructuring (OECD 1987). To this end, the Japanese government has been trying to change specific sectors of the economy through policy reform and has been working to change its economic institutions. The Maekawa Group (a group commissioned in 1985–86 and devoted to the study of economic structural adjustment) and the Administrative Reform Council (1981–83 and 1987–) were formed to make recommendations on how to meet these challenges. Both groups, which included opinion leaders in the private sector and former government officials, were formed at the request of the prime minister. After intensive study and discussion, the two groups submitted their recommendations to the prime minister, who in turn committed himself to incorporating them into actual policies. The recommendations mainly advocated changes in macroeconomic policies and economic institutions.

The Maekawa Report recommended the following:

- Improved access to the Japanese market and the promotion of manufactured imports
- Separation of fiscal policy management from the strict balanced budget rule
- Further promotion of the adjustment of declining industries
- The liberalization of financial and capital markets
- Furthering development cooperation with developing countries

The Administrative Reform Council's first report recommended reducing the size of the central government by consolidating or abolishing ministries and agencies, and privatizing three state-run enterprises (tobacco, telephone and telegraph, and the railroad). Both recommendations were implemented by the government. The Administrative Reform Council's second report in 1988 proposed administrative deregulation in seven areas (the distribution system, transportation, information, the financial markets, oil, rice and other cereals, and civil aviation).

Other forms of institutional reform include tax reform, which was promoted by the Ministry of Finance. A low consumer tax was introduced over a wide range of commodities and services to correct for the overly heavy reliance on income taxes. Moreover, it is widely anticipated that some form of land reform to correct distorted land prices is imminent.

The reports by the Maekawa Group and the Administrative Reform Council, which were partly intended to soften criticism of Japan's persistent trade imbalances, have given Japan's trading partners a sense of the direction of Japanese restructuring. Implementation of the institutional changes recommended in these reports has not been easy, not only because the changes are opposed by groups with vested interests, but also because radical changes are often difficult to implement. Thus, although the United States has expressed its dissatisfaction with the pace of implementation of the recommendations and has criticized the reports as paying lip service to serious problems, it must also be realized that institutional reforms take time. The slow pace may reflect the cautious attitude toward institutional reform, which is irreversible, but, in the long run institutional reform will promote the restructuring of the Japanese economy.

JAPAN'S NEW INTERNATIONAL ROLE

As the Japanese economy grows and the trade imbalances continue, Japan will increasingly be called upon to play a greater role in promoting growth and stability in the world economy. It appears that national consensus has been reached in Japan on the country's new international role.

It has often been pointed out that Japan should recycle its trade surplus in the form of DFI and official direct assistance (ODA), and encourage import expansion through boosting domestic demand and market liberalization measures. This chapter has described the commitment and efforts of the Japanese government in pursuing these goals. Although trade imbalances cannot be attributed to the policies and performance of a single country alone, Japan has stepped forward and committed itself to playing a more active role—and one that is befitting of Japan's economic stature—in the global economy.

But the restructuring of the Japanese economy, which is already under way in the formulation of government policies and the private sector's performance, is also needed to achieve this goal. However long the restructuring takes, it will eventually resolve the trade imbalance and contribute to the further development of the Japanese economy.

Part IV

Japan's Development Experience and Contemporary Developing Countries

Ten

Is the Japanese Model Applicable?

Does the Japanese model of industrialization offer anything useful for contemporary developing countries? International market conditions and initial requirements for industrialization now differ considerably from those of the late nineteenth century. Nevertheless, pre–Second World War Japan and contemporary developing countries share basic similarities in their industrialization processes and mechanisms that go beyond the differences in their initial conditions. Thus, the Japanese model may have relevance for developing countries. After reviewing the Japanese development experience on both the microeconomic and macroeconomic levels, two topics from preceding chapters—general trading companies and CPC development in modern industries—are examined for their applicability to developing countries.[1]

UNIVERSALITY VERSUS UNIQUENESS OF THE JAPANESE EXPERIENCE

The model presented in this book is based on the industrialization process of a late-developing country—Japan. Contemporary developing economies now face some of the same problems of late-developing industrialization that Japan faced as a late-developing country. These problems and the similarities between Japan and contemporary developing countries are described in this section.

When a country begins to industrialize, there exists a huge technological gap between the developing country and the advanced industrialized countries. The gap for Japan was almost of an incomparable magnitude, unlike that of late-developing European countries. For example, in the initial stages of industrialization in the nineteenth century, both Germany and Great Britain had at that time a few industries, such as the chemical industry, that were among the most advanced in the world. Unlike these countries, Japan had to import each new industry, which then had to follow the typical catching-up process.

Pre-industrial Japan and the developing countries today have in common large, indigenous, traditional sectors, from which the industrialization process receives significant support. These sectors are what makes up what is often collectively referred to as Japan's non-Western initial condition and account for the so-called dualistic development pattern. As explained below, the successful move from light to heavy industrialization in the production and trade structures could not have occurred without a flexible indigenous sector. Thus, the industrialization processes of pre–Second World War Japan and some of the contemporary developing countries are not fundamentally different. This is especially true for developing countries that, like Japan, are lacking in resources and, therefore, are primarily dependent on processing trade.

The differences in initial conditions should not, however, be overlooked. First, the development of science and technology in the first three quarters of this century has given rise to many new industries in the advanced industrialized countries. This development has created a gap between industrialized countries and developing countries today that is even wider than that which existed between the industrial world and Meiji Japan. As a consequence, more external resources are now required for the establishment of new industries. The wider gap has, however, also created more opportunities to utilize accumulated knowledge, which may account, in part, for the faster overall growth of the developing countries.[2]

Second, the backward economies of East and Southeast Asia provided a market for Japan when its new industries reached the export stage. Today's developing countries, in contrast, have difficulty finding similar economically backward markets for their exports. It may be argued that this and the developed countries' protection of their less competitive industries leave developing countries in an unfavorable position to expand exports.

In order to overcome these formidable obstacles and establish new industries, many developing countries have to date relied heavily on DFI. Private sector experience and existing channels in export marketing can, however, be useful assets in export expansion. Heavy reliance on DFI, which basically is a package transfer of such scarce resources as capital, technology, and management, may be regarded as an institutional device by which a late-developing country can overcome obstacles to industrialization, as suggested by Gerschenkron (1966). Japan's general trading companies, for example, were established to help late-developing Japan expand its trade in competition with its developed rivals. But Japan's reliance on DFI was limited to a few industries within a certain period of time.

Third, contemporary developing countries suffer from their colonial heritage. Although colonial rule, or quasi-colonial rule, brought about some modernization, such as railways, it obstructed or even repressed the emergence of socioeconomic factors necessary for the development of an independent national economy. The legacy of this heritage can still be seen in the international relations and domestic affairs of developing countries. Indeed, a feeling of antineocolonialism prevails in the developing countries, and this has bred mistrust of market economy solutions. That feeling is manifested most strongly with respect to DFI and prevents developing countries from taking full advantage of this type of investment in the industrialization process.

Because of these differences in initial conditions and the international environment, the Japanese model cannot be applied to developing countries in the 1990s and beyond without modifications. Nevertheless, it can provide useful insights into the mechanism and problems of their catching-up industrialization process.

CPC DEVELOPMENT IN DEVELOPING COUNTRIES IN THE 1990s AND BEYOND

CPC development is an appropriate strategy of industrial development for a late-starting industrializing country with a domestic market of a certain size and potential comparative advantage in industrialization. First, domestic demand for a new product is created by imports; efficiency in domestic production is then improved through import substitution; and finally, exports increase as the product becomes competitive in foreign markets. If import substitution is slower than expected, it is either because the country lacks comparative advantage in the industry or because improvements in production efficiency are obstructed. The CPC development model provides a framework by which the development performance of individual industries can be assessed. Of course, it should take into account different international market conditions and greater participation of multinational corporations (MNCs) in the developing countries.

CPC Development in Asian Developing Countries

The promotion of industrialization and the introduction of modern industries began in East and Southeast Asia during the 1950s and 1960s. Due to their potential comparative advantage in labor-intensive textile production and their high domestic demand for imported textiles, the countries of the two regions introduced the textile industry as their first modern industry. In Taiwan and Korea, for example, the textile industries were introduced in the 1950s and by 1970 the industry in these two countries had achieved import substitution and were beginning export expansion. In the 1970s, they proceeded to adopt import substitution and export expansion in the heavy industries such as shipbuilding and steel making.

The ASEAN member countries began industrializing in the 1960s. In Thailand, the modern textile industry began with cotton and then synthetics in the mid-1960s, and achieved import substitution and began export expansion in the 1970s. Development of Indonesia's modern textile industry began in the late 1960s and the industry achieved import substitution in the 1970s.

Figure 10.1 illustrates the CPC development of both synthetic fabric and crude steel production for four Asian countries. Production/demand ratios are indicated on the vertical axis. The increase in these ratios beyond unity shows the attainment of import substitution and export expansion for individual industries (also see Figure 2.1, Panels B and C). Rising production/demand ratios were observed for the two industries and in all four countries, which supports the role of CPC development of the two major industries in these countries. But CPC development occurred at different times for the two industries in all four countries and among the four countries for each industry.

Synthetic fabric weaving was introduced and developed after cotton fabric weaving in all four Asian countries. Taiwan was the first to begin production and began to export before 1970. Korea followed closely and reached Taiwan's level of export expansion by the mid-1970s. Thailand's production/demand ratio exceeded unity in the early 1970s, and Thailand followed both Taiwan and Korea in export expansion by partly taking advantage of the earlier development of the cotton textile industry. For Indonesia, only a long-run trend is shown in Figure 10.1 due to the lack of consistent time series data for the industry's development. The development of the Indonesian synthetic fabric industry was delayed until the mid-1970s and exceeded unity only after 1980.

Two characteristics of production/demand ratios of the four countries should be noted. First, domestic demand for textile goods (estimated by production plus imports minus exports) was largely made up of goods in the intermediate stage of production. The intermediate goods were consumed by the textile industry to produce finished textile products such as clothing, bags, and other accessories, most of which were directly exported. This characteristic implies that the production/demand ratio for intermediate goods would tend to be very low relative to the same ratio for finished textile products. Second, the share of indirect exports was relatively high at 70 to 80 percent in Korea and Taiwan. This tended to raise the overall production/demand ratio for the synthetic textile industries (including unfinished fabrics as well as finished products) higher than it would be otherwise by reducing the apparent domestic demand estimate without increasing production. In Thailand and Indonesia the indirect export of synthetic fabric began in the 1980s and has reached around 15 percent only recently.

Development of the steel industry, which lagged behind synthetic fabric production by five to ten years, occurred in the mid-1970s in all four coun-

Figure 10.1
Catching-Up Industrialization of East and Southeast Asian Countries

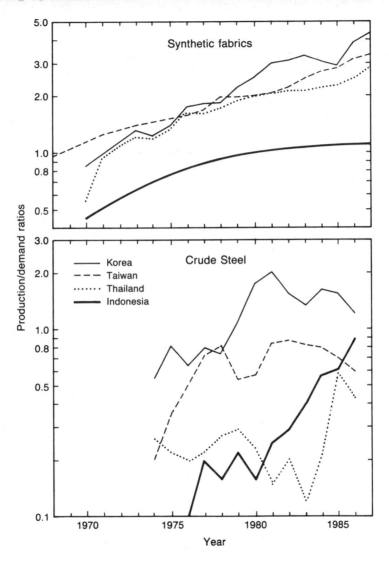

Notes: Production/demand ratios tended to increase for these industries. The import substitution stage is reflected as the ratio approaches unity; the export expansion stage, as the ratio continues to increase above unity. Although the general trend is depicted, there were observed time lags between the two industries and among the four countries, which indicates time differentials in CPC development.

Sources: Calculated from statistics obtained from the Japan Chemical Fiber Association and the Japan Iron and Steel Federation. Because of the unavailability of consistent time series data, the curve for Indonesian synthetic fabrics (top) depicts only a long-run trend based on ad hoc information of the import substitution and export expansion stages of the industry's development.

tries (see Figure 10.1). For steel, the production figures measure domestic production of crude steel, whereas the demand figures include finished steel products converted to a crude steel basis. The production/demand ratios include indirect exports in the form of steel products. Furthermore, the ratios fluctuated in response to both domestic and world market business cycles. Korea quickly developed its steel industry and succeeded in reaching the export expansion stage by 1980, whereas Taiwan still remained below unity throughout the 1980s, due, in part, to being handicapped by the small size of its domestic market. The production/demand ratios of both Thailand and Indonesia stayed below 0.3 until the mid-1980s but have recently begun to increase rapidly.

Both the textile and steel industries have typically followed CPC development in countries with abundant labor and a sizable domestic market. Although MNCs participated at the early stage of development, with local firms entering at a later stage, both groups aimed at import substitution from the beginning. In contrast, finished clothing production and the electrical machinery industry, although labor-intensive and introduced earlier, relied on export expansion from the beginning without experiencing import substitution. There are also many such cases in Hong Kong and the export-processing zones of Taiwan and the Philippines.

This particular pattern is made possible by MNCs, which import capital, technology, and packaged parts and materials, use local labor for sewing and assembling, and export abroad through their own distribution networks. Export expansion is possible from the beginning because the production technology of MNCs is standardized, so that skilled labor, continuous learning, and the adoption of new technology are not required. This situation describes a typical process in the product cycle (PC) theory, by which technology and production are transferred to developing countries through DFI (Vernon 1964). Industrial development of the PC type provides developing countries with labor employment and foreign exchange, but both the educational effects on local firms and laborers and the linkage effects on other industries are inevitably limited.

Kinked Efficiency Improvement in CPC Development

The primary force underlying CPC development in Japan was improved production efficiency—that is, better utilization of labor, a larger scale of operation, advanced technology and equipment, and a general improvement in production and management techniques. Both cost reduction and quality improvement occurred, which allowed for the substitution of domestic products for foreign ones, first domestically (import substitution) and later abroad (export expansion). Figure 10.2, Panel 1, illustrates the declining import/demand ratio (import substitution) and the increasing export/produc-

Figure 10.2
Alternative Mechanisms Underlying CPC Development

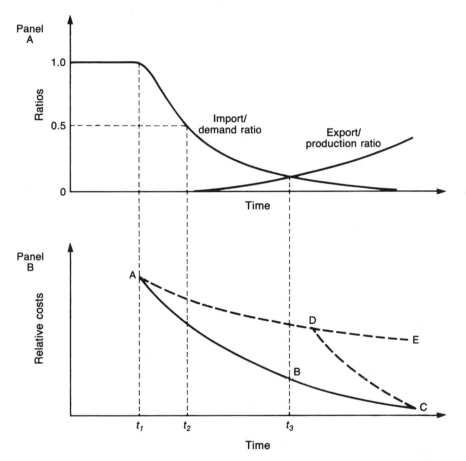

Notes: Panel 1 illustrates the process of CPC development—import substitution followed by export expansion, by means of a decreasing import/demand ratio and an increasing export/production ratio. Panel 2 illustrates alternative mechanisms underlying CPC development—the ABC curve illustrates a continuous reduction of domestic production costs relative to foreign production costs, whereas the ADC curve illustrates a kinked path of relative costs. Under the latter mechanism, import substitution is achieved not so much by small reductions of relative costs as under import restrictions (the AD curve), whereas export expansion, which is subsidized only in the beginning, is mainly achieved through rapid reduction of relative costs (the DC curve).

Source: Reproduced from Yamazawa and Tambunlertchai (1985: figure 16.1).

tion ratio (export expansion) in CPC development, whereas Figure 10.2, Panel 2, charts the reduction of the underlying relative costs. The AC curve in Panel 2 shows the continuous improvements in efficiency and decreasing domestic costs relative to foreign costs that are required for successful import substitution and export expansion in the marketplace. Quality improvements may be included as a factor contributing to the nonprice competitiveness of domestic products. It was observed in Chapters 4 and 5 that both a productivity increase and a relative price decline accompanied the successful import substitution and export expansion of cotton textiles and steel products in Japan.

In contrast, in contemporary developing countries, industrial development has been supported by protection rather than by improvements in efficiency. Once imports have created domestic demand, domestic production is encouraged to meet that demand through restrictions on imports. Import substitution is achieved even without sufficient productivity improvement and cost reduction (see the AD curve in Figure 10.2, Panel 2). That is, import substitution and export expansion are possible with limited improvements in efficiency if high tariffs, import bans, and export subsidies are effectively imposed.

This kind of government intervention is common in many developing countries, and it has been widely observed that these countries continue to impose high tariffs even after import substitution has apparently been achieved and export expansion has begun. The ADE curve in Figure 10.2, Panel 2, illustrates the effects of this strategy. It is too costly in the long run, however, to continue export expansion without improvements in efficiency, but it may also be an exaggeration to say that no improvements in efficiency are achieved in this process. It is plausible to contend that import substitution can be achieved under tariff protection and that export expansion can begin with the introduction of export subsidies, but that improvements in efficiency and cost reduction are only brought about by the competition of exports in foreign markets.

The ADC curve illustrates the kinked path of improvements in efficiency. The domestic product becomes competitive at point C, so that true import substitution is achieved (assuming there is no rush to import in the absence of import restrictions), and export expansion can continue without subsidization. As Figure 10.2, Panel 2 shows, kinked rather than linear improvements in efficiency seem to better explain the import substitution and export expansion of textiles in Asian developing countries.

Changes in Business Behavior at the Export Stage

It is not easy to substantiate the kinked path that results from improvements in efficiency as found in textile industries in Asia because of the lack of reliable data on productivity and costs throughout the import substitution and export expansion stages. However, Yamazawa and Tambunlertchai (1985) provide evidence to support the belief that Thai textile firms undertook behavioral changes as they began the process of export expansion.

During August and September 1979, the authors conducted interviews in major textile firms in Thailand to examine the relationship between the export performance (measured by the percentage of production exported) of individual firms and their production, management, and marketing characteristics. All the sample firms began with import substitution, and none exported before 1971. Although the export/production ratio for all firms combined had increased to more than 30 percent in 1978, the ratios for the individual firms differed greatly.

Product type is the crucial factor in the export/production ratio, a finding that is consistent with the difference in comparative advantage among product categories. The export/production ratio is larger for cotton and polyester-cotton blend fabrics because of the large domestic market, making production on a larger scale practical. The ratio is smaller for polyester-rayon blends and synthetic yarn fabrics because of the small domestic demand and the resulting smaller scale of production and the increased difficulty in transferring technology.

Among firms with the same products, however, the principal determinant in making behavioral changes is the ability to make changes in production and management techniques. The shift from domestic sales to exports and the establishment of marketing and distribution channels abroad require such changes, but not every firm can make them. Standards of quality, packaging, and timely delivery are usually higher for exports than for domestic sales. Textile finish, for example, is classified into categories—A+, A, B, and C— according to the number of frays and streaks in the goods. Normally only A+ and A goods can be exported; B goods are sold locally, and C goods are rejected. Quality control inspection is required for exports, but the distinction between A and B goods is less important when production is geared to the domestic market. Those firms that exported established stricter internal quality control measures when they began exporting regularly. Changes in the product mix and concentration on fewer items enabled them to realize economies of scale, and marketing and production controls were integrated more closely to permit quicker responses to changes in world demand.

All these changes in production and management strategies were introduced regularly, and the firms that achieved a greater export/production ratio were the firms that made greater efforts in these areas. Changes in production and management strategies seem to have contributed to improvements in efficiency at the export expansion stage, although this is difficult to quantify. Nevertheless, the strategy of kinked improvements in efficiency is a rational one for developing countries grappling to achieve CPC development.

Not every industry can pass through import substitution to export expansion. Many, such as the metals, machinery, and chemical industries, have not been able to export after achieving import substitution under protection. Because they are protected and because they are also constrained by small-scale production due to the small size of domestic markets and the greater need for technology transfers, these industries can only meet domestic demand. The formation of larger regional markets through regional integration agreements will help promote the CPC development of these industries.

APPLICABILITY OF JAPANESE
GENERAL TRADING COMPANIES

Motivated by the need to increase foreign exchange earnings, many developing countries are eager to develop new exports and explore new markets for their traditional exports. Aware of the difficulties involved, they have become interested in Japanese general trading companies (GTCs) because the GTCs significantly contributed to the expansion of Japan's foreign trade (see Chapter 6). Some developing countries, including Korea and Thailand, implemented GTC promotion policies with the expectation that sales of their exports would rapidly increase. Because their GTCs have only recently been set up, it is too soon to fully evaluate their performance or to forecast their future with any degree of confidence. However, it is possible to assess their early development and, because they are modeled after Japan's GTCs, to compare development experiences.

Some insist that GTCs evolved out of Japan's social, economic, and cultural background and that Japanese-style GTCs cannot be introduced into many developing countries. They argue that entrepreneurship is present only in countries with a Confucian tradition and that sociocultural factors or different environmental factors in countries without a Confucian tradition can delay industrialization; they suggest that developing countries fitting this description ought to utilize Japanese GTCs rather than try to create their own. However, despite questions regarding the applicability of the GTCs' functions under different social, economic, and cultural conditions, a case can be made for promoting indigenous GTCs. This is discussed below in the context of Korean GTCs.

Korean Promotion of GTCs

In 1963, Korea adopted an export-oriented growth policy, under which manufacturing firms, not intermediary firms, became eligible for preferential export financing from banks at half the prime rate. Because of this incentive, the export of labor-intensive manufactures expanded rapidly in the

1960s. By presidential decree in 1972, Korea began to promote its heavy and chemical industries and used monetary and fiscal incentives to encourage domestic firms to explore new areas such as shipbuilding, steel manufacturing, and chemicals production. These Korean domestic products eventually would be exported but to do so meant finding new distribution channels. To this end, another presidential decree promoting GTCs was handed down in 1975.

Two types of trading channels existed in Korea before 1975. One was made up of small and medium-sized trading companies, which generally specialized in a limited number of commodities. Because their major markets were in North America and Western Europe and because they could not afford to maintain their own information and marketing networks in those distant markets, they exported their goods through foreign trading companies (including Japanese GTCs). Large manufacturers exporting directly represented the other channel. For instance, large textile or electrical manufacturers established branches or sales agents in major markets and exported products through them. Non-Korean trading companies were not interested in the new exports, and Korean manufacturer traders lacked the skills required to develop new markets. Thus, large, effective, domestically owned trading com-

Table 10.1
Eligibility Requirements and Preferential Treatment for Korean GTCs

Qualification criteria	Eligibility requirements
Capital	2 billion won (minimum total assets)
Annual export performance	2 percent increase in total exports over previous year
Number of export items	5 (US$1 million or more in total sales per year)
Number of overseas branches	20

Preferential treatment benefits
Preferential treatment in international tender
GTCs can import major raw materials even if they serve as intermediary
GTCs can use more than two banks for letters of credit for importing major raw materials
Overseas branches of GTCs can hold more foreign exchange than other trading companies
GTCs can have more than two branches in one country
Tax reduction and exemption for GTC export and import commissions

Source: Presidential Decree on the Implementation of the Foreign Trade Transaction Act, Republic of Korea, 1975. Seoul.

panies were needed, which led the Korean government to hand down the 1975 presidential decree to begin promoting GTCs.

The eligibility requirements and types of preferential treatment accorded GTCs in Korea are listed in Table 10.1. These GTCs were also eligible for general benefits for export promotion. The requirements listed in Table 10.1 reveal the Korean government's intention to promote trading companies that exported many types of products and had global information networks. In this manner, the Korean government could encourage the development of heavy manufactures for export.

By 1978, 13 companies had been declared eligible for preferential treatment. They were affiliated with major manufacturing groups, such as Sam Sung, Dae Woo, and Hyun Dai, and 60 percent of their exports came from within their own groups. They were required to renew their status every year. Three firms eventually failed to meet the eligibility requirements and withdrew their applications. In 1982, ten companies continued to maintain eligibility, and one of these, which had been created especially for small and medium-sized manufacturing firms, was operated by the government.

The expansion of the designated Korean GTCs was remarkable. Their combined share of total Korean exports was 26.4 percent in 1977, 33.9 percent in 1979, and more than 50 percent by 1982. GTC exports of heavy industrial goods also increased remarkably and represented 47 percent of GTC exports in 1979, compared to the share of 21 percent of such exports by Japanese trading companies in Korea.

Korean GTCs have also been active in exploring new markets, particularly in Latin America and Africa. Their performance so far has justified their promotion by the Korean government.

Problems with Korean GTCs

Although it is too soon to fully assess the effects of the Korean GTCs, a comparison with Japanese GTCs is helpful in identifying problems.[3]

By 1979, Korean GTCs had reached a scale of operations comparable to that of the Japanese GTCs in 1960, when the latter began to diversify (see Table 10.2). For this reason, Korean GTCs are compared with the Japanese GTCs of FY1960 rather than with the Japanese GTCs of the late 1970s. Japanese figures for FY1960 in Table 10.2 are converted at 360 yen to the U.S. dollar, whereas, in 1979, the rate was 219 yen and the export price index had risen by 38 percent. This means the Japanese figures for FY1960 must be multiplied by 2.27 to correspond with the FY1979 Korean data. Total Japanese sales in 1960 adjusted in this manner are US$933 million for the average of 12 GTCs and approximately US$1,977 million for Mitsubishi; sales per employee are US$5.0 million and US$6.4 million, respectively, all of which are

Table 10.2

Comparison of Korean and Japanese GTCs

	Korea (FY1979)		Japan (FY1960)		Japan (FY1978)	
	Average (9 GTCs)	Dae Woo[a]	Average (12 GTCs)	Mitsubishi[a]	Average (9 GTCs)	Mitsubishi
Overseas branches (number)	29	56	41	55	103	138
Overseas staff[b]	51	116	189	308	647	873
Total sales[c]	561	1,120	411	871	11,969	21,314
Sales per branch[c]	19.3	20.4	10.0	15.8	116.1	154.4
Sales per employee[c,d]	5.2	4.3	2.2	2.8	18.5	2.2

	Korea (FY1979)	Japan (FY1960)	Japan (FY1978)
GTC share of total exports (%)	33.9	47.6	48.1
GTC share of total imports (%)	4.7	63.9	51.2

Notes:

a. Dae Woo Industrial and Mitsubishi Corporation are the largest GTCs in their respective countries.

b. Number of expatriate employees only; Korean data are for 1977.

c. In millions of U.S. dollars. Korean figures include only exports and imports; Japanese data also include offshore trade and domestic (within Japan) transactions.

d. Total sales divided by the worldwide total number of employees.

Sources: Financial statements of the companies.

comparable to the Korean figures (see Table 10.2). Thus the Korean GTCs are not very different from the Japanese GTCs at the start of rapid economic growth.

The Korean GTCs still need to resolve the following problems:

1. Despite their rapid expansion in recent years, Korean GTCs act as trading arms of parent manufacturing groups, and the GTC figures, which include existing exports by parent manufacturers within the respective groups, cannot be expected to increase at the same rate in the future. Expansion of their activities outside their own groups is the biggest task confronting Korean GTCs.

2. Korean GTCs specialize in export trade. Although their share of total exports has become more similar to that of the Japanese GTCs, their share of imports remains much smaller than that of their Japanese counterparts. Domestic sales represent only a small share of Korean GTC earnings. Dae Woo's exports, for example, were 528 billion won in 1979 and represented 85 percent of Dae Woo's total sales. In contrast, the shares of exports, imports, and domestic and intra-country trade in the total sales of the Mitsubishi Corporation in FY1960 were 17.4 percent, 29.9 percent, and 51.3 percent and 1.4 percent, respectively. These shares show that Mitsubishi's reliance on domestic trade was over 50 percent. Taking into account the commission fees, risks, and handling costs of each type of transaction, it is often said that the order of profitability is domestic, import, export, and intra-country trade. During the pre–Second World War period, Japanese GTCs mainly profited from domestic and import trade and bore the costs incurred in export trade. Since only export values are considered under the Korean eligibility requirements, a Korean GTC tends to handle only the export trade for other members of the same group, and other members retain their own import and domestic trade capabilities. Thus, in expanding their business, Korean GTCs are restricted to the less profitable export transactions.

3. Large Korean manufacturers tend to export their products through their own channels. Before the Second World War, Japanese manufacturers lacked personnel skilled in foreign transactions and thus had to rely on trading companies. But today in Korea, manufacturers have this type of personnel and can engage in direct exports independently. This situation resembles the practices of Japanese automobile manufacturers and electronics firms exporting either directly or through affiliated special trading companies. Large manufacturers today will continue to export and import directly as long as there is no incentive to do otherwise.

4. The promotion of GTCs has been implemented on a competitive basis, and little preferential treatment is shown. Ten GTCs are too many for the

Korean economy given its present size. Three or four GTCs would be closer to the optimum number. However, the promotion policy in effect at present is consistent with the promotion of efficient GTCs; that is, the policy itself does not attempt to limit the number admitted. Instead, it allows competition to narrow the field.

Indigenous Korean trading companies have closer contact with domestic producers and consumers. Considering the quick shift to export expansion of heavy industrial products, they have been as eager to develop new export items as the Japanese GTCs were during the high-growth period of their economy. Korean GTCs are credited with their contribution to the diversification of export products and expansion of markets. The promotion of indigenous GTCs is thus justified despite the high costs to maintain overseas networks at present.

Japanese industrial policy and technological borrowing as well as the CPC model and GTCs have attracted the interest of foreign economists. An attempt by developing countries to copy Japan's GTCs is not recommended. Nevertheless, analysis of the Japanese experience can aid in the development of appropriate policy measures and the identification of rational responses consistent with accepted economic principles.

Notes to Chapters

CHAPTER ONE

1. Toyo Keizai Shinposha's *Long-Term Economic Statistics* series on Japan's economic development enables this overview. Volume 14 (Yamazawa and Yamamoto 1979a) especially provides time series statistics of manufacturing production and exports and imports classified by common industry groups, which allows for the analysis of the interaction between production and trade.

2. It should be noted that exports and imports include only commodities and that exports are FOB and imports CIF.

3. Kuznets (1967) gives a higher foreign trade ratio for Japan than the estimates presented here.

4. The distinction between light and heavy industries is based on factor proportions of production and end use, but it has a weak theoretical basis. It does, however, fit well into the sequence of industrial development and is often used in Japan and centrally planned economies.

5. This expansion of the export market by stages is discussed in Nawa (1937), who hypothesizes it as a "three-stage development" of Japan's foreign trade, and in Kojima (1965), who describes it as an "expanding export frontier." For cross-classification of commodity by geographical region, see Yukizawa and Maeda (1978).

6. See Yamazawa and Yamamoto (1979a, Pt. 1, chap. 1, and Pt. 3) for detailed statistics and an analysis of the geographical structure of Japan's foreign trade.

7. This phasing approximately coincides with that described by Fei, Ohkawa, and Ranis (1985) in their analysis of Japan's economic development.

8. Elasticities are computed from an estimation of raw material import functions of the log-linear type.

CHAPTER TWO

1. Akamatsu apparently obtained the idea from W. Hoffman (1931) during his stay at the Kiel Institute of World Economics in the late 1920s but assimilated, expanded, and gave the concept a poetic name. Readers having difficulty trying to imagine a flock formation of flying wild geese may refer to the illustration in Laura Ingalls Wilder, *Little House on the Prairie*, Harper and Row, 1953, p. 263.

2. See the estimation of the constant price series of production, imports, and exports of cotton fabrics in Chapter 4, pp. 71–73.

3. Changes in the organizational structure of the expanding industry certainly affect its CPC performance. Owing to the relatively large size of Japan's domestic market, major industries had at least a few competing firms. Competition among domestic producers brought about rapidly decreasing costs, and accelerated import substitution and export expansion. Because of the small domestic markets and lack of competition among domestic rivals in the Asian developing countries, there is typically a lack of incentive to reduce costs, which tends to delay CPC development. However, competition in the domestic market can be strengthened through government policies that encourage more competition with the introduction of imports. This topic presents an intriguing question for the study of industrial organization but is mentioned only occasionally in the following chapters.

4. Despite the decline in world prices of rayon and some chemicals, which was due to rapid expansion and greater economies of scale, Japanese prices of these products declined at an even faster rate.

    The differences in domestic and export prices do not indicate dumping practices but reflect product differentiation within manufacturing industries such that productivity increases and decreasing costs are greater in the export-producing sector than in the rest.

5. Shinohara (1972:30) was the first to analyze the correspondence between the growth cycle and balance of payments. He concludes that export booms, through an improved balance of payments and favorable demand conditions, generated long swings in pre–Second World War manufacturing. His explanation is consistent with the second type of correspondence in the analysis presented here, but it does not explain the interaction between production and the balance of payments over the entire period.

CHAPTER THREE

1. Myint (1958), Caves (1965, 1971), and Meier (1976) review studies on the role of primary goods exports in generating economic growth in North America and Southeast Asia.

2. Fujino (1965) and Fujino, Fujino, and Ono (1979) analyze the development of Japan's silk-reeling industries, focusing on productivity improvement, employment creation, and other domestic economic impacts.

3. The constant market share (CMS) approach, which allows for the identification of the sources of export growth, has frequently been used by analysts since the 1950s. Richardson (1971) summarizes the formulation of the CMS analysis and its economic implications. Empirical applications of the analysis are also reviewed.

4. Time series data of Japanese and Chinese exports of hand and steam filature to the United States were constructed by Niyomka (1975) under the assumptions that (1) both Japan and China exported all production of steam filature before 1910, (2) the two countries exported hand and steam filatures to the United States in the same proportions as their total exports to the world, and (3) the United States imported hand filature from these two countries alone.

5. Lockwood (1954), Baba and Tatemoto (1968), and Shinohara (1962) attributed the expansion of Japan's exports to the depreciation of silver. But as shown in the following analysis the effects of silver depreciation need to be examined with care.

6. A similar point was made by Fujino (1965).

7. Equation 3.2 was estimated alternatively by applying individual consumer expenditures of the United States to y.

$$\log_e M = 0.0003 + 1.7930 \log_e y - 0.2976 \log_e L - 0.8085 \log_e P$$
$$(8.34) \qquad\qquad (1.36) \qquad\qquad (1.92)$$

$$\bar{R}^2 = 0.9371, \ DW = 1.93$$

Cumulative consumption of silk fabric (L) was included in order to measure the learning effect of silk fabric consumption, which increased rapidly after 1870 but proved to be statistically insignificant.

8. See Kajinishi (1964) for an analysis of the financing of the silk-reeling industry in Meiji Japan, and Fujino (1965, chap. 19) for the impact of the industry on the development of Japan's banking system.

CHAPTER FOUR

1. The analysis in this chapter is based on Kajinishi (1964), but the periodization presented here is the work of this author.

2. Conventional tariffs are those that are agreed upon with trading partners.

3. The most severe competition in the commercialization of acrylic took place among five firms because of the absence of a basic patent and possible independent development.

CHAPTER FIVE

1. *Zaibatsu* were powerful family-controlled business conglomerates involved in manufacturing, trading, and financial activities. Each *zaibatsu* was centered around

a holding company (under family control), which in turn controlled the main operating companies of the group, which in turn controlled smaller companies.

2. Fogel and Engerman (1969) presented a short-run equilibrium model in which equilibrium price and quantity are determined by the intersection of annual short-run demand and supply curves. The short-run demand curves were moved to the right by domestic income increases and supply curves were shifted in the same direction by increases in productive capacities. A similar approach was tried in an earlier study on which this chapter is based, but the present model was eventually adopted because of data requirements. Reliable data on productive capacity over the whole period are not available for Japan's steel industry.

3. The price was deflated by the GDE deflator to adjust for the inflationary trend that characterized Japan's economic growth (Yamazawa 1972).

4. Differentiation of equations (1) through (5) with respect to time t enables a system of log-linear equations in growth rates of variables to be derived. The linear equation system is solved for the equilibrium growth rate for each endogenous variable. It can be proven, making a few plausible assumptions, that the model generates a path of successful import substitution and export expansion but tends to move in the other direction for small values of S/D.

5. Yamazawa (1972) gives the details of final tests and simulations.

6. This section is based on MITI (1970).

7. Tecson (1985) gives a detailed analysis of the first and second reorganization programs and an appraisal of their contribution to the development of industry.

CHAPTER SIX

Chapter 6 is based on two studies jointly undertaken by Ippei Yamazawa and Hirohisa Kohama (Yamazawa and Kohama 1984).

1. In 1888, the number of foreign merchant houses in Yokohama totalled 127, which, by represented nationality, included English (41), Chinese (25), American (18), German (17), French (10), Swiss (8), other European (5), and Indian (3). Among the largest foreign merchant houses were Jardine, Matheson and Co. (English), Walsh, Hall and Co. (American), and Siber Brenwald and Co. (Swiss).

2. The term *direct* (i.e., *direct* trade, and *direct* imports and exports) is used here to describe trade conducted by Japanese nationals rather than foreigners. In other words, direct trade excludes foreign merchants as go-betweens.

3. Extraterritoriality was admitted in foreign settlements, a situation described by Takahashi as "quasi-colonial" (Takahashi 1968: vol. 2, pp. 167–193).

4. See Takahashi (1973: vol. 3, chap. 2) for a description of the disadvantages to Japanese merchants. Takahashi also cites an editorial that appeared in *Tokyo Keizai Zasshi* (Tokyo Economic Journal), 10 January 1881, in which direct trade policy

was criticized by free traders on the ground that the government was driven too much by nationalism when it forced, at great cost to the national economy, the substitution of Japanese for foreign merchants.

5. Old exports and imports are those that had already been traded before 1875 when direct trade promotion was announced. New exports and imports are those goods that began to be traded only after 1875. Indigenous goods were produced and consumed domestically before the opening of trade, whereas modern goods were introduced to Japan through trade, with production in Japan beginning later. Imports are all modern goods by definition and are classified into six groups by end use.

6. G. C. Allen contended that Western merchants and Japanese branches of foreign banks contributed greatly to the expansion of Japan's foreign trade in the Meiji period (1868–1912). See Allen and Donnithorne 1954:196. Data in this chapter, without refuting the contribution of Allen and Donnithorne, substantiate the proposition that Japanese merchants expanded so as to replace foreign competitors and accelerate the expansion of Japan's foreign trade.

7. See Takahashi 1973: vol. 3, p. 138.

8. This is consistent with Allen's explanation of the competence of Japanese merchants in comparison with Chinese merchants (see Allen and Donnithorne 1954:204). He pointed out that Japan's mercantile activity rested on a secure institutional basis and an industrial hinterland that had been developed mainly by native initiatives.

9. The author is indebted to Yasukichi Yasuba for pointing out the significance of this regulation to this discussion. However, because of the lack of documentation in either Japanese or foreign sources, the restrictive effect of the regulation cannot be accurately assessed. But this author disagrees with the view that this regulation was the driving force in increases in the direct trade ratio.

10. See Takahashi 1973: vol. 3, chap. 2.

11. Differences in average values between major pairs of categories turned out to be statistically significant.

12. $R_1 = R_2 = 0$ for exports to or imports from Europe and North America; $R_1 = 1$ and $R_2 = 0$ for exports to and imports from East Asia; $R_1 = 0$ and $R_2 = 1$ otherwise.

13. In order to avoid the effect of extreme values in log-linear formulation, zero and near-zero values of the DER and DIR are replaced uniformly by 0.001 throughout the estimation.

14. In the absence of interaction terms, the coefficients of both N and M are positive and the coefficient of N is statistically significant.

15. In other regressions not shown here, however, the coefficients of R_1, the category Old and R_1, and the category Indigenous had a negative effect on DER, which partly refutes hypothesis 1 (part 3).

16. See Chap. 4, page 78 of this volume; also see Takahashi 1973: vol. 3, pp. 173–197.

17. See Yasuba (1979) for details on the development of ocean transportation.

18. See Takahashi 1973: vol. 3, p. 63.

19. Until a merger reduced the number to nine, the major GTCs in Japan had been referred to as "the ten GTCs." The companies include Mitsubishi, Mitsui, C. Itoh, Marubeni, Sumitomo, Nissho-Iwai (formed by a merger in 1968), Toyo Menka, Kanematsu-Gosho (merged in 1967), Nichimen, and Ataka (which was absorbed by C. Itoh in 1977).

CHAPTER SEVEN

1. Although the Special Emergency Tariffs (1904–05), as well as the Luxury Tariffs (1924), were motivated by the need to increase tariff revenue, these laws were exceptional in the history of Japan's tariff laws.

2. Excerpt from the speech delivered by Minister of Finance Osachi Hamaguchi on the proposal for the revision of the Tariff Law at the 51st session of the Japanese Diet (Ministry of Finance 1963: Vol. 13, p. 46).

3. The protection effects of tariffs on domestic manufacturing activities are properly measured not in terms of nominal rates, but in terms of their effective protection rates (ad valorem equivalents). These rates, however, are not available for the prewar years because of the prohibition on the release of data for security reasons. Chapter 8 provides estimates of the effective protection rate for the years after the Second World War.

4. The data presented here are based on data originally published in "Quantity and Value of Merchandise Imported by Each Port," *Dainihon gaikoku boeki nempyo* (Foreign Trade Annual of the Empire of Japan), Ministry of Finance, various years.

5. Note that when the ratio of tariffs collected on import value is calculated for an aggregated commodity group, such as total commodities or manufactures, the arithmetic mean of the tariffs collected on individual commodities in the group is weighted by the value of imports. But very high tariffs on individual commodities tend to restrict imports and lower the weighted arithmetic mean of tariffs. Restrictive tariffs are therefore given low weight. Data for tariffs on individual commodities, on the other hand, are fairly free from this bias because simple arithmetic means are calculated as average tariffs for groups classified by industry and economic use.

6. Japan lagged behind the other developed countries in the adoption of restrictions. Quantitative restrictions had not been adopted as a permanent feature of government policy by any country until 1931 when the world began to see the rise of protectionism. In 1931, France adopted quantitative restrictions, and the main European countries followed suit.

7. Great Britain, Department of Overseas Trade (1930).

8. Before 1899, although DFI was allowed outside the foreign settlements, it did not significantly affect industrial development. Within the foreign settlements, however, DFI was active in such activities as tea processing, ship-repairing, iron-making, paper manufacturing, and the installment of gas lighting immediately after the opening of trade.

9. Although Hitachi independently developed the technology to produce electric dynamos, it purchased the technology for producing related machinery, such as boilers and turbines, under patent contracts (see Aihara 1973).

CHAPTER EIGHT

1. Japan joined the International Monetary Fund (IMF) as an Article 14 country in August 1952 (which entitled Japan to impose foreign exchange controls on transactions). Japan became an Article 8 country in April 1964.

2. For a detailed discussion on these measures see Komiya et al., eds. (1988).

3. "Excessive competition" has a special meaning in Japan. See Komiya et al., eds. (1988).

4. The Foreign Trade and Foreign Exchange Control Law was enacted in December 1949 and continued unchanged until January 1982.

5. The Foreign Exchange Concentration Rule was eliminated in 1969. See MITI (1982).

6. AIQ is not different from AA in practice, but is still an interim form between IQ and AA and may be changed back to IQ if necessary.

7. The unsuccessful passage of the Machinery Industry Encouragement Act in 1963 and MITI's failure to strengthen its leadership over business are often cited as indicators of changes in MITI's industrial policy. See Tsuruta (1982) for details.

8. Economic Planning Agency, *Master Plan for Trade and Foreign Exchange Liberalization* (June 1960), reprinted in Kanamori, ed. (1974).

9. These import quota restrictions remained despite their prohibition under the GATT rule. Both rice and barley are categorized as state trading items and are exempted from this rule.

10. The tariff on cheese and butter was raised from 35 to 45 percent, that on boilers and electric generators from 15 to 20 percent, and those on lathes and other machinery from 15 to 25 percent.

11. The government classified liberalized industries as either category 1 or category 2 and allowed different degrees of foreign participation.

12. A similar rediscounting facility for import financing was provided by the Bank of Japan.

13. The numerator does not include foreign exchange fund loans, whereas the denominator includes export financing in the form of overdrafts provided to trading companies by foreign exchange banks. See MITI, *Tsusho Hakusho* (1972:191, 339).

14. Rediscounting at the basic official rate by the Bank of Japan is still available for qualified export bills.

15. The quantitative appraisal of the export privileges provided by the Korean government is based on Yen (1983: table 3).

CHAPTER NINE

1. Thailand's growth was set back much less than other ASEAN countries in 1985 and 1986, and it recovered quickly to 6.6 percent in 1987 and 9.0 percent in 1988. Although other ASEAN countries, with the exception of Singapore, recovered, their growth rates were 2–3 percent lower than Thailand's.

2. $Y = (C + I + G) + (X - M) = D + B,$

   where Y denotes national income, C denotes consumption, I denotes investment, G denotes government spending, $(X - M)$ denotes net exports, D denotes national expenditure, and B denotes the current external surplus in the national account (that is, exports minus imports of goods and services), which is the current account balance minus the net transfer payment. Changes in B nearly reflect the changes in the current account balance.

   $$dY/Y = (D/Y)dD/D + (B/Y)dB/B$$

   Since the ratio (D/Y) is around 1, the growth rate of national expenditure in Table 9.2 closely reflects the changes in the contribution of national expenditure to overall growth.

3. Figures for 1978 and 1986 are not consistent with this relationship. This is because both prices and the exchange rate changed drastically in these years so that the current account balance, expressed in billions of current dollars, departed substantially from the contribution of foreign demand.

4. Komiya (1988) provides a detailed analysis of Japan's macroeconomic policies during the period covering the two oil shocks.

5. Due to the continued boom in 1987–88, the steel- and ethylene-producing industries exceeded their existing capacities and this has led to persistent excess demand for iron. While some iron-producing firms are said to be planning expansion capacity, many are exercising extreme caution in resuming capacity expansion at the same rapid pace that occurred before the oil shocks.

6. Leasing machinery and equipment is new to many firms. Firms now prefer to rent instead of purchase machinery and equipment to avoid depreciation of the value of the machinery and equipment. This practice has become popular with factory and office equipment, especially because technical progress is so rapid that purchased machines become obsolete much earlier than their designated life

period. Factory and office equipment valued at about US$30 billion comprised three quarters of the total amount of lease contracts in 1986 (MITI 1988a).

7. Cheap labor costs were cited as a prime motivation for DFI by 60.9 percent of the firms operating in the Asian NIEs and 46.1 percent of firms in ASEAN. However, the number of firms motivated by the desire to be present in local markets for these areas is also large at 58.3 and 51.7 percent, respectively.

8. *Nihon Keizai Shinbun* (The Japan Economic Journal), 11 November 1988. The MITI White Paper (MITI 1988c) was based on a questionnaire survey conducted in September 1988 on the globalization of Japanese firms' R&D activities.

9. Peck, Levin, and Goto (1987) provide the most detailed analysis of the industry adjustment laws.

10. Peck, Levin, and Goto (1987) suggest that these eight industries were highly concentrated, and that it was anticipated that capacity reduction would be difficult to achieve if left to individual firms.

CHAPTER TEN

1. The basis for this chapter began with the author's participation in the Comparative Analysis Project, which was jointly coordinated by Kazushi Ohkawa and Gustav Ranis at the International Development Center of Japan from 1975 to 1981. The studies by Yamazawa and Hirata (1978), Yamazawa and Kohama (1984), and Yamazawa and Tambunlertchai (1985) all originated from this project, and both Chapter 6 and this chapter were based on these studies. The comparative analysis methodology used by Fei, Ohkawa, and Ranis (1985) influenced that used by the author when comparing the economic history of Japan with the recent economic performances of various developing countries.

2. This is what Ohkawa (1976) called the "compressed process" of catching-up development.

3. This section utilizes information from discussions with Rhee Chong Inn, and from his doctoral dissertation (Rhee 1984).

Bibliography

Japanese statistics sources often include English explanations and are accessible to English-language readers.

Aihara, H. 1973. "Nihon niokeru Gaikokushihon no Yakuwari [Role of Foreign Capital in Japan]," *Keizai to Boeki* [Economy and Trade], No. 110 (September). Yokohama-shiritsu Daigaku (Yokohama City University).

Allen, G. C., and A. G. Donnithorne. 1954. *Western Enterprise in Far Eastern Economic Development: China and Japan*. Winchester, MA: Allen and Unwin.

Akamatsu, Kaname. 1943. "Shinkou Kogyokoku no Sangyou Hatten [Industrial Development in Newly Industrializing Countries]," in *Ueda Teijiro Hakushi Kinen Ronbunshu* [Essays in Honor of Dr. Teijiro Ueda], Vol. 4. Tokyo: Kagagushugi Kogyosha.

_____. 1961. "A Theory of Unbalanced Growth in the World Economy," *Weltwirtschaftliches Archiv*, 86(2):196–217.

Asahi Shinbunsha. 1930. *Nihon Keizai Tokei Sokan* [Statistical Abstracts of the Japanese Economy]. Tokyo: Asahi Shinbunsha.

Baba, M., and M. Tatemoto. 1968. "Foreign Trade and Economic Growth in Japan: 1868–1937." In L. Klein and K. Ohkawa, eds., *Economic Growth: The Japanese Experience Since the Meiji Era*. Homewood, IL: Richard D. Irwin.

Balassa, B. 1965. "The Tariff Protection in Industrial Countries: An Evaluation," *J. Political Economy* 73(6):573–594.

Bank of Japan [Nihon Ginko]. 1956– . *Keizai Tokei Nempo* [Economics Statistics Annual]. Tokyo: Bank of Japan.

Bensusan-Butt, D. M. 1954. "A Model of Trade and Accumulation," *American Economic Review* 44(4):511–529.

Bergsten, Fred, and W. R. Cline. 1987. *The United States-Japan Economic Problem.* Rev. ed. Washington, D.C.: Institute for International Economics.

Caves, R. E. 1965. "Vent for Surplus Models of Trade and Accumulation." In R. E. Baldwin et al., eds., *Trade, Growth, and the Balance of Payments*, pp. 95–115. Chicago and Amsterdam: North Holland.

————. 1971. "Export-led Growth and the New Economic History." In J. Bhagwati et al., eds., *Trade, Balance of Payments and Growth*, pp. 403–442. New York: North Holland.

Caves, R. E., and R. W. Jones. 1973. *World Trade and Payments*, 2d ed. Boston, MA: Little.

Chen, E. K. Y. 1989. "The Changing Role of the ANICs in the Asian Pacific Region Towards the Year 2000." In M. Shinohara and Fu-chen Lo, eds., *Global Adjustment and Future of Asia-Pacific Economies*, pp. 207–231. Tokyo: Institute of Developing Economies and Asia Pacific Development Centre.

Destler, I. M., H. Fukui, and H. Sato. 1979. *The Textile Wrangle: Conflict in Japanese-American Relations 1969–1971.* Ithaca, NY: Cornell University Press.

Fei, J. C. H., K. Ohkawa, and G. Ranis. 1985. "Economic Development of Korea, Taiwan and Japan in Historical Perspective." In K. Ohkawa and G. Ranis, eds., *Japan and the Developing Countries: A Comparative Historical Analysis*, pp. 35–64. New York: Basil Blackwell.

Fogel, R. W., and S. L. Engerman. 1969. "A Model for the Explanation of Industrial Expansion During the Nineteenth Century, With an Application to the American Iron Industry," *J. Political Economy* 77(3):306–328.

Fujino, Shozaburo. 1965. *Nihon no Keiki Junkan* [Japan's Economic Cycle]. Tokyo: Keiso-shobo.

Fujino, Shozaburo, Shiro Fujino, and Akira Ono. 1979. *Sen-i Kogyo* [Textile Industry]. Choki Keizai Tokei [Long-Term Economic Statistics of Japan], Vol. 11. Tokyo: Toyo Keizai Shinposha.

Gerschenkron, A. 1966. *Economic Backwardness in Historical Perspective.* Cambridge, MA: The Belknap Press of Harvard University Press.

Great Britain, Department of Overseas Trade. 1930. *Economic Conditions in Japan.* London: His Majesty's Stationary Office.

Haberler, G. 1964. "Integration and Growth of the World Economy in Historical Perspective," *American Economic Review* 54(2):1–22.

Hayami, Y. 1972. "Rice Policy in Japan's Economic Development," *American J. Agricultural Economics* 54(1):19–31.

Helleiner, G. K. 1981. *Intra-firm Trade and the Developing Countries.* New York: Macmillan.

Henmi, K. 1969. "Primary Product Exports and Economic Development: The Case of Silk." In K. Ohkawa, B. F. Johnston, and H. Kaneda, eds., *Agriculture and Economic Growth: Japan's Experience.* Tokyo: University of Tokyo Press.

Hoffman, W. 1931. *Stadien und Typen der Industrialisierung.* Jena, Germany: G. Fischer.

Inada, K., S. Sekiguchi, and Y. Shouda. 1972. *Keizai Hatten no Mekanizumu–Sono Riron to Jisho* [Mechanism of Economic Development: Its Theory and Practice]. Tokyo: Sobunsha.

International Monetary Fund (IMF). 1988. *International Financial Statistics.* Various issues.

Japan Tariff Association. 1962. *The Customs Tariff of Japan.* Tokyo: Japan Tariff Association.

Johnson, H. G. 1968. *Comparative Cost and Commercial Policy Theory for a Developing World Economy.* Stockholm: Almqvist and Wiksell.

Kajinishi, M. 1964. *Gendai Nihon Sangyo Hattenshi: Sen-i* [History of Industry Development in Modern Japan: Textiles]. Tokyo: Kojunsha.

Kanamori, Hisao, ed. 1970. *Boeki to Kokusai Shushi* [Trade and Balance of Payments]. Tokyo: Nihon Keizai Shinbunsha.

Key, B. 1970. The Role of Foreign Contribution in Prewar Japanese Capital Formation—with Special Reference to the Period 1904–14. Unpublished Ph.D. dissertation. University of California, Berkeley.

Kobayashi, U. 1930. *The Basic Industries and Social History of Japan: 1914–1918.* New Haven, CT: Yale University Press.

Kojima, K. 1958. *Nihon Boeki to Keizai Hatten* [Japan's Trade and Economic Development]. Tokyo: Kunimoto-shobo.

_____. 1965. *Sekai Keizai to Nihon Boeki* [World Economy and Japan's Trade]. Tokyo: Keiso-shobo.

_____. 1973. "Reorganization of North-South Trade: Japan's Foreign Economic Policy for the 1970s." *Hitotsubashi J. Economics* 13(2):1–28.

Komiya, R. 1988. *Gendai Nihon Keizai* [Modern Japanese Economy]. Tokyo: Tokyo Daigaku Shuppan Kai.

Komiya, R., M. Okuno, and K. Suzumura, eds. 1988. *Industrial Policy of Japan.* Tokyo: Academic Press Japan Inc.

Kuznets, S. 1967. "Quantitative Aspects of the Economic Growth of Nations: X Level and Structure of Foreign Trade: Long-Term Trends." *Economic Development and Cultural Change* 15(2), Part II:1–140.

Linder, S. B. 1961. *An Essay on Trade and Transformation.* New York: Wiley.

Lockwood, W. W. 1954. *The Economic Development of Japan: 1968–1938*. Princeton, NJ: Princeton University Press.

Mason, F. R. 1910. "American Industry and Tariff," *American Economic Association Quarterly* 11(4):1–182.

Meier, G. M. 1976. *Leading Issues in Economic Development*, 3d ed. New York: Oxford University Press.

Ministry of Finance [Okurasho]. 1882–1943. *Dainihon Gaikoku Boeki Nempyo* [Foreign Trade Annual of the Empire of Japan]. Tokyo: Ministry of Finance.

———. 1938. *Meiji Taisho Zaiseishi* [Fiscal History of the Meiji and Taisho Periods]. Tokyo: Zaisei Keizai Gakkai.

———. 1950. *Zaisei Kinyu Tokei Geppo* [Fiscal and Financial Statistics Monthly], 5 (May).

———. 1951– . *Nihon Gaikoku Boeki Nempyo* [Foreign Trade Annual of Japan]. Tokyo: Ministry of Finance.

———. 1963. *Showa Zaiseishi* [Fiscal History of the Showa Period], 13. Kokusai Kinyu to Boeki [International Finance and Trade]. Tokyo: Toyo Keizai Shinposha.

———. 1982. *Zaisei Kinyu Tokei Geppo* [Fiscal and Financial Statistics Monthly], No. 365 (September).

Ministry of International Trade and Industry (MITI) [Tsusho Sangyo-sho]. 1951– . *Tsusho Hakusho* [White Paper on International Trade and Industry]. Tokyo: Tsusho Sangyo Chosakai.

———. 1952–60. *Boeki Gyotai Tokei* [Trade Business Statistics, by Industry]. Tokyo: Tsusho Sangyo Chosakai.

———. 1970. *Shokou Seisakushi* [History of Commercial and Industrial Policy]. Tokyo: Tsusho Sangyo Chosakai.

———. 1982. *Tsusan 30 Nenshi* [Thirty-Year History of MITI]. Tokyo: Tsusho Sangyo Chosakai.

———, Industrial Policy Bureau [Sangyo Seisaku-kyoku]. 1988a. *Susumu Kozouchosei to Sangyo Kozou no Tembou: Kozou Chosei Bijyon* [Progress of Structural Adjustment and Prospect for Industrial Structure: Vision for Structural Adjustment]. Tokyo: Tsusho Sangyo Chosakai.

———. 1988b. *Tsusan Tokei Handobukku* [Handbook of Industrial and Trade Statistics]. Tokyo: Tsusan Tokei Kyokai.

———. 1988c. *Gaishikei Kigyou no Doukou* [Activities of Foreign Corporations in Japan], Vol. 19. Tokyo: Keibun Shuppan.

Morikawa, H. 1976. "Sogoshosha no Seiritsu to Ronri [Evolution of General Trading Companies and Their Business Principles]." In M. Miyamoto, ed., *Sogoshosha no Keiseishi* [Business History of General Trading Companies]. Tokyo: Toyo Keizai Shinposha.

Myint, H. 1958. "The Classical Theory of International Trade and the Underdeveloped Countries," *The Economic Journal* 68(270):317–337.

Nakagawa, K. 1967. "Nihon Kogyo-ka Katei Niokeru Soshikikasareta Kigyouka Katsudo [Organized Entrepreneurial Activities in the Process of Japan's Industrialization]," *Keizai-Shigaku* [J. Business History], 2(3)(November).

Nawa, T. 1937. *Nippon Bosekigyo to Genmen Mondai* [Japanese Cotton Spinning Industry and the Raw Cotton Issue]. Osaka: Daido-shoin.

Nihon Boseki Kyokai [Japan Spinners' Association]. 1982. *Bokyo Hyakunenshi* [A Century of History of the Japan Spinners' Association]. Osaka: Nihon Boseki Kyokai.

Nihon Kagaku Sen-i Kyokai [Japan Chemical Fiber Manufacturers' Association]. 1974. *Nihon Kagaku Sen-i Sangyoshi* [History of Japan's Chemical Fiber Industry]. Tokyo: Nihon Kagaku Sen-i Kyokai.

Nihon Kanzei Kyokai. 1965. *Boeki Nenkan* [Trade Annual]. Tokyo: Nihon Kanzei Kyokai.

Nihon Tekko Renmei. 1957– . *Tekko Tokei Yoran* [Iron and Steel Statistics Abstract]. Tokyo: Nihon Tekko Renmi.

Niyomka, P. 1975. Japanese Silk Exports and Economic Development: 1860–1910. Unpublished master's thesis. Hitotsubashi University, Tokyo.

OECD. 1978. *The Impact of Newly Industrializing Countries on the Pattern of World Trade and Production in Manufacturing.* Paris: OECD.

_____. 1979. *The Case for Positive Adjustment Policies.* Paris: OECD.

_____. 1981. *Structural Problems and Policies Relating to the OECD Textile and Clothing Industries.* Paris: OECD.

_____. 1987. *Structural Adjustment and Economic Performance.* Paris: OECD.

_____. 1988. *Economic Survey: Japan 1987/1988.* Paris: OECD.

Ohkawa, K. 1976. *Keizai Hatten to Nihon no Keiken* [Economic Development and Japan's Experience]. Tokyo: Taimeido.

Ohkawa, K., and H. Rosovsky. 1973. *Japanese Economic Growth: Trend Acceleration in the Twentieth Century.* Stanford, CA: Stanford University Press.

Ohkawa, K., N. Takamatsu, and Y. Yamamoto. 1974. *Kokumin Shotoku* [National Income]. Choki Keizai Tokei [Long-Term Economic Statistics of Japan], Vol. 1. Tokyo: Toyo Keizai Shinposha.

Ohkita, S. 1987. "The Outlook for Pacific Co-operation and the Role of Japan," *The Indonesian Quarterly* 15(3). Jakarta: CSIS.

Ono, A. 1968. "Gijutsu Shimpo to 'Borrowed Technology' no Ruikei [Technological Progress and Typology of Borrowed Technology]." In J. Tsukui and Y. Murakami, eds., *Keizai Seicho Riron no Tenbo* [Prospects of Economic Growth Theories]. Tokyo: Iwanami Shoten.

Pasha, W. 1987. *On the Contribution of Phasing to the Analysis of East Asian Economic Development.* Discussion Paper, Nagoya University, Nagoya, Japan.

Patrick, H., and H. Rosovsky. 1976. *Asia's New Giant: How the Japanese Economy Works.* Washington, D.C.: The Brookings Institution.

Peck, M. J., R. C. Levin, and A. Goto. 1987. "Picking Losers: Public Policy Toward Declining Industries in Japan," *J. Japanese Studies* 13(1):79–123.

Rhee, C. I. 1984. Kankoku no Boeki Hatten to Sogoshosha Katsudo [Korea's Trade Development and General Trading Companies]. Unpublished doctoral thesis presented to Hitotsubashi University and later published in Korean language under the same title in 1987.

Richardson, J. D. 1971. "Constant Market Share Analysis of Export Growth," *J. International Economics* 1(2):227–239.

Sautter, C. 1973. *Le Prix de la Puissance* [The Price of Power]. Paris. Le Sevil.

Shinohara, M. 1962. *Growth annd Cycles in the Japanese Economy.* Tokyo: Kinokuniya.

_____. 1972. *Ko-Kogyo* [Mining and Manufacturing Industries]. Choki Keizai Tokei [Long-Term Economic Statistics of Japan], Vol. 10. Tokyo: Toyo Keizai Shinposha.

_____. 1982. *Industrial Growth, Trade and Dynamic Patterns in the Japanese Economy.* Tokyo: University of Tokyo Press.

Shionoya, Y., and I. Yamazawa. 1973. "Industrial Growth and Foreign Trade in Prewar Japan." In K. Ohkawa and Y. Hayami, eds., *Economic Growth: The Japanese Experience Since the Meiji Era*, pp. 515–555. Tokyo: Japan Economic Research Centre.

Takahashi, K. 1968. *Nihon Kindai Keizai Keiseishi* [History of the Formation of the Modern Japanese Economy]. Tokyo: Toyo Keizai Shinposha.

_____. 1973. *Nihon Kindai Keizai Hattatsushi* [History of the Development of the Modern Japanese Economy]. Tokyo: Toyo Keizai Shinposha.

Takeuchi, H. 1972. "Denki Kogyo [Electrical Industry]." In K. Kojima, ed., *Nihon Boeki no kozo to Hatten* [Structure and Development of Japanese Trade]. Tokyo: Shiseido.

Tamura, S., and S. Urata. 1988. "Changing Pattern of Technology Policy in Japan." Paper presented at the 17th Pacific Trade and Development Conference, Bali, Indonesia.

Tecson, G. R. 1985. Industrial Policy for International Competitiveness: A Case Study of Industrial Policy in the Iron and Steel Industry of Japan. Unpublished Ph.D. dissertation, Hitotsubashi University. Summary published in *Hitotsubashi Review* 94(2):113–118 (August 1985).

Toyo Keizai Shinposha. 1935. *Nihon Boeki Seiran* [Foreign Trade of Japan: Comprehensive Statistical Survey]. Tokyo: Toyo Keizai Shinposha.

Tran, V. T. 1985. "Vertical Integration of Japanese Firms in Southeast Asia: Case Study of the Synthetic Fiber Industry [Nihon kigyo no Tonan Ajia deno keiretsuka-gosen kogyo no kesu]," *Nihon Keizai Kenkyu* [J. Japanese Economic Research], No. 14, March.

_____. 1988. "Foreign Capital and Technology in the Catching-up Process of Developing Countries: The Experience of South Korea's Synthetic Industry," *The Developing Economies* 26(4):386–402.

Tsuruta, Toshimasa. 1982. *Sengo Nihon no Sangyo Seisaku* [Japan's Industrial Policy after the Second World War]. Tokyo: Nihon Keizai Shinbunsha.

United Nations. 1947- . *Monthly Bulletin of Statistics*. New York: United Nations Statistical Office.

Vernon, R. 1964. "International Investment and International Trade in the Product Cycle," *Quarterly J. Economics* 80(2):190–207.

Yamaguchi, K., et al., eds. 1974. "Mitsui Bussan Kaisha Hyakunenshi" [Hundred-Year History of Mitsui and Co.]. Unpublished draft.

Yamamoto, Y. 1969. "Kokusai Shushi Tokei no Choki Sogoka Ni Tsuite [Long-term Estimate of Japan's Balance of Payments Statistics]," *Jinbun Gakuho*, Kyoto University, 28 (March).

Yamamura, K. 1976. "General Trading Companies in Japan: Their Origins and Growth." In H. Patrick, ed., *Japanese Industrialization and Its Social Consequences*, pp. 161–199. Berkeley: University of California Press.

Yamazawa, I. 1969. "Kanzeikozo to boekihogo [Tariff Structure and Trade Protection]." In I. Yamada, K. Emi, and T. Mizoguchi, eds., *Nihonkeizai no Kozohendo to Yosoku* [Structural Changes and Forecast of the Japanese Economy]. Tokyo: Shunjusha.

_____. 1972. "Industry Growth and Foreign Trade: A Study of Japan's Steel Industry," *Hitotsubashi J. Economics* 12(2):41–59.

_____. 1975. "Industrial Growth and Trade Policy in Prewar Japan," *The Developing Economies* 13(1):38–65.

_____. 1984. *Nihon no Keizai Hatten to Kokusai Bungyo* [Japan's Economic Development and International Trade]. Tokyo: Toyo Keizai Shinposha.

_____. 1988a. "The Textile Industry." In R. Komiya et al., eds., *Industrial Policy of Japan*, pp. 345–367. Tokyo: Academic Press Japan, Inc.

_____. 1988b. "Japan-U.S. Economic Conflicts and Their Impacts on the Pacific-Asian Region." In R. A. Scalapino, ed., *Pacific-Asian Economic Policies and Regional Interdependence*, pp. 219–239. Berkeley: University of California Press.

Yamazawa, I., and A. Hirata. 1978. "Industrialization and External Relations: Comparative Analysis of Japan's Historical Experience and Contemporary Developing Countries' Performance," *Hitotsubashi J. Economics*, Vol. 18 (February).

Yamazawa, I., and H. Kohama. 1984. "Trading Companies and the Expansion of Foreign Trade: Japan, Korea and Thailand." In K. Ohkawa and G. Ranis, eds., *Japan and the Developing Countries: A Comparative Analysis*, pp. 426–446. New York: Basil Blackwell.

Yamazawa, I., and S. Tambunlertchai. 1985. "Manufactured Exports from Developing Countries: The Thai Textile Industry and Japan's Historical Experience." In K. Ohkawa and G. Ranis, eds., *Japan and the Developing Countries: A Comparative Analysis*, pp. 369–388. New York: Basil Blackwell.

Yamazawa, I., and Y. Yamamoto. 1979a. *Boeki to Kokusai Shushi* [Trade and Balance of Payments]. Choki Keizai Tokei [Long-Term Economic Statistics of Japan], Vol. 14. Tokyo: Toyo Keizai Shinposha.

_____. 1979b. "Trade and Balance of Payments." In K. Ohkawa and M. Shinohara, eds., *Patterns of Japanese Economic Development: A Quantitative Appraisal*, pp. 134–156. New Haven, CT: Yale University Press.

Yasuba, Y. 1979. "Meijiki Kaiun Niokeru Unchin to Seisansei [Wages and Productivity of the Marine Transport Industry in the Meiji Period]." In H. Shimpo and Y. Yasuba, eds., *Kindai-Ikoukino Nihon Keizai* [Transition of the Japanese Economy in the Modern Period]. Tokyo: Nihon Keizai Shinbunsha.

Yen, K. W. 1983. "Export Assistance Regimes in the Pacific Asian Developing Countries: The Case of South Korea, Taiwan, the Philippines, and Thailand." Unpublished paper presented to the Pacific Economic Cooperation Conference Task Force on Trade in Manufactured Goods. Seoul: Korea Development Institute.

Yukizawa, K., and S. Maeda. 1978. *Nihon Boeki no Choki Tokei: Boeki Kozoushi Kenkyu no Kiso Sagyo* [Long-Term Statistics of Japan's Trade: A Groundwork for the Historical Study of Trade Structure]. Osaka: Dohosha.

Index

7407